THE ESSENTIAL GUIDE TO JUDGING DOGS

ANDREW H. BRACE

RINGPRESS

RINGPRESS

Published by Ringpress Books Ltd,
Spirella House, Bridge Road,
Letchworth, Herts, SG6 4ET, United Kingdom.

Discounts available for bulk orders.
Contact the Special Sales Manager at
the above address. Telephone (0462) 674177

Distributed to the Book Trade in the United Kingdom by
Bookpoint Ltd.
39 Milton Park, Abingdon, Oxon OX14 4TD
Telephone 0235 835001

First Published 1994
© 1994 ANDREW BRACE

ISBN 0 948955 04 X

Printed and bound in Singapore.

Contents

Acknowledgements

My life with dogs has been a rewarding one, yet it would never have been possible without the indulgence of my long-suffering parents, who finally relented and enabled me to fulfil a childhood dream when they bought me my first pedigree dog – a Boxer – as a reward for passing the 'eleven-plus' examination. In subsequent years they turned parental tolerance into an art form!

One of the greatest influences in my life has been my fellow Welshman, Nigel Aubrey Jones, whose contribution to the dog world in both Britain and the American continent has been inestimable. Over the years Nigel has been a source of inspiration and encouragement, yet he has never been afraid to offer advice and direction just when it was needed.

The canine societies who have invited me to officiate for them have given me the opportunity to do what I enjoy most. I thank them for that.

The greatest satisfaction of all has come from the privilege of meeting so many dogs at close quarters, in many cases when they were fresh, wide-eyed young puppies. Many of these have been of such exceptional quality that the impact they made upon me when I first set eyes on them will never be forgotten. I thank their owners for the pleasure these dogs have given me. Several of the dogs who I had the privilege of judging as promising youngsters are featured in this book alongside others of whom I have special memories.

I also wish to thank the owners of the beautiful dogs whose photographs appear in the book for their co-operation, along with the photographers involved.

It is the dogs who have made it all worthwhile – and I dedicate this book to them.

ANDREW H. BRACE.

In an attempt to avoid verbosity and clumsy grammar in this book, I have taken the liberty of referring to judges in the male gender. I apologise in advance to any readers of the fairer sex who may take offence at this, and I am the first to concede that some of the finest dog judges I have met have been ladies. Happily, there is no sex discrimination in the world of dog judging where both men and women enjoy totally equal opportunities.

Introduction

At the age of eleven I was given my first pedigree dog, a Boxer named Bruce, who kindled in me a passion for the fascinating world of dog showing and breeding, which has never waned.

In my late teens I began judging dogs, an activity which I enjoy enormously. Over a period of more than twenty-five years I have had the privilege to know many capable dog judges, and I have learnt something from each of them. As a schoolboy I ring-stewarded for some of Britain's finest all-rounder judges, and I will always be grateful to those who took the time and trouble to discuss their decisions with me afterwards.

Judging dogs has taken me to many different countries where I have experienced several judging systems, and in each I have discovered something new and beneficial to my greater understanding of the global dog world.

This book is a collection of my thoughts on judging dogs. It is a personal, and in some cases, an unorthodox view, but it is written as a result of the strong feelings I have about the sport. It is not aimed at the absolute beginner, but at the enthusiastic breeder/exhibitor who has perhaps just begun judging, or who is contemplating it for the first time.

No one will ever become a great dog judge simply from reading books, but I hope that those who read this title will feel that, having done so, they are better equipped to cope with the rocky road ahead than when they started.

Chapter One

WHY JUDGE DOGS?

REASONS FOR JUDGING

For dog shows to be run, there must be dogs, there must be exhibitors, there must be show officials and organisers, there must be ring stewards, and there must be judges. Given that there always appear to be plenty of established judges in existence, why should anyone want to add to their number? It is a simple question which prompts many varied answers. Some would say that their experience and knowledge of a breed is such that their opinions on that breed would contribute to its progress. Some would answer that it is a logical progression from owning, exhibiting and breeding dogs. Others nobly suggest that judging is their way of "putting something back" into the dog game. A few, if they were honest, might admit that approval for a number of different breeds is their passport to world travel.

Personally, I look on judging dogs as a challenge. It presents the opportunity to walk into a ring faced with a number of dogs, and to make a decision as to which of these is the best. One of the greatest thrills of judging is finding an unknown dog, maybe a Junior or even a Puppy, who is superior to the competition on the day, and awarding such a dog top honours. It is a source of great personal satisfaction to see that dog then go on to many more successes, and have your own opinion endorsed by more experienced judges.

Judging is all about assessing quality. Great dogs are a joy to behold and a privilege to judge. Unfortunately, you have to wade through a lot of inferior stock to find the stars, but having large numbers of also-rans is what makes the economics of dog shows work in Britain. It would be fair to say that if I was ever told that I would only ever be asked to judge mediocre dogs, I would quit tomorrow. There is no pleasure in judging dogs of indifferent quality, many of whom should not really be competing at Championship events. It is the hope of finding a truly outstanding specimen that keeps us going. That, to me, is the incentive to judge dogs.

THE JUDGE'S ROLE

The judge's lot is not always a happy one. The centre of the ring is the loneliest place in the world, and having agreed to undertake a judging appointment, I hope that any would-be judge realises the responsibilities and the implications of that appointment. To begin with, the object of the exercise is to find the best dog, be it in the Breed, in the Group, or in the final Best in Show line-up. We should be looking for the best dog, regardless. All we should be relying on when making our decisions is our understanding of correct type for the breed, sound anatomical construction, and typical temperament coupled with the basic "eye" for quality and balance which all outstanding judges possess.

There is very little chance that any judge's decisions on any day will prove universally popular, but his brief is to please just one person – himself. It is not easy, bearing in mind human frailties, to blot out from your mind the form of winning dogs, the breeding of exhibits (when you are judging as a breed specialist and regularly in competition yourself), and the fact that some of the exhibitors showing under you will, in the near future, be judging your own dogs. All that matters is that you make the right decision and can sleep easy with your conscience. No judge is perfect. We have all made mistakes, but provided those mistakes are made in all honesty, and they are learnt from, they are not major disasters.

But why should so many people want to get on the judging bandwagon? There seems to exist the mistaken belief that becoming a judge brings with it some mythical power. In reality, you are simply being asked to award prizes to dogs you think worthy. Power can only be conceived in the minds of those who choose to abuse it. Some aspiring judges may, in all honesty, wish to pursue their careers in the hope that if they award a dog top honours, then the owner of that dog will reciprocate when they themselves judge. This is diseased thinking, and any judges who have this frame of mind should do everyone in the sport a favour and take up some other hobby.

Far from being powerful, the judge is vulnerable. He has agreed to put his neck on the line and make decisions in front of a ringside of people, many of whom will know far more about the breed than he does. He is exposing his knowledge, or lack of it, and will have to face the consequences.

THE CHANGING SCENE
Unfortunately, mainly due to the economic changes of the past decades, there are fewer and fewer true "fanciers" exhibiting dogs, and more and more competitors. There is a world of difference between the two. In years gone by, this country boasted many large kennels, owned by wealthy enthusiasts, who kept vast numbers of dogs, and several staff to look after their every need. Today, few people in Britain have the financial backing to run such establishments, and dog showing is dominated by hobbyist exhibitors who own one, or a handful of dogs.

The fanciers of yesteryear were connoisseurs, very much immersed in their breed and their breeding, and they possessed intimate knowledge of a breed with all its bloodlines, and understood all its nuances and subtleties. They were invariably members of the upper classes, living in beautiful homes, and surrounding themselves not only with beautiful dogs, but equally lovely porcelain, works of art and the other trappings of family wealth. They had standards of quality which they applied to all aspects of their life, and it followed, logically, that they would only settle for the very best in their livestock.

It might seem ridiculous to even mention this fact in a book which is being written in the 1990s, but the demise of this element in the dog world, as our "classless" society has evolved, has had an effect on the shows of today. This backbone of what some will view as snobbery, has been replaced by enthusiastic amateurs, seventy-five per cent of whom will show dogs for no longer than five years. They choose to show what are essentially pet dogs, and I do not mean any disrespect when using this term. The dog is, first and foremost, a companion, and that role is of prime importance especially in today's political climate where dogs are perceived as an enemy by certain sad factions of society.

We live in an "instant" age where we want everything now or sooner. Today, people who have maybe shown just one dog with moderate success decide they want to judge. They have no deep knowledge of the breed they own, they have done little to study anatomy, they have never bred a litter, and – remarkably – they may not even own a book on their breed. Yet they want to pass opinions in public on other exhibitors' dogs. They get themselves on committees and soon find themselves in a position where they can influence the sport in some small way, if only by inviting judges or having a say in the approval or otherwise of judges who have vastly more experience than themselves. Far too many hobbyist competitors will assess a judge purely by whether or not they themselves won under him. Their depth of knowledge of the breed is not sufficient for them to have any other yardstick. This is bad for the sport. The only understandable reason for such people wishing to judge is that they believe they know far more than they actually do, and in that case they are a lost cause.

RECOGNISING YOUR SHORTCOMINGS

Unless you recognise your own shortcomings, you can never improve, and the one thing which judging dogs has taught me is to realise how much I don't know rather than how much I do.

It is generally accepted that once you have been approved by the Kennel Club to award Challenge Certificates in a breed, you have "arrived" and made it to the top of the tree. Many judges feel that this accolade is synonymous with their knowing all there is to know about a breed. My own feeling is that, the first time you award CCs in a breed, you realise that you didn't know as much as you thought. It is only after judging a breed at top level three or four times that I really begin to feel comfortable with that breed. That might sound contradictory and rather ridiculous, but it is true. As for the aspiring judges who feel that being in a position where they themselves can award CCs, will bring CCs in return, this is sheer folly. Statistically, you will find that the majority of CCs awarded in any year are won by owners who are not, themselves, Championship show judges. Many people begin judging dogs for the wrong reasons.

Judging dogs is not necessarily a natural progression from owning, exhibiting and breeding. Some highly successful breeders and exhibitors never contemplate judging, no matter how others might attempt to persuade them. It is no small coincidence that such people are often far more popular than their peers who occasionally pin on the judge's rosette!

Chapter Two

WHO SHOULD JUDGE DOGS?

CREDENTIALS FOR JUDGING

My own feeling is that it is expecting rather a lot of experienced exhibitors to ask them to respect the opinion of a judge who has not, himself, been at least moderately successful as a breeder or exhibitor. It is true that there have been exceptions. The late Stanley Dangerfield springs readily to mind as someone who never sought to establish a successful kennel himself, yet rose to the top via administration and journalism to become, more than anyone in recent years, the person who brought "style" to the British All-Rounder.

It would be stupid to attempt to lay down a definite time-scale of when an individual should embark on a judging career. It is impossible to generalise, and no two people are the same as regards ability and potential. Having said that, I do not think it is untoward to suggest that no-one should contemplate judging until they have been actively exhibiting and breeding for at least five years. Those first five years will pass very quickly, and they will provide ample opportunity for the mistakes we all make when we are flushed with the enthusiasm and novelty of it all.

As I have said before, it used to be that breeders and exhibitors did not automatically judge dogs. Few even thought of it, and when they did it was only at the suggestion of one of the "breed elders" who often controlled a breed to a large extent. Today, showing and judging seem intertwined, and the "them and us" relationship of judges and exhibitors has been replaced by a situation where almost everyone who has been showing for a year or so starts judging.

STATUS

A by-product of the popularity of dog shows, and the need for more and more judges at lower levels, has been a cheapening of the judge's status. There was a time when judges were revered, respected and held in awe. Today, as in all walks of life, there is great familiarity, and the average exhibitor seems to feel quite at liberty to address a judge he may never have met before by his Christian name! This is probably due to the fact that the majority of exhibitors officiate as judges, to some degree.

Time and time again we read of disciplinary actions being brought against exhibitors who have chosen to abuse judges, usually verbally, after an appointment. This kind of behaviour is unforgivable. Always remember that no-one forced you to enter under a particular judge. It was your decision; your money. If you do not like what that judge did, you need never show under him again. You paid for his opinion and, hopefully, that is what you got. Sadly, few exhibitors today fully understand the implications of entering under a judge. Exhibitors should be seeking the judge's opinion of their dogs, and before entering a show, they should think about this in context.

A judge should have enjoyed some success as an exhibitor before attempting to assess other people's dogs. I am handling my Beagle, Ch. Too Darn Hot for Tragband, to win the CC and BOB. at a Midland Counties Championship show under the late all-rounder, Joe Braddon. This CC gave her the breed record and she retired from the show ring with forty-two CCs won under forty different judges, taking the Bitch CC at Crufts on each of the three occasions she competed there. She also won seven Hound Groups and was an All Breeds Best in Show winner at Championship level. "Ada", as she was universally known, took time out from the show ring to produce two litters, returning after both to take further CCs. She has many Champion progeny in Britain, Scandinavia and Australia. One grand-daughter won Best in Show at the Windsor Championship show of 1993. David Dalton.

However, it would be idealistic to say that exhibitors still enter a show for a judge's opinion – in most cases, they enter in the hope of winning. Provided they have the red card in their hand, they are not really interested in what the judge thought of their dog. Indeed, many take great exception to the few published judges' critiques which aim to tell the truth – warts and all. Far more popular is the judge who writes that everything in the garden is rosy and shies away from ever faulting anything.

SERVING AN APPRENTICESHIP
So, we are looking to a brief "apprenticeship" of around five years for our would-be judge. During that period I would expect the individual to be reasonably successful at Championship shows, and if this is with home-bred stock, then so much the better. I would hope that any litters that are bred have been produced after much forethought and planning, and not simply to fulfil some crazy

requirements to get on a Club judging list. In these times, it is not advisable to encourage unnecessary breeding.

ANALYSING THE BREED STANDARD

During the pre-judging period, it is essential that anyone who aspires to officiate in the future makes every attempt to learn as much as possible about their breed. Start with the Breed Standard. It may appear at first as merely a faceless list of requirements: dark, oval eyes; medium length; well-arched neck; slightly sloping pasterns and so on. Reading (and even memorising) it is one thing; understanding it is another. Take the Standard to pieces, phrase by phrase, and ask yourself *why* your breed should have a slightly undershot mouth, well-sprung ribs, or whatever.

Finding out the reasons why your breed has evolved in a certain way can be a great adventure. Get hold of as many books on your breed as possible, and the older the better. I am constantly surprised at the lack of breed literature in the average exhibitor's library. Many breeds have long-established works available, considered to be "the bible" of the breed. Some such treasures may be out of print, but the real enthusiast will run one to ground and persuade the owner to lend it, if only for long enough to photocopy! Many of today's exhibitors seem to be interested only in books which contain photographs of contemporary specimens; their natural interest in the history and origins of the breed is nil – and yet it is only knowledge of the past that can provide a foundation for creating the future.

Having got to grips with the Breed Standard, and begun to understand *why*, the aspiring judge should look at old photographs of dogs which were outstanding at the time. In many cases, breeds will have changed dramatically, sometimes for the better, sometimes, alas, very much for the worse. Study these photographs alongside the Standard and assess the dogs accordingly. While type might have evolved and become more refined, it is important to recognise the changes which have taken place and decide whether these represent progress or regression. It can be a sobering experience to look dispassionately at dogs of days gone by, and conclude that present-day dogs have strayed considerably from the ideal described in the original Breed Standards.

I deliberately mention original Breed Standards, because the present-day examples, published by the Kennel Club, are streamlined versions of the originals. Many breed experts bemoaned the "sterilising" of their Breed Standard, feeling that the original was much more graphic and elaborate than today's replacement. Simple word changes can dramatically alter the sense of a phrase. As an example, the original Pekingese Standard called for a "massive" head. Today's Standard merely requires that head to be "large". The two words convey completely different meanings to the reader, and it is important that all enthusiasts acquaint themselves with the older versions of their Breed Standard if they are to fully understand the modern equivalent.

BREED ESSENTIALS

As a newcomer, it is important to listen to as many different viewpoints concerning your breed as possible, and then to make up your own mind as to your own list of major priorities within the breed. In a breed, you can often find quite diametrically opposing views on correct type, especially if the breed is one which has experienced a large volume of imported stock in recent years. You will hear "American type", "German type", "Dutch type", for example, being discussed in Boxer and Dobermann circles. Often these generalised expressions may be based on only a handful of dogs, which may not necessarily be representative of the breed in their native country, and it is important to remember that the breed should call for the same essentials, no matter where a dog happens to be born. In extreme examples – like the German Shepherd – the breed may have become polarised into two quite distinct types. In the Shepherd's case, "Alsatians" and "Germanic" dogs bear little similarity to each other.

Listen to as many *experienced* people in your breed as possible. You will hear conflicting views and arguments, but provided they are all rationalised and explained logically, this will provide you with much food for thought in sorting out in your own mind how you view perfection in your breed. It is not a good idea to pay much heed to the relatively inexperienced exhibitor (albeit accidentally successful) who is keener to discuss exhibitors than dogs. They contribute nothing to their breed and will only serve to distract the genuine enthusiast from what really matters.

AT THE RINGSIDE

It is important to study the judging of as many judges as possible within your breed. By studying, I do not mean watching a couple of classes, showing your dog, then going home. I find it astounding that exhibitors, who aspire to judge, leave a show before their breed-judging is completed. How can they possibly learn anything if they do not bother to wait to see what is, in theory, the cream of the breed competing for the Challenge Certificates and Best of Breed?

Apart from the time spent preparing, exercising and showing your own exhibit, every spare minute of a show day should be spent at the ringside, learning – not in the bar, in the hope that you might bump into a show secretary who just happens to be looking for a judge for your breed at the next Open show!

You can never get a true judge's eye view of dogs from the ringside, but it is the next best thing. Get yourself into a judge's frame of mind. Look at the class as it assembles. Is there a dog there who immediately takes your eye? If there is, ask yourself why it attracts you? Study each dog as carefully as your vantage point allows, watching movement as well as stacked outlines. You may surprise yourself by finding a dog who did not have immediate impact impressing you when you look closely. Ask yourself why such an apparently correct dog did not appeal the minute he stepped into the ring. An interesting exercise is to jot down brief thoughts on a dog, keep your notes, and see how they compare to subsequent judges' critiques on the same dog. All these informal exercises serve as excellent grounding for the day you judge your first show.

THE JUDGE'S CHARACTER

It is generally assumed that, provided an individual has sufficient knowledge of the breed concerned, anyone can judge dogs. On the surface that may be the case, but in reality there are other less obvious qualities which are important in making an excellent judge.

Firstly, it is essential that a judge has great strength of character, and is capable of judging without fear or favour. It is no good attempting to judge dogs if you are the type of person who doesn't like upsetting others. Some people are just too nice to be dog judges! They worry about hurting exhibitors' feelings, and it is very hard to put people at the wrong end of the line with dogs which their owners adore. But judging must be free of sentiment. It is neither an art nor a science, yet a combination of both, and it should be as clinical as possible.

Over-sensitive people do not make good judges as they worry about the brickbats they may receive if they put down an exhibitor who is known for showing his displeasure. I have yet to encounter a judge who has stepped away from his ring free of criticism, and I doubt that I ever will. If you talk to enough people, you will find someone who thought he did a lousy job! So, criticism is par for the course and judges must have a thick skin. That is not to say that they should not be responsive to constructive and well-meaning criticism. Indeed, it can be most helpful and reassuring to have a more experienced judge point out where he feels you may improve in your assessment of a breed. However, this is a far cry from the carping and back-biting which emanates from bitter exhibitors who have not had a good day, and judges must be able to rise above that.

Impartiality is also something which must be exercised from that very first appointment onwards. Novice judges are often tested in their early days, and many fall into the trap of "playing safe". It takes a considerable amount of fortitude to put up an unknown exhibitor with an outstanding young dog, over a less-than-exciting Champion, shown by the judge who is judging you the following week – when you are looking for a third CC. Yet, it has to be done. In the early days of judging, there is sometimes the temptation in this situation to play safe, firmly believing that the next time you judge you will do it all absolutely straight down the line. But you never will. Once you have made that fatal mistake and compromised yourself, there is no turning back. You have tasted the forbidden fruit of convenience-judging, and thereon in you will never be able to break the habit.

The best piece of advice I was ever given, and it was freely offered by someone for whom I have the utmost respect, is this: "Judge as if today is your very last appointment. Judge as if you will never have the opportunity to judge again, and judge as if this is the appointment you would like to be remembered for." Think about it. In the centre of the ring, it may be helpful to remember these words of wisdom. You will see things more clearly, and will soon make up your mind about which is the right dog to put up.

Judges need a degree of self-confidence, though not to the extent that they are convinced they are God, and can do no wrong. The sort of self-confidence I am talking about is such that you should not automatically doubt your own judgement when you discover that you have "missed" a Champion, for example. Not all Champions are great dogs, and any Champion is only as good as the judges who awarded its Challenge Certificates.

A lack of self-confidence is very apparent to exhibitors and other judges who may choose to take advantage of the fact. Beware of the well-meaning advisor who, knowing you are shortly to judge a breed, deliberately enthuses wildly about one dog and mercilessly "rubbishes" another. There is usually a vested interest lurking in the background, and it is not very flattering to think that such a person believes he can influence you – it does not say too much about your reputation as a judge.

Judges will, if worthy of the name, discuss in depth with their peers the dogs they have judged, or maybe seen ringside, and which have impressed, or disappointed them. Such discussions do not necessarily involve either promoting or hatcheting a dog – among judges who have respect for their colleagues, this is all part of the never-ending learning process. Respect means listening to opinions, but not necessarily being influenced by them. There is a sense of mutual respect which means that every individual will listen to different viewpoints, but will have the confidence to make up their own mind.

WRITING A CRITIQUE

The ability to express yourself in print succinctly and articulately is a great asset to the dog judge, if not an essential. The gift of writing is not given to all, but every judge should be capable of explaining in print why he placed the First dog over the Second. Grammar is incidental, but the reasoning is important. Writing critiques on dogs from photographs can be excellent practice for the would-be judge. The trap many novice judges fall into (myself included) when they first start judging, is detailing a dog from nose to tail. Having said that, many of this country's greatest judges of yesteryear were true stockmen who were basically illiterate. With education not available to all, things were very different in those days, and while some of these characters may not have been able to read or write, they could spot a good dog at 100 yards!

In Britain, judges are only requested to write critiques on their First prize winners at Open shows and First and Second at Championship events, these being forwarded to the weekly canine newspapers, which publish them. In Europe, however, every dog shown has to be graded for quality against its Breed Standard by the judge (1st, 2nd, 3rd or Zero), who then gives each dog a fairly detailed critique.

This is, in my opinion, an excellent system; it is educational for both exhibitors and judges. At the end of the day, every exhibitor leaves the show having received the judge's opinion. That is not the case in Britain where you can be thrown out of a strong class of thirty with an excellent dog, whom the judge actually rated quite highly, yet win a First in a very weak class in which the judge hated them all!

The critique should, in my view, list the subject dog's major attributes, and its major faults. I know that some judges feel it is unfair to criticise a dog, because future judges may latch on to a failing which they may have not otherwise noticed. That is poppycock. If judges base their decisions on past critiques they have read, they should not be judging in the first place. Your critique should reflect how you saw the dog. It is your opinion on the day, and should not be coloured by the dog's past record or what influence it might have on future "judges". You can be critical in a critique without being brutal. "Preferred the more refined head of the winner" is much more palatable than "Head like a bucket", though they both, in reality, might mean exactly the same!

I think critique-writing is an important part of any judge's job, and it is a task which should be approached seriously. The "Nice head, moved well, unlucky to meet one above" is a worthless waste of space. It says absolutely nothing about the dog, and merely states the obvious in that the dog was unlucky to meet the winner. Of course it was, otherwise it would not have stood Second!

IN THE RING

Another asset to the judge is a clean and smart appearance. I like to see judges well-dressed and stylish, yet practical. Ladies who judge in stiletto heels seldom make a good job of it, and an abundance of jewellery can be as off-putting to dogs as large hats. Personally, I can see nothing wrong with a little individuality in a judge's dress, provided it doesn't go over the top. Gentlemen have little choice in the fashion department, but a smart and colourful jacket with contrasting slacks seems to me to be a quite acceptable alternative to the rather drab two-piece suit.

A good memory is invaluable to the dog judge, and not for exhibitors' faces, as some cynics would suggest! It is essential, judging under the British system, to be totally aware of what is what in your ring, and that involves being able to assimilate dogs you have seen in a previous class with "new" dogs appearing in that class for the first time. You have to be able to know how you placed your "seen" dogs earlier, and this calls for definite and consistent judgement and a good memory. Do not rely on your stewards to place "seen" dogs in order. You must be responsible.

Most dog judges are in some way extrovert by nature. If they were not, why would they choose to subject themselves to close scrutiny by a ringside week after week? Shrinking violets seldom make impressive dog judges as they are naturally self-conscious and look rather uncomfortable in the ring. They may be extremely knowledgeable about their breed, but their bearing in the ring does not inspire confidence, seeming to be rather apologetic about their very presence! A good judge must be in complete control of his ring, and he should be capable of coping with the occasional bossy steward. Good ring stewards are worth their weight in gold – bad ones are a nightmare. The ringside should be able to see immediately who is the judge and who is the steward. Sometimes it isn't that obvious!

*A good memory is
essential when
judging breed
classes.*

Smith.

*Large working breeds need large rings if their movement is to be assessed efficiently. Here a
large class of Bullmastiffs is being evaluated in a ring of appropriate size by the highly
respected young Molosser-breeds expert from Germany, Christopher Habig.*

Carol Ann Johnson.

Physical stamina is another essential of the aspiring dog judge. Judging dogs is tiring, both mentally and physically. Those who only judge occasionally usually return home after a day's judging with muscles aching which they never even knew existed, as a result of the walking and bending. You don't need to be an Olympic athlete to judge dogs, but if you're in pretty good shape it helps. You may recall that earlier I spoke of the need for a judge to have a certain self-confidence. Without it he will not only dither in the ring and create the impression that he does not really know what he is looking for, but he will be easy prey to forward exhibitors, who will happily promote their own dogs before he judges, and other judges who are only too keen to have anyone endorse their opinions. However, it is important that a judge is well aware that he is capable of making honest mistakes.

At the end of an assignment, it intrigues me to find some judges whose major concern is their next appointment. Having sorted out a breed, they never give their day's judging a second thought and are reluctant to discuss their placings with anyone who is sufficiently interested to engage them in conversation on the subject. Personally, I have yet to leave a show without having slight misgivings about one or more of my placings. They may be very minor positions about which the exhibitors concerned have already forgotten, but there can be a nagging doubt that maybe I was a little harsh on a particular dog because its handler persisted in moving it too fast, or perhaps the winner of Minor Puppy was unnervingly forward for its age?

ASSESSING A CLASS

A judge has just two minutes, according to Kennel Club guidelines, to assess a dog. That is not very long to really "get inside" that dog, but it is all we have. It is, however, sufficiently long enough to establish the overall quality of a dog, and the experienced judge will know as soon as his dogs come into the ring which dogs have aroused his interest, and which he would rather not be there. However, judges should be ever mindful of the fact that, whilst they have just two minutes to evaluate a dog, the exhibitor has had weeks to prepare the dog and plan how he can best hide a fault and fool the judge!

Speed and technique will vary from judge to judge. There is a widespread belief in today's climate of hobby exhibitors whose dog-showing activities are mainly a social activity, rather than a by-product of their breeding, that it is important that every exhibitor should be given their "money's worth" and to a certain extent this is true. Dog showing may not be as expensive a hobby in Britain as it is elsewhere in the world, but we are still talking about a not inconsiderable amount of money for each dog entered at a Championship show.

The Kennel Club guidelines' suggestion of two minutes per dog is, I suspect, quoted as an average, but in certain quarters this is interpreted as being literal. My belief is that any judge who takes his job seriously should spend longer on the better-quality dogs in a class than on the obviously inferior ones. This philosophy has got me into hot water with both our Kennel Club and some breed clubs, but I maintain that dog shows should be about evaluating the very best, the crème-de-la-crème if you like, and it is the judge's responsibility to sort out the better dogs as best he can.

If, for the sake of argument, you are faced with a class of twenty dogs, and as soon as the class assembles, you find ten which you think are interesting, quality dogs, and another ten which are obviously inferior, then my contention is that the job dictates that your major consideration should be getting the better ten in the right order. I am not saying that you should ignore the ten that you know, almost immediately, are not going to figure in your placings. They are entitled to a hands-on examination and their individual movement should be studied, but I find it surprising that anyone should advocate that a judge should waste unnecessary time on obviously inferior dogs, when there are excellent dogs in the same class, who collectively pose a difficult decision.

At Championship shows today we see many dogs which are basically "class fillers", and whose quality is not sufficiently high for them to be competing at that level. That is not to say that they are bad dogs, but they are outclassed, and it is sad that so many exhibitors thrust their dogs into competition of that degree when they would be far better off patronising the ill-supported Open shows. This sounds harsh and unfeeling, but as I have said before, judging dogs is not a charitable activity. The object of the exercise is to establish the best, not flatter the worst.

In my experience, the "faith healer" type of judge, who feels obliged to man-handle every square inch of a dog's surface area, believes that excessive handling suggests great thoroughness. Yet, it could indicate a lack of knowledge, depending on your viewpoint. I am not saying that my feelings on the subject are right; this is simply what I believe.

The beauty of the judging system in Scandinavia, for example, where every dog receives both a quality grading and a written critique from the judge, is that this problem does not arise. The dogs in which a judge is interested (in my example above, the "good" ten) would be given Firsts for quality, the others (my "bad" ten) a Second, Third, or Zero, depending on their overall merit. Having assessed the dogs, it is only those who have won a First for quality which return for the actual placings, so a judge does not have to worry about getting bogged down with mediocre dogs. They have had his written opinion and his quality assessment and so they leave the ring, never needing to be seen by the judge again. That, I feel, is an excellent system, but it is one which would be extremely difficult to implement in the UK. Our judges are able to cope with up to 250 dogs a day. With the critique system, the recommended average is 75. For us to bring in a grading and critique system, we would need many more judges, our shows would go on for longer, and at the end of the day, it would be the exhibitor who would be expected to pay drastically increased entry fees.

I am a great admirer of the Scandinavian dog scene for many reasons. Their system, with much smaller numbers than ours, is such that if you are interested in a breed, the chances are that there will be two or three more breeds in the same ring as yours. Consequently, there is the opportunity to see at close quarters, other breeds being judged. Watching other breeds can often teach you about your own, in a relative sense, and is good for broadening the outlook towards dogs in general. In our country, if you are involved with a numerically strong breed, and exhibit regularly at Championship shows, all you will ever see is your own breed and so your outlook tends to become rather insular.

Another advantage of the critique system is felt by the exhibitor. He will begin showing in "Puppy Shows" where dogs are not quality graded, merely given written critiques. From Day One he goes to shows and gets the judge's opinion. If, after ten shows, he has had ten fairly indifferent critiques, he will conclude that perhaps his dog is not as wonderful as he at first thought. He may then think hard about whether it is really worth spending a lot of money to go to Championship shows.

With our system, the equivalent exhibitor will show his puppy at ten shows, never get placed, never get a critique, no-one bothers to tell him what is lacking in the apple-of-his-eye, and he concludes that all dog shows are "fixed", the same "faces" always win, and he becomes bitter and twisted. Our system is really rather unfair to such people, and they cannot be blamed for their ignorance as there is no structure through which their puppy can be evaluated. It would be much kinder in the long run, and make for much more pleasant exhibiting at Championship level, if these Davids never tackled the Goliaths.

Chapter Three

WHEN TO START JUDGING

RING-STEWARDING

In the previous chapter I looked at ways in which the aspiring judge should attempt to acquire a very basic grounding in his breed, as an active exhibitor who uses his time at dog shows wisely. There are other ways in which a potential judge can try to equip himself for his first appointment. In my opinion, no-one should ever be allowed to judge at Open show level until they have some ring-stewarding experience. There are three things that stewarding will teach you – experience in the centre of the ring, experience of organising the ring, and the opportunity to learn how to use the judge's book – all of which will prove invaluable when you do eventually start to judge.

The very experience of ring stewarding will allow you to become accustomed to standing in the middle of a ring and exercising a degree of authority. This might sound trivial, but a lot of novice judges, who begin officiating without any stewarding experience, get to their first appointment, arrive at the ring and suffer from "stage fright". It can be a daunting experience, judging for the first time – you get out into the ring and see all those eyes on you, and your knees begin to shake! Getting in a few sessions as a steward will at least ensure that the sensation of being centre-stage is not a new one when you come to judge.

Canine societies of all levels are always looking for stewards, and start at the bottom. Write to your local societies, explaining that you have not stewarded before, but that you would like some experience in that field. They will be only too happy to hear from volunteers and will probably offer to place you with an experienced steward who will show you the ropes. After about half-a-dozen shows you should be fairly proficient and capable of stewarding single-handed, and you should then attempt to do so for a few more shows before you think of judging.

Stewarding will ease you into a ring-organising situation. You will need to instruct the exhibitors where to stand, and you will need to arrange the "seen" dogs from previous classes on one side of the ring. However, always consult the judge before attempting to do this. Some stewards blithely line up all First prize winners at the top end of the line, then all Seconds, then Thirds and so on. Personally, I prefer to have my "seen" dogs grouped into classes. In other words, those who met in Minor Puppy should be placed in order at one end, then those from Puppy next, then Junior and so on. It is very likely that a dog who won Third in Junior will be superior to Second in Minor Puppy, so the lining-up in order of previous wins is not very logical.

You should not order exhibitors around for the sake of it when stewarding. You are there to assist the judge. At the start of your stewarding assignment ask the judge if he has any special requests. Remember to line up the winning dogs in the centre of the ring, from left to right, as this is a Kennel Club rule. (Further essential information can be obtained from the Kennel Club's leaflet detailing the duties of stewards. You should be familiar with this before you ever steward.)

The third area where stewarding will help is in familiarising yourself with the judge's book. It is the judge's responsibility to mark up his winners and absentees, and sign the book. You should seize your stewarding opportunity to study how this is done. Some judges take on their first appointment when they have never even seen a judge's book and can easily make mistakes.

TRAINING OPPORTUNITIES

The majority of licensed shows in the UK tend now to consist of Open and Championship events. The smaller Limited and Sanction shows (which were considered excellent training grounds for judges of yesteryear) are very few and far between. Consequently, there is every chance that when you first begin judging, your first licensed show will be an Open event, and you will be judging just your own breed.

Judging just one breed is an exact form of judging in that all the exhibits are being measured against the same Breed Standard. Judging variety classes (in which more than one breed can compete) is an entirely different matter. You have to assess each dog against its own Breed Standard, and then evaluate the competition accordingly. It calls for quicker thinking altogether. It is variety judging which is called for in judging Exemption Shows (which are run for charitable causes and can be entered on the day) and Matches (where up to 64 dogs compete in a knockout type of competition, meeting in pairs). These events are invaluable training opportunities for judges, and my advice would be to certainly accept any invitations to judge such competitions before tackling your first Open show. The exhibitors will not expect the judges at these events to be experts, but they will give you the chance to look at a dog and sum up its overall merits quite quickly, without getting bogged down in "detail judging". They are, in my opinion, a very valuable part of the whole dog scene in Britain, and many a top dog has first been discovered as a raw youngster at such events.

In Britain there is no formal system of education for dog judges. Championship show judges are only approved by the Kennel Club by virtue of their level of previous judging experience, their direct involvement with the breed, and the opinion of the relevant breed clubs to whom the governing body refers. There is no hard and fast rule as to what is necessary in order for a judge to be approved to award Challenge Certificates. If there were, there might not be such widespread dissatisfaction at the approval of judges. In the absence of any formal training, it rests very much with the individual as to how he can train himself as a judge - if he has the inclination to do so, and I trust that he will. RTC Associates is a private company which organises a Judging Diploma Course which aims to teach the basics of judging, anatomy, ring procedure etc. Successful candidates graduate with a diploma, but this has not, as yet, been recognised by the Kennel Club.

BREED SEMINARS

As we assume that all judges begin judging "their" breed first, it is just one breed which they will initially want to study. These days more and more breed clubs are organising seminars which are aimed at educating judges. These vary in quality from the painfully inadequate to the quite brilliant, and there is no way of telling how beneficial any seminar will be until you have actually attended it. However, no matter how lacking any such function may prove, it is a pretty poor student who does not learn at least one thing during the day.

There are ways of evaluating beforehand the possible success of a breed seminar. Firstly, ask the club secretary for a programme so that you can see what topics are to be discussed, and who the speakers will be. It is important that the majority of time is given over to *the breed*. Far too many seminars tend to allow peripheral subjects to detract from the very thing most supporters have come to learn about. Listening to a Kennel Club official explaining the rules and regulations, and a vet discussing infertility may be very interesting, but they do little to improve your understanding of the breed. A little discreet market research on your part will soon reveal how capable, or inept, the speakers are likely to be. Not too many people in the dog world are experienced public speakers, but there are lots of successful breeders who have mastered the art of conveying their message articulately.

Go to as many breed seminars as you can, and please go to listen and learn. It is important that you should understand what you are being told, so if a point is mentioned which confuses you – *ask*. Far too many people hear something which they do not understand, and sit there and suffer in silence, too embarrassed to ask lest they should appear foolish. The irony of this situation is that there are usually a dozen or so other people in the audience who are equally baffled, yet they too endure their embarrassment. Have the good sense to raise your hand and ask for the point in question to be clarified. If nothing else you will emerge as the champion of the silent sufferers!

It is also important to remember that any seminar you attend will only be as good as its speakers, and as you listen to viewpoints which are put across so forcibly that you might be tempted to assume they were written in tablets of stone – always remember that what you are hearing is one person's opinion.

THE QUESTION OF "TYPE"

In many breeds, where "Type" is concerned, you will find that the breed may have several "camps", each of which advocates a slightly different type from the others. It is wise to remember that any breed may have several slightly different types (in this context, I would prefer the word "styles") within that breed, and provided they all conform to the basic requirements of the Breed Standard they should be equally acceptable. At the end of the day, such subtle variations boil down to personal preference and interpretation. It is wise to listen to as many different viewpoints as you can on "type", and then make up your own mind.

I have seen judges ridiculed for using the expression "my type" when complimenting a dog. Their critics claim that there is only one type – the one that is called for in the Breed Standard. However, Breed Standards allow considerable room for manoeuvre in interpretation of certain requirements, and just because a breeder may favour a line which produces dogs which correspond with his own interpretation of the Standard, there may be others who, if not identical, are equally correct within the context of the Standard. I have no difficulty understanding a judge opting for "his type" when faced with two slightly different animals which may be otherwise equally acceptable.

ATTITUDE

One of the most important aspects of any dog judge is his attitude - not his attitude in the ring which is something quite different – but his attitude to the job. A judge's approach to judging must be positive. He must look for dogs which he can put *up* because of their virtues, not for dogs which he can put *down* because of their faults. This is a fundamental point, and it is one which should be carefully and consciously developed from the earliest exhibiting days. It is a state of mind which can be cultivated through handling your own dogs and looking at those who have beaten, and lost to, them.

The first essential of a successful exhibitor is that he must know his own dog and be capable of assessing it totally objectively. You must know where your dog excels, and where he fails. When

I awarded Morag Boulton's Whippet, Ch. Pencloe Dutch Gold, his third and qualifying CC, and with it Best of Breed, when I first awarded Challenge Certificates to the breed. "Dutch" went on to win a total of fourteen CCs, all in the space of nine months, the last of which was won at Crufts 1992 when he went on to win Best in Show.

John Hartley.

you go into the ring, you must immediately be able to emphasise your dog's major virtues, but at the same time make every effort to conceal the dog's weaker points. This is not sharp practice. It is good handling. The best handlers are those who can, instantly, "collect" a dog and throw out an impressive outline which is guaranteed to catch the judge's eye. They know what to draw the judge's attention to, and they know what to disguise as best they can. The attitude of this type of successful handler is one of capitalising on virtues and minimising faults, and it is an attitude which is carried forward to judging. In my experience, it is often the judges who have been outstanding handlers who become equally outstanding judges. In the USA, for example, many of the top multi-breed judges were at some stage professional handlers, and the same level of professionalism which they exercised as handlers tends to be carried forward into their judging activities.

This positive approach should be applied to other exhibitors' dogs too. Do not home in on an obvious fault which may be quite minor in relation to the overall animal. Look for its good points, for it is these which create a dog's value, not its shortcomings. All dogs have faults, to a greater or lesser degree. Falling into the trap of seeking them out as a priority is the first step on the road to nowhere. Any fool can see if a dog has light eyes or is cow-hocked. It takes a connoisseur to appreciate its exquisite balance, exceptional head and expression, and the like. Some judges seem to derive a macabre satisfaction from finding something wrong with an otherwise outstanding dog, and having done so thrust it to the heavens like buried treasure!

I vividly remember one judge of my acquaintance, assessing a particular dog who was enjoying a remarkable run of success. The dog was exceptionally typical of his breed, wonderfully constructed, and his movement was very impressive. The judge concerned placed this dog Second below another which, to the eyes of the average ringsider, was considerably inferior in overall quality. After he had finished judging, he could not wait to tell me that the big winner had two dropped incisors, whereas the dog he had placed First had a perfect mouth. I will never forget the relish with which he told me of those two teeth! I need hardly tell you that the "perfect mouth" subsequently had a career which was less than spectacular. Indeed he never made his title. The "dropped incisors" lived to fight another day. This was a classic example of fault judging. Allowing one obvious fault to blind you to a dog's multitude of virtues is a sign of totally negative judging. Fault judges soon become known for it, and they never prosper. In time they tend to contribute as much to the breeds they judge as the mediocre dogs (but lacking obvious faults) they invariably put up. Both lack quality.

IMPARTIALITY

I have discussed the mental approach to faults and virtues, and now I must say something about the attitude towards friends, acquaintances and enemies. Before anyone judges, they should be clear in their own mind that they are capable of treating all exhibitors equally. Given the failings of human nature, I know this is not easy, but it is a great help to look at a dog you really admire, and imagine it is owned and handled by your arch-enemy. Do you still admire it as much? Similarly, study a dog you really do not like at all. Imagine that dog handled by your bosom pal. Is it now really quite so awful?

Judges are often faced with a well-known exhibitor who may be handling a rather indifferent dog. In their formative years, some judges might try to talk themselves into thinking the dog is better than it appears, simply because of who is on the other end of the lead. Just imagine that dog with a complete newcomer. Now, would you really be giving it a second look under those circumstances? OK, so why are you agonising over whether or not to use the dog now? These mental approaches can never be underestimated in the whole make-up of the successful dog judge, and they should be worked on from the time you first become involved

THE PSYCHOLOGY OF JUDGING

Over the years much high-minded material has been committed to print on the subject of dog judging, yet seldom have I ever read anything which addresses the psychology of the subject. Most writers on the topic write as if dog judges are outside the human race, and immune to human weaknesses. However, it is worthwhile looking at the demands made on a dog judge and his reactions to them.

THE PRESSURES

In an ideal world, anyone who judged dogs would do so totally impartially and the results with which he came up would be the same, regardless of who handled which dog. In many cases I am sure that this is so, but anyone who believes that this always happens is being incredibly naive. In the "good old days" of the stockmen judges who regularly assessed all manner of livestock, fur and feather as well as dogs, tales abounded of established judges who varied from less than scrupulous to downright corrupt. When I began showing dogs it was rumoured that certain all-rounder judges had their "price lists" and some had even been known to divert a Challenge

The show must go on! I am judging Best of Breed in Bull Terriers at a show in South Africa in the late seventies. The reason for the plaster cast is that I had been the victim of an armed mugging in Johannesburg shortly after arriving, which resulted in all the tendons in my right hand being severed with a knife. Emergency surgery was performed, which proved 100 per cent successful, and thus South Africa saw its first one-armed judge. Happily, none of the breeds judged were trained for man-work! Laurie Bloomfield.

Certificate in favour of a bottle of whisky! I firmly believe that this sort of corruption, if ever it really existed, has been stamped out, but to pretend that all dog judges are devoid of any political inclinations would be silly. It is important to recognise this fact so that well-intentioned, younger judges avoid falling into the same trap.

JUDGING APPOINTMENTS

One of the blights on the present-day dog scene, which has apparently caused considerable concern at the Kennel Club, is the often quite blatant exchanging of judging appointments between show secretaries and officials. Given a large enough ring of co-operative show societies, who may have rather weak committees and ambitious officers, it is all too easy to spread judging appointments around to such an extent that the participating "judges" can swiftly build up an extensive portfolio of classes which, on paper at least, may be sufficient to satisfy the Kennel Club Judges Committee that they are experienced enough to award CCs.

This is where referral to breed clubs can be helpful, and they tend to be quick to point out that certain proposed Championship show judges of their breed are not sufficiently interested or capable to be placed in a position from which they can create Champions. At the same time, it is hoped that the Judges Committee is sufficiently worldly to realise that some breed clubs tend to be a little biased in their assessment of non-specialist judges and, on principle, will not support anyone who is not one of their number. The "job swap" problem is causing untold damage to the standard of judging and hopefully the Kennel Club will one day find a way of eliminating it.

As I have mentioned earlier, the best dog judges must have great strength of character and must be able to treat exhibitors equally. They will find the best dog, regardless of age, breeding or ownership, and reward it accordingly. They will not pander to breed club officials who exhibit under them, as do some judges in the hope of getting their names on breed club judging lists. The breed clubs have a degree of power, and it is fascinating to watch some ambitious multi-breed judges as they plot their campaigns. A visit to a ring to watch certain "targeted" breeds becomes a regular occurrence, they chat to as many exhibitors as possible, tell them that their dogs are wonderful and that they either won deservedly or were "robbed". Soon they have discovered the identity of the major breed club officials in the breed, and off they go to ingratiate themselves in the right quarters. Many see through it, but a surprising number fall for the "sweetness and light" treatment and before you know it, our enterprising judge has his breed club show invitation!

HONEST JUDGING

It is the hope of all conscientious judges to create the impression of doing a good job. They are not unduly bothered about criticism which stems from "sour grapes", but they are anxious to appear capable and honest. The perception of honesty varies, and it is my contention that many judges do not judge to the best of their ability because, subconsciously, they are attempting to appease the ringside and prove how unbiased they are. There have been many occasions when I have witnessed excellent dogs going down to inferior dogs, simply because the judge of the day happens to be known as a good friend of the owner of the superior dog. The thought process goes something like this: "The ringsiders know how friendly I am with Mary Jane and that our bloodlines are very similar; they are all expecting me to put her dog up in this class, so I'll show them how straight I am."

Consequently, poor Mary Jane gets dumped to second, her best friend having studied her dog until she has found something which displeases her. The judge is confident that the defeat is justified, and she convinces herself that she has done a good "honest" job. You hear a lot of twaddle talked ringside about judges who put up their friends. In my experience, more exhibitors suffer by being put down under their friends than win unfairly. I really believe that most judges try their best, and that few are really dishonest. The biggest problem is that so many judges tend to be rather weak, and lacking in self-confidence. They do not have the necessary belief in their own opinion to go out on a limb, and give top honours to a dog they have never seen before, handled by an exhibitor they have never seen. In its own way, this is a kind of dishonesty, because they are failing to judge dogs "cold" with no regard for ownership or reputation, presumably due to a self-admitted lack of knowledge?

It is very easy for a judge to develop a perfectly respectable reputation as an adequate judge. From the start of his career he puts up good dogs, never does anything too radical, usually finds his Best of Breed winner in the Open class, never puts big winners too far down the line, and does his best to share the awards around among exhibitors, never being overly generous or harsh towards any one in particular. He tries to be all things to all men, endeavours to keep all "camps" happy, and never awards Best of Breed to a bad dog which causes those watching the group to throw up their arms in horror. Yet, this can be the type of judge who regularly misses a really outstanding youngster if it is not "well-owned", so busy is he trying to keep everyone happy. He is generally accepted to be a "nice man", never upsetting anyone and never criticising anything or anyone. He is not the worst kind of judge, but sadly he will never have an original thought in his life, and when judging he finds it difficult to look at dogs in isolation.

The fact that so many judges are preoccupied with what others might think of, or rather how they might interpret, their judging can also be to their detriment. No judge likes to be accused of playing "follow my leader", but when an outstanding dog appears who has enjoyed a deserved run of success, it is quite stupid to approach such a dog with the sole intention of trying to demote it. There is nothing clever about putting a good dog down. That is more of a crime than putting a bad dog up. Once a judge becomes established, he can very swiftly acquire a reputation based on his past performance. Some judges are known as "giant killers" as they seem to habitually knock big winners. Others appear to be "star finders", often delighting in finding a new dog from obscurity.

JUDGING YOUNGSTERS

Some judges seem to have a penchant for awarding top honours to young Juniors or even Puppies. I have been criticised in the past for giving CCs to youngsters who are not fully mature. Critics of such actions maintain that you have to judge "on the day" and an immature dog should not be able to beat a fully mature rival. My answer to that is that maturity in itself is no virtue. Quality and type do not change with age. The knowledgeable judge should know how a dog of a particular breed should look for its age. You would not expect a Dobermann or Boxer of ten months to be as "finished" as an adult, there will be a certain looseness and some scope – somewhere for the puppy to go. Given an outstanding, if immature youngster up against fully mature dogs of inferior quality, I would opt for the young dog every time. Time will not improve the older dogs; it could be the making of the youngster. This is not judging based on how you think the dog will finish up – that is utter folly, for none of us have crystal balls – but it is making a reasoned decision based on the dog on the day at a certain age.

CONSISTENCY

When you begin judging your breed, you should have a fairly clear picture in your mind of how you perceive ideal type in that breed. You should always try to find that type in your winners, though it is not always easy. A judge hopes for a line-up of unbeaten dogs, which are even and basically out of the same mould, but remember, you can only judge what the exhibitors put in front of you, and sometimes you will find yourself having to place dogs which fall short of your ideal type. If you judge honestly, and consistently, always trying to find the same type, when you have judged for a few years exhibitors will know the sort of dog you are looking for, and the experienced amongst them will be able to work out for themselves which dogs you should, or should not, like. Over the years you will probably find that your entries may get smaller. Far from being a criticism of your judging, this is often a compliment in that the consistency of your judging enables exhibitors to have a good idea of the sort of dog you most admire. It is an irony of the sport, but the best (and most consistent) judges do not always attract the biggest entries. The judge who judges to one type one year, and a completely different type the next, or who never seems to have a type in mind at all, will be better supported by those exhibitors who will feel that anything could go up, so it's worth an entry. Such judging can be a lucky-dip, but an inconsistent track record can often result in a big entry. Strange, but true!

Chapter Four

THE BASICS OF CONSTRUCTION

It is perhaps largely due to the fact that, in Britain, there is no formal system for the training of judges that so many who attempt the job are surprisingly ignorant of one of the most fundamental aspects of the dog – its basic construction. Few, if any, other animals appear in so many diverse shapes and sizes as the dog, having been modelled to fulfil various functions through man's selective breeding. Yet, the fact remains that all dogs, whether they be Chihuahuas or St Bernards, have basically the same bone structure and a skeleton which is made up of the same number of bones. This is something which many judges seldom think about. True, these bones will be of different shape and size, but each dog will have the same basic number, apart from in the tail where there can be some variation. While it is not necessary to have a vast knowledge of anatomy to become a capable dog judge, it is unthinkable that anyone should wish to judge dogs without some basic comprehension of the canine skeleton. Without wishing to go into too much technical detail, I would like to discuss the skeleton in terms of judging dogs.

THE SKELETON

The spinal column consists of five groups of vertebrae: the cervical vertebrae, the thoracic vertebrae, the lumbar vertebrae, the sacral vertebrae and the caudal (or coccygeal) vertebrae. The seven cervical vertebrae make up the neck. The first two, the atlas and axis, differ considerably in form from the other five as they are specifically adapted to allow for almost total freedom of head movement in all directions. The form of the cervical vertebrae will dictate length and shape of neck. The thirteen thoracic vertebrae form the upper part of the chest and provide anchorage for the ribs. They help set the pattern for the topline.

The lumbar vertebrae number seven, and they form the upper part of the loin or coupling, and may commonly be referred to as the back. They act as a support both for and to the abdominal muscles. In conjunction with the thoracic vertebrae, they contribute largely to outline. The three sacral vertebrae are fused and, therefore, they cannot move independently. They provide an area of firm attachment for the bones and muscle of the pelvic girdle, and their location is referred to as the croup. In terms of judging, they can affect tail-set to a marked degree. The caudal or coccygeal vertebrae form the tail, gradually reducing in size from the sacral junction to the tip of the tail.

The forequarters essentially consist of the scapula (shoulder blade), humerus (upper arm), radius and ulna (fused to form the lower arm), carpus (wrist), metacarpus (pastern), and phalanges (toes). The hindquarters begin with the pelvic girdle, two fused halves attached to the sides of the sacral vertebrae. In the pelvis lies the acetabulum (hip socket) into which the femoral head fits. The hind "legs" consist of the femur (thigh), tibia and fibula (lower thigh) - the stifle or knee joint

The Skeleton

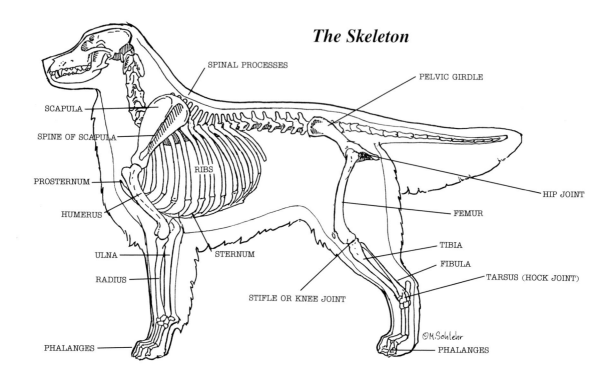

SPINAL PROCESSES

PELVIC GIRDLE

SCAPULA

SPINE OF SCAPULA

RIBS

PROSTERNUM

HUMERUS

ULNA   STERNUM

RADIUS

PHALANGES

HIP JOINT

FEMUR

TIBIA

FIBULA

TARSUS (HOCK JOINT)

STIFLE OR KNEE JOINT

©M.Schlehr

PHALANGES

Marcia Schlehr

comprising the lower end of the femur, the patella (kneecap) and the upper portions of the tibia and fibula – along with the tarsus (hock), metatarsus (rear pastern), and phalanges (toes). The dog has thirteen ribs on each side of the thoracic vertebrae. Below the ribs is the sternum (or breastbone), consisting of eight sternebrae, the foremost of which is the manubrium (prosternum), which is very prominent in breeds such as Dachshunds.

It is the relative positioning of the various bones in the fore and hindquarters which will have a large part to play in determining movement in a dog, as their correlation form angles which will enable ease of action. With a few exceptions, the shoulder blade in most breeds should slope upwards and backwards at an angle of approximately 90 degrees or more with the upper arm. With insufficient angulation in this area, a dog will be incapable of extending its forequarters efficiently and will lack "reach". The stifle angulation called for by most Breed Standards will vary from around 110 degrees to 130 degrees, and insufficient or excessive angulation will result in either lack of extension, or a rather stilted movement lacking drive.

It is the efficient construction of the skeleton, enhanced by correct muscular development, which will produce a balanced, sound dog. Imbalance of any one area will detract from the efficiency of the overall animal as a functional machine and, therefore, judges must be able to work out in their own minds the reasons for physical shortcomings. As far as dog judges are concerned, the combination of skeletal muscles, especially in their upper layers, is important because it

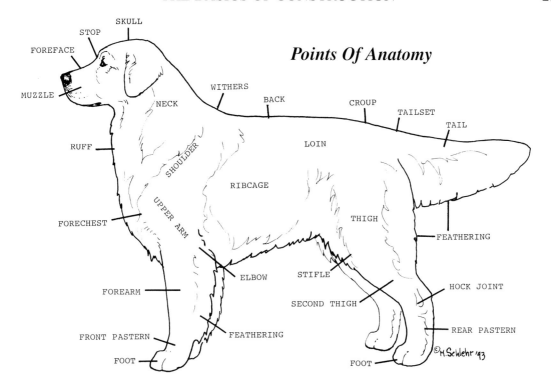

Points Of Anatomy

Marcia Schlehr

contributes greatly in creating the dog's external appearance or "finish", as well as being largely responsible for movement. Muscle development and strength are particularly significant in the forequarters, as these are attached to the ribcage by muscles only. Without strong muscular development, shoulders become loose, backs can soften, and the whole dog's capacity for efficient and sound movement will be reduced and impaired.

It is important that judges should familiarise themselves with the skeletal construction of dogs in general, and the breeds they undertake to judge in particular, as the make-up of the various breeds will differ dramatically. Furthermore, it is the differences within the construction of the breeds which are the starting point of breed type. A Whippet with the bone structure of a Scottish Terrier would just not be a Whippet.

Two of the major causes of unsoundness to be found when judging dogs are hip dysplasia and patella luxation. Without an understanding of correct construction, a judge could never expect to recognise such conditions when faced with them. It should also be remembered that the skeletal conformation of each breed helps to establish breed type, in other words, making each breed an individual, which brings me to the whole question of type with all its complexities.

Chapter Five

WHAT IS TYPE?

You will have noticed that in earlier chapters of this book, I have repeatedly referred to "type". So what is "type", and why is it so important? Type is one of those infuriating words which is exceedingly difficult to actually define. My own understanding of the word is that it refers to the combination of all the component characteristics which make a breed unlike any other. In other words, if you consider a Newfoundland, for example, with its broad and massive head with barely perceptible stop, small deeply-set eyes and short, clean-cut muzzle, its massive bone and large webbed feet, its deep and broad chest, and oily water-resistant coat, all these features help to make it a Newfoundland rather than a Flat Coated Retriever or a St Bernard. A Newfoundland which lacks these major breed characteristics can never be considered wholly typical.

ESSENTIALS OF TYPE

In a large number of breeds it can be said that, above all, the head and expression tend to dictate type. This is not to say that when judging such breeds we should judge on heads alone, as we should always be conscious of the need to assess any dog on its overall picture. Having said that, no matter how magnificently constructed a Boxer for example, may be, and how excellent its movement is, if its head lacks rise of skull, is too long in foreface and the nose has no "tilt" to it, that dog can never possess type for its breed.

It is important to be clear in your own mind as to what virtues are directly related to type, and which aspects are not so important in determining type. Let us consider a Pekingese which is well boned, has a body of the correct shape and construction, and a wide, shallow face. If that dog has light eyes, it does not render the dog untypical. The light eyes are a fault of a cosmetic nature, but they do not detract from the overall picture of a typical specimen. On the other hand, if we have a similar Pekingese who has darker eyes, and yet who is extremely light and shelly in bone, the dog loses type as the great bone and substance in a small frame is one of the essentials of this breed.

Type is the first impression a dog gives. It is the overall picture of the animal. Type allows a dog to walk into a ring and say "I am a Dobermann," or, "I am a Chihuahua". When a dog walks into your ring you should ask yourself: "Is this what the breed is all about?"

CHARACTER

Inextricably linked to type is disposition, character or "attitude". The mental approach of any dog is as much a part of its breed type as head, expression, tail carriage etc. Just imagine finding an Afghan who, stacked, creates an impression of quality and balance, with a beautiful head and eye and correct conformation. Suppose that, when the class first moves around the ring, the dog

Bearing is very much a part of type, as illustrated by Chris and Julie Amoo's Afghan Hound, Ch. Viscount Grant. I qualified this dog for the finals of the Dog World/Spillers "Pup of the Year" competition when judging at Richmond Championship show. "Gable" then went on to win the finals and ended up winning Best in Show at Crufts. In all he won six Hound Groups and was the top winning Afghan Hound of 1986 and 1987.

Marc Henrie.

slouches about, head and tail down. What do you do? Personally, if the dog also moved in this manner when it was gaited individually, I would not place it.

The Afghan Standard calls for "strength and dignity", "head held proudly", and it should move "with a style of high order". An Afghan who fails in these fundamentals, and does not have that goose-bumps exotic quality just isn't an Afghan. When an Afghan takes off, you should almost be able to visualise it turning its head, and flicking its hair, like some upper-class model before a camera-shoot. So you see, bearing is very much a part of type.

Terriers without a typically game temperament are unworthy of the name. Toys (bred specifically to be companions) who are shy or sharp cannot be typical.

CONSTRUCTION

Construction, make and shape are also related to type, but maybe not to such a marked degree. Dogs can have constructional shortfalls, and yet still be essentially typical – a slightly long back, slightly straight shoulders or stifles, less than ideal spring of rib – are faults which should be recognised, but they do not detract dramatically from type in an otherwise excellent dog.

It is important to know, long before we start judging, why the breed we are judging is constructed as required in the Breed Standard. I have already mentioned the importance of going through the Standard and finding out "why?" When we understand why a neck should be of a certain length, pasterns of a certain angulation, loin and couplings of a particular type, we will be able to evaluate conformation more positively. If a physical shortcoming would prevent the dog from fulfilling its original purpose, then its seriousness should be considered greater than another fault, which may appear equal, but which does not, in fact, affect the dog's functional duties to any degree.

I have already discussed the attitude towards faults, and I hope that I have stressed sufficiently the need to dwell on virtues much more than faults. However, it is essential that the judge already has his perception of faults (and their seriousness) in perspective, before he judges.

FETISH JUDGING

This brings me to the subject of "fetishes", a particular failing of some breed judges. When judging as a breeder-judge, it is only natural that your major likes and dislikes will have been coloured by your own experiences as a breeder. If, for the sake of argument, you have had a problem for generations with straight shoulders, and have eventually managed to improve that aspect of your own stock, the chances are that when you judge an obviously straight-shouldered dog, you will be particularly hard on it. You have experienced the problem and know how hard it can be to get rid of, therefore, you are not going to encourage the fault. That is quite understandable, and it makes differing opinions equally plausible.

However, you may be rather critical of another judge who is equally tough on gay tails, for example. It may be a problem you have never had to cope with, so it does not bother you unduly. All judges will have slightly different priorities, and there is nothing wrong with that. If we all thought the same, what would be the point of dog shows? It is, however, a totally different matter to develop a "fetish" for certain breed faults and to allow them to totally blind you to a dog's attributes. Much as you may dislike a particular fault, it must always be seen in perspective.

I remember some years ago listening to a Boxer breeder who announced to a bar full of tired exhibitors that she would never, ever, place a Boxer which had an unpigmented third eyelid. Some months later, I made a point of watching the lady judge. She was true to her word. In her prize winners there was not a pink haw in sight, but there were wry mouths, straight shoulders, and roach backs in abundance!

In my view, the most serious faults are those which can be described as "type faults". Constructional faults, unless they are severe, may not be so serious. As an example, in a breed which calls for moderately well-angulated hindquarters, if a dog is slightly straight in stifle, yet is balanced, and wonderfully typical with lots of other qualities, I would be forgiving of his slight lack of angulation. In my experience, dogs who have a tendency towards straightness will always

breed and reproduce her like, or hopefully still better, she needs to be out of the ring for up to six months – often longer in heavily-coated breeds. For a dog to reproduce himself, all he needs is a few moments of passion in an exercise-pen! The point of heavily campaigning a bitch, never taking a litter off her, and sometimes never even allowing her a normal season, until she is well past her "sell-by" date escapes me. If we accept that the show ring is a measure of breeding success, and the two are inextricably entwined, the worth of an outstanding bitch can only be proved if she herself is bred from. Is a wall full of rosettes really more important than a litter of potential stars?

Judges too can get caught up in the battle of the sexes. Here, the temptation to judge "for the Group" can often prove too hard to resist. Given an extremely good male in magnificent coat, full of "attitude" (which may stem more from his hormones than his breed type!) and a slightly superior, more classically typical bitch, who may be carrying a perfectly adequate jacket for her sex, and showing steadily, if not with the excitement of the intensely extrovert male, who should win? The purist would take the bitch, but I suspect that the vast majority would go with the male and keep the crowd happy. After all, "he's the one to send into the Group"!

It is true that, as dog lovers, we tend to anthropomorphise our animals. We like our dogs to be big and butch, and our bitches to be feminine and elegant, but when you read through the Breed Standards, how many actually call for dogs to be particularly masculine and bitches feminine? (Usually, the only specified differentials are those of height or weight, though the German Shepherd Dog and Bull Terrier Standards do call for obvious masculinity and femininity.) This really stems from our human conception of sexuality, and it is something we have imprinted on our dogs. We should, however, always be conscious of our perception of masculinity in the show dog, and not confuse it with coarseness and a lack of quality. It is possible to have masculinity with quality, as many of the male dogs featured in this book show.

In reality, many breeders will confirm that their best litters have been bred from bitches who have been rather strapping girls with plenty of substance, whose more precious sisters (who may well have been more successful in the beauty stakes) frequently prove disappointing as producers. Indeed, in the Toy breeds, most strive for a pretty, rather refined male, and a "dual purpose" bitch who, aesthetically, may appear more "masculine" than the male.

The term "elegant" is a word which can, and often does, cause misunderstanding in canine circles. Some assume it to mean over-refined or generally underdone, yet have you not seen Shire Horses which could be described as elegant? It is a word I would regularly consider using in relation to Great Danes, Boxers and Dobermanns for example, yet in its true sense it is in no way incompatible with substantial and strong.

Judges should always bear in mind that overt sexuality in the dog is not as important as correctness in relation to the Standard. Too many insist on ultra-masculine dogs and very feminine bitches, and as a result may miss an exceptionally good specimen simply because it is not sufficiently masculine or feminine to conform to their perception of the breed. Often, such dogs which may be overlooked by some judges, can be of great value to their breed.

Chapter Six

HOW TO JUDGE

YOUR FIRST APPOINTMENT

Having obtained some experience of ring stewarding, and, hopefully, having judged a few dog matches or exemption shows, you will eventually receive your very first invitation to judge your breed at a Kennel Club licensed show. It will probably come from a society fairly local to you, your name having been put forward by a committee member or official who has noticed that you have been winning in your breed fairly consistently. Societies are often keen to give a "new name" a chance as, being an unknown quantity, a first-time judge will attract a numerically good entry.

The society should invite you in writing. If you receive a telephone call from the secretary, asking if you will judge, it is important that you ask them to confirm the invitation in black and white. The Kennel Club is very strict on societies keeping to the rules, and there is an accepted procedure for formulating a judging contract. When you have received your written invitation, reply by return with your acceptance. The invitation should ask for details of your expenses, though many shows which are inviting lots of judges will ask you to judge "in an honorary capacity" (i.e. for nothing!). I will leave it to you to decide whether this is acceptable to you. Most judges begin judging in this way, considering it a great honour to be asked as a novice, and are therefore only too happy to offer their services free of charge.

Often, Open shows will ask if you are able to bring your own steward. Sometimes it is helpful to have a familiar face with you in the ring for your debut, but this can be a two-edged sword. If you are a little nervous (and if you are not, you wouldn't be human!) and spend too long talking to the spouse/friend/relative who has agreed to act as your steward, you may find exhibitors jumping to all manner of unsavoury conclusions as to why you needed to get in a huddle with someone who has a catalogue in his hand! My advice is, take a friend for moral support, but make sure they stay out of harm's way. Having a stranger to steward for you might be better, in the long run, for a novice judge.

Your reply to the secretary should confirm that you are happy to accept the appointment. It should also indicate that either you will be pleased to judge without expenses or, if not, you should state clearly what you require by way of remuneration. Specify either a definite sum of money, or travelling expenses in terms of a specified quantity of gallons of petrol at the current price. All these things might sound trivial, but there should be no room for misunderstanding on either side. Furthermore, be sure to ask in your letter of acceptance that the secretary subsequently confirms the appointment in writing. This is a Kennel Club requirement, but it is one area of show-running where many secretaries lapse.

Start a judging file in which you can keep all relevant correspondence. For each appointment you

should have:
1. The initial invitation.
2. A copy of your letter of acceptance.
3. The secretary's confirmation of the appointment.

PREPARATIONS

Nearer the day, you should receive from the secretary a schedule for the show with details of your entry, your admission passes and the time at which you are expected to arrive. Make a point of studying the schedule to ascertain whether or not there is a telephone at the show venue. If so, highlight the number. Should anything untoward happen on your way to the show, it is important that you are able to telephone the secretary to warn him of your delay. You do not want to create a bad impression on your first appointment.

The night before the show, read through your Breed Standard again. It can be surprising how easy it is to forget certain clauses. Take the Standard with you to the show. It is no disgrace to place it on your table so that you can check anything about which you have doubts. At least exhibitors will realise that you are taking your job seriously. Decide what you are going to wear. The outfit should be smart but sensible, and comfortable shoes are absolutely essential. Never, ever, buy new shoes for a judging appointment. Take wet weather gear with you too. You never know when you will be called on to judge in the rain, so be prepared. Make sure that you have a pen (which writes!) to mark up your judging book, and then try to get a good night's sleep. It won't be easy. I can still recall the sleepless night I had before my first-ever show!

Be sure to allow yourself plenty of time for the journey. Gauge your time of departure to arrive at the requested time, and leave an hour before! Traffic can cause untold delays, and sitting in a traffic jam, panicking that you might miss your first appointment, is not to be recommended.

AT THE SHOW

On arrival at the show, report to the secretary. You will be given your judge's badge and book, and probably envelopes from the weekly dog papers, which contain letters asking you to submit your critiques in the pre-paid envelopes, which are included. Most shows will offer you a cup of coffee in the hospitality area where you will meet your co-judges. Make sure you know where your ring is.It is a good idea to have a look at it beforehand so you can work out in your own mind where you want the dogs to line up. You can discuss this with your steward, who you may have met over coffee, or will meet for the first time at the ring. Well before your start-time pay a visit to "the smallest room"!

When you get to your ring, discuss procedure with your steward, and make sure that you are happy with the position of the judge's table if your breed is a small one which needs to be examined on a table. Check that it is secure and does not wobble, and that it has a non-slip surface. If this is not the case, politely ask the steward if he can do something about it. Most shows provide rubber mats for examination tables. In cases where they do not, it is surprising how many exhibitors are only too keen to provide mats or carpet-pieces for the judge's table!

The chances are that you will see many exhibitors whom you know very well. Cutting them dead is stupid, but so is engaging them in deep conversation. A polite "good morning" should keep everyone happy. Study your judging book so that you know how many dogs are in each class, paying particular attention to those which contain repeat entries of dogs seen in earlier classes. You will have to concentrate extra hard in these cases if you are not to reverse a decision unwittingly. You must also make sure that you know exactly what awards are to be made. Apart from Best of Breed, you may be required to declare a Best Opposite Sex, a Reserve Best of Breed or a Best Puppy, or any combination thereof. The steward calls in the first class. The exhibitors line up their dogs around the ring, and now it's up to you ...

IN THE RING

Never assume that your steward is infallible. He might offer to mark your absentees for you, but especially as a novice judge it is a good idea to go around the ring with your judging book, ticking off those numbers which are present, and then marking the remainder "Abs" at the end of the class. Do not be too keen to mark a dog absent as some stragglers might turn up late. We are not as keen in Britain to implement the "third shout" rule as the Australians are, for example. In that country if an exhibitor has failed to show up after the statutory steward's calls, they are marked absent. Maybe that is why, in Australia, exhibitors are so wonderfully prompt at getting into the ring!

If you sit at the judge's table and watch the dogs coming into the ring, one by one, you should immediately have a good idea of which dogs you really like. Study the exhibitors setting up their dogs. They will assist you no end, as they invariably concentrate on their dog's major fault. Just try it – notice how many of them spend ages fiddling around, trying to sort out a dodgy front or a weak topline. This is a very useful tip, and one which usually holds true. Most exhibitors know what is wrong with their dogs, and it is always the first thing they try to put right before you leave the table! Once everyone has their dogs standing in traditional show pose, take a leisurely look along the line, studying each dog in profile from a distance (you can never accurately assess a dog's outline if you are standing on top of it), and then look at its head, expression, general forehand and hindquarters at close quarters. You have probably already seen some dogs which made a particular impact at first glance.

Standing in the centre of the ring, ask the class to move around the ring once, or maybe twice. I find that as the first class is invariably Puppy, most of the exhibits will lack experience. Consequently, a second circuit of the ring will give them more of an opportunity to get into their stride. Is there anything going around which takes your eye? Make a mental note of it for the individual examination. Sometimes, depending on the size of the ring, your breed, and the number of entries, circuiting a whole class at the same time may not be terribly practical. Twenty young Rottweilers in a relatively small ring are not conducive to a trouble-free "send around". Remember that you are in charge. Split the class up if you like, and send it around in two batches of ten, or four of five, if you feel that would be more advantageous for the dogs and your assessment of them. You have now seen all your dogs moving around the ring. You know which caught your eye when stacked, and which appealed going around. If there is one dog who impressed you in both situations, the chances are that he is going to figure somewhere in your final placings.

INDIVIDUAL EXAMINATION

You will now need to assess each dog individually. Do not rush the handler. Give him time to set up his dog as he thinks fit. Be firm but sympathetic when approaching the dog. First, stand back and look at the profile. Is it balanced? Is it typical? Is it as you would expect of this breed in this class? Stand in front of the dog and study expression. Many breeds' expression will change when alert, as when in repose their ear carriage will be relaxed and the keenness is not there in the eyes. In such breeds, it is quite acceptable to make some sort of noise to see the dog's reaction. Just a little squeak will often bring the ears up, and the whole head becomes much more typical and expressive.

Some judges first offer their hand to the dog. Personally, I do not think that is such a good idea. I

Even in the smaller breeds it is important to check a dog's bite. Here judge Olga Hampton examines the mouth of a Lhasa Apso, handled by Juliette Cunliffe.

Carol Ann Johnson.

prefer to place one hand on the dog's skull and run it back down the neck in a stroking motion. That usually relaxes the dog and establishes contact. If the reaction is a grumbling from below, it is advisable to ask the handler to show you the dog's mouth, and be on your guard. Judges need to have fairly speedy reflexes with some dogs! On this point, if a dog attempts to bite you, the judge, you should excuse it from the ring and make the appropriate report to the Kennel Club. There is no room at dog shows for dogs with poor temperament.

I automatically ask the age of every dog I judge, even in the non-age classes. I think it is important to know how old a dog is if we are to make a plausible assessment of its merits. As I have mentioned in an earlier chapter, a ten-month-old puppy should not have the finish and substance of a three-year-old. I also find that asking the age establishes some verbal contact with the exhibitors, some of whom may be rather nervous and apprehensive. Just that brief exchange of words can serve to relax them a little. Check the dog's mouth, ascertaining that the dog's bite is correct for its breed, and remembering that there is more to a mouth than incisors. I must admit, I am not unduly bothered about the occasional missing premolar in the smaller breeds, but in the sporting and working dogs I think missing premolars must be considered a fault (though not a disqualification, as some would suggest).

By now, through your match meetings and exemption shows, I hope you have established a routine of "going over" a dog. No two judges adopt the same procedure. Having dealt with expression and bite, I tend to run my hands down a dog's throat to its forechest, check bone and feet, then carry on with neck, shoulders, ribbing, loin, hindquarters, tail-set and coat, also checking for entirety in the males. There will be certain breed characteristics which need to be looked at

When judging Pekingese it is important to ascertain that the dog is "amazingly heavy when picked up" and that the weight is correctly distributed, with the centre of gravity being nearer the front than the rear. Here I am assessing Marjorie MacDonald's Ch. Guzmac Be My Desire who later won Reserve in the Toy Group.

While any dog should be able to move soundly, head and expression should also be studied carefully in all breeds. Here, I am assessing the forehand of Alison Price's Griffon Bruxellois bitch, Ch. Marquant Miss Scarlet, to whom I later awarded the Toy Group.

Carol Ann Johnson.

closely in some breeds, but not in others. The webbed feet of breeds like the Newfoundland, the black tongue of the Chow Chow, the double dew-claws of the Briard and Pyrenean, the varied shades of blue and tan in the Yorkie's coat and so on. There are also ways of handling different breeds. It is customary in Britain to carefully pick up a Pekingese and study its head face-to-face, as it were. This is not because so many Pekingese judges were at one time rather short-sighted, as one wag once announced, but because the weight and substance of the breed should be such that a Pekingese is surprisingly heavy when picked up, and it is also necessary to determine when picking one up that the weight is distributed correctly. In other words, the dog's centre of gravity is much nearer the front than the rear if it is correctly constructed. These little breed idiosyncrasies will be familiar to you if you are "in" that breed. It is when you come to judge other breeds that they can cause embarrassment as they can so easily reveal a judge's lack of knowledge.

So, you have "gone over" your first dog in your first class. Your handling of it should be thorough without being excessive. In my view, some breeds need less "hands on" assessment than others. In a short-coated breed like, for example, the Whippet, it should only really be necessary to check mouth, muscle tone, coat and skin condition and testicles in the male. Everything else should manifest itself when the dog is gaiting and, being a running hound, movement should be considered of prime importance. In such a functional breed, outline, shape and movement will obviously be far more important than an exquisite headpiece.

With heavily-coated breeds it is obviously necessary to handle a dog more, as the coat can disguise lack of body condition and, to a certain extent, constructional shortcomings, yet even in the hairy dogs construction will reveal itself in its true colours when the dog is gaited at the correct speed. My mention of correct speed is deliberate. Moving a dog too fast can help to disguise constructional faults which are all-too-obvious if the dog moves more slowly. Feel free to ask a handler to move again, but at a slower pace, if you feel there is something which may be masked by speed.

ASSESSING MOVEMENT

Having "gone over" your first dog, ask the handler to move it. Now the majority of British judges automatically ask for a triangular pattern of movement. Personally, I have never favoured what I call "The Great British Triangle", but rather I prefer to see a dog moved straight up and back, and then around the ring in a circle, continuing its circle back to its line-up position. Let me explain why ...

It is relatively easy to assess accuracy of "up and down" movement within a few strides, so by using a straight line in opposite directions we can determine how true a dog is in front and rear. However, it is the profile movement which I consider to be of greater importance, for it is by studying side-gait that we can see if a dog retains balance in its whole outline, whether it exhibits reach and drive, whether it is unusually high-stepping, and whether or not its topline and head carriage is as excellent as the handler suggests when it is stacked.

In the "triangle" form of movement I find that, largely due to some rings being rather small for the breed concerned, dogs will see the ring-rope ahead, and begin to put on the brakes well in advance. They also have to negotiate two sharp corners in the triangle, and therefore their stride will be interrupted. Using the circular method of gaiting, however, the dog has no corners to deal with, and a much greater length of circuit without any breaks or speed changes. This affords a much more fluid action and presents the judge with the opportunity to study the whole dog, rather than simply its forehand or hindquarters. As the secret to dog judging is the perception of the overall picture, it makes perfect logic to me to spend time studying a dog going around, rather than watching it deal with a rather restricting triangle. I will say, not for the first time in this book, this may not be the view of the majority of judges, but it is how I see things.

Some judges, I know, still prefer the triangle because they say in this way each dog gets the same minimum treatment, and they can then dispense with the also-rans before getting down to the business of judging the real ones. The decision is yours, of course, as to how you wish to see dogs move individually. Only you will know what will prove most revealing to you.

Having completed your detailed assessment of the first dog, make a brief mental summary of it. Something along the lines of: "Liked the type, lovely head, a bit long in body, moves well in front but close behind, covers the ground well and has excellent topline on the move". Some judges when they start off like to make a few brief notes after each dog. I think this can be a mixed

Liz Dunhill, the talented Rottweiler breeder and handler, moves Ch. Fantasa Clockwork Orange to illustrate her outstanding profile action which shows freedom, reach and drive along with the correct and typical topline. It is vitally important that judges study profile movement where they will obtain a far better perception of the overall dog in motion, rather than with simply "up and down" movement. I awarded this Rottweiler bitch her first CC when she was still a Junior.

blessing. What ringsiders hate to see is judges referring to their notes when making their actual placings, rather than looking at the dogs. It suggests that they are not capable of assessing the overall animals, but are running the list of their component parts through a mental computer and adding up the scores.

However, I have found that when dealing with very big classes of twenty-plus dogs, it can be helpful to note the standard of movement in each dog. This way you will not be taken in, and be tempted to pull in a stunningly outlined dog who moved abysmally. At one time, dogs were judged on a points system, but I have never found this to be a very constructive method, as those valuable intangibles such as quality, balance and attitude were never given points!

Move on to your second exhibit and repeat the same basic procedure. Try to be consistent in your examination of dogs. Never start at the head with one dog, and the tail with the next. This

Sharon Pinkerton gaits her German Wirehaired Pointer bitch, Sh. Ch. Bareve Beverley Hills, in the Group ring at Crufts where she demonstrates the exceptional movement and carriage which has accounted for so many top honours. The only bitch in an American-sired litter of thirteen, she was the top winner in her breed for 1988/90/91, and currently holds the breed record with twenty CCs, sixteen of them being with BOB. Her CCs were won between seventeen months and seven and a half years of age. She was Best of Breed at Crufts four years running and is a Gundog Group winner. She was overall Runner-Up when I was judging the Pedigree Chum Champions Stakes at the 1988 Welsh Kennel Club Show.   David Dalton.

looks awful from ringside, and it does little to aid your logical thinking. Work your way through the class until you have seen every dog at close quarters and moved them individually. Now comes the hard part. Making your decision.

THE PLACINGS

Depending on the size of the class, it may be that you would prefer to make a "short-list", in which case, go around the class selecting those dogs you wish to remain for further consideration. But before you pull anything into the centre of the ring, say aloud to the exhibitors "I am making a selection, but am not placing". It can be rather disappointing for an exhibitor to be pulled in first, only to end up at the other end. Always let your exhibitors, and your ringside, know what you are doing. Before making your short-list, do check with the stewards how many actual prize cards are available. These days it tends to be either four or five. In a class where you have five cards to give out, it is most unfortunate if you have a short-list of six, so that just one poor soul leaves the ring empty-handed.

Your first class will probably be Puppy, and it is safe to assume that as this is your first appointment, you will be judging a breed which you have both owned and bred. You will be faced with a ring full of exhibitors, many of whom will be familiar to you. Some will be friends, some may be strangers. The chances of your sworn enemies showing under you will, in fairness, be slim, but should they do so remember that they are there for your opinion of their dog, and not to give you the chance to settle old scores. In a Puppy class you will find puppies of between six and twelve months at the majority of Open shows. In theory, some of the exhibits can be twice as old, and therefore twice as mature, as some of the others. As I have said earlier in this book, it is important that you – as a breed judge – should fully understand how your breed should look at a certain age and stage of development. The physically bigger the breed, the less mature it will be. Some of the Toy breeds frequently win CCs from the Puppy class. In Great Danes or St Bernards it would be unthinkable, unless in very exceptional circumstances.

As you have been going over the dogs in your first class, all sorts of things might be coming into your head. You will be aware of the fact that some of these exhibitors will be judging your own dogs in the near future. You will be acquainted with the winning some of the dogs have done, because they have been in competition with – and probably beaten – you at some stage. You will doubtless know the breeding of several of the dogs you are judging. Some may even be sired by your own stud dog, or out of a bitch of your breeding. You will be conscious of these facts, and you would not be human if you did not admit that fact, but it is essential that you try as best you can to block such things out of your mind.

Look at it in context. Some of the dogs you are judging will be shown by unfamiliar handlers. You know nothing about them or their dogs. For you to be even considering the past history of those exhibits who are known to you, is to place those strange handlers at either a disadvantage, or an advantage, depending on how you look at it. The impartiality of judging is a discipline which can be self-taught, and the exercise of imagining a dog with a different handler, which I mentioned earlier, can often prove invaluable. It is not that difficult to pretend that you have just arrived from the Planet Mars and are meeting these dogs and handlers for the first time. Through constant practice it is quite easy to judge dogs "cold", but it must be worked at.

When evaluating puppies in your breed you, as a breeder, will know how much can be forgiven in the name of immaturity, and how certain aspects of a dog will hardly ever improve, no matter how old the dog is. It is this knowledge which is vitally important and can often give you the advantage over a non-specialist judge. Your experience in this field is terribly valuable to you, and you should utilise it. I have covered elsewhere in this book the different approaches to judging dogs against bitches. As a breeder-judge you should be in a position to judge your breed positively and seek out the best specimen in your entry, rather than getting bogged down thinking which stands the best chance in the Group and beyond. You have a certain experience in your breed, showing and breeding dogs of quality. You are familiar with your Breed Standard. You know how dogs should move and why. This is all you require – if you have the right temperament and attitude – to judge dogs well.

In my opinion, an individual's interpretation of a breed is governed very definitely by the best specimen of that breed they have ever seen. In other words, if you have been surrounded by mediocre dogs, and have never taken the time and trouble to look closely at superior dogs – hopefully the top winners in your breed – and tried to understand what makes them big winners, your standards when judging will not be that high. If, on the other hand, you have made a concerted effort to look at the very best available, and to analyse their exceptional merit in your mind, you will carry with you, in your mind's eye, the picture of the best example you have ever seen.

Breed Standards are all very well. They are the written descriptions of perfection. But you have to be able to relate them to real dogs, and I know, in my own case, my mental perception of any breed I judge is based on the best example of that breed I have ever seen. You tend to carry with you a mental picture of a dog you considered great when you began to learn. Sooner or later, an even greater one will appear who may then make your original yardstick seem less than perfect. This is all part of the learning process. As we continue in this fascinating world of dog showing, we are constantly upgrading that mental picture of our ideal as we see better and better dogs. Sometimes, alas, we may be forced to stick with our original ideal as nothing seems to compare, but here the memory can play tricks.

I learnt a valuable lesson when I was researching an article some years ago. For a very long time I had carried with me a mental ideal of a particular breed, feeling sure that nothing since had ever matched one long-since dead bitch for overall quality. During my research, I stumbled across a photograph of the bitch in question and suddenly found myself questioning her dubious shoulder placement, and was her head really that plain? In truth, when we are in our formative years we are less discerning and more easily pleased, as we have limited knowledge and experience. As we learn more, we become more critical and less forgiving. In reality, I concluded that should this bitch appear in today's show rings she would be lucky to make her title.

But going back to your first appointment, and your first class. You have evaluated your Puppies and placed them in order of merit. A good indication of a dog's worth is whether you would like to take it home with you, and hopefully you are able to find dogs of sufficient quality that you could happily own them. Work your way through the classes systematically, at all times concentrating on the dogs rather than any other factors, and always trying to find the best one regardless. Please do not treat your judging appointment as a chance to share the cards among as many exhibitors as possible.

If you find yourself faced with an exhibitor who consistently brings in the type of dog you admire, and they happen to be the best in their classes, put them up – even if they have to win every class. Logically, if they are established breeders who have been successful with formulating a line which breeds to type, if you like one you should like the others. I see far too many judges putting up a male of one type, then the same exhibitor comes in with the feminine replica of the male, only to be beaten by something inferior and quite off-type, simply so that the judge can say he "shared it around". This is not judging dogs. You may be accused of favouring a particular line or kennel. However, if that produces the dogs you think are the best representatives of their breed, you have no cause for concern. You are judging *dogs*.

As you are starting judging at Open show level, you will not be flooded with outstanding dogs. You will have many dogs of moderate quality which are very close in overall merit. You will be faced with dogs which may be otherwise equal, one moving badly in front, one moving badly behind. You will have excellent movers with indifferent heads, and indifferent movers with excellent heads. In situations such as this, simply stand back and ask yourself which is more representative of the breed? If you are judging a breed which is essentially functional, would its slightly plain head really affect its ability to do its original job? If you are judging a breed which was bred specifically for its aesthetic and companion values, would its rather straight hindquarters actually impede its life as an elegant pet? These are the sort of decisions you will have to make,

An obviously delighted Anne Wells receives a first CC from me with her imported Bernese Mountain Dog, Fero v. Buetingen of Glanzberg at Bernfold, after a run of several Reserve CCs. Interestingly, at the same show, all the unbeaten puppies who challenged for the Best Puppy award were sired by him.

Carol Ann Johnson.

and many judges tend to get bogged down with analysing detail, and end up failing to see the wood for the trees. Given two dogs in a close decision, which one best says: "I am this breed". It can be an interesting exercise in situations such as this to simply silhouette the dogs and judge them on outline. When you have to decide a minor placing between two dogs, neither of which is outstanding, this I find is the best way to come up with an answer.

As you get through your classes, you may find a really excellent dog which is totally new to you. As you are involved with this breed, you may find yourself wondering why you haven't seen it before, and may begin to doubt your own judgment. You may even be considering putting a well-known, if rather inferior, winning dog First, and playing safe by putting the exciting newcomer Second, "just in case" you might have missed something.

Forget it! Go with your instincts every time. If that dog is as good as you think it is, sooner or later some other more courageous judge is going to find it and start it off, and when he does, rest assured, you will be kicking yourself and regretting not having the bottle to follow your gut feeling. You may not always be right, but when a dog appears who gives you that indescribable "buzz", go with it. If you make a mistake, you have made it honestly and you will learn from it, but never ever go against your natural instinct, for following their instincts is what makes the great judges great.

BEST OF BREED
When you are judging for Best of Breed, remember the wording on the award: "Best of Breed", not "Best Bet for the Group" or "Flashiest Dog in Show", but Best of Breed. In other words, the best specimen of the breed who will do most good for the breed. In your winner you should be seeking a dog which has excellent breed type, who immediately hits you as a specimen of its breed. It should have the correct disposition for the breed, it should be as sound in construction as possible and it should present a balanced picture either standing or moving. It should also have

"quality", a degree of refinement with all the integral parts blending into an harmonious whole where no one virtue seems to overshadow the others. You should be proud of the dog you are sending into the Group.

AFTER JUDGING

Having completed your assignment, made all the required awards, signed all the paperwork and thanked your steward, take yourself off for lunch and when you have time, study your judging book and re-read your comments which will form the basis for your critique. You can study the catalogue too, having finished, and you may be in for some pleasant surprises when you analyse the breeding of the dogs you have put up.

Do make a point of watching your Best of Breed winner in the Group. I cannot understand judges who finish their breed and lose interest. Watch how your representative fares under the All Rounder, and when he has finished judging, feel free to ask for his opinion. There are not many judges who will not discuss the dogs they have judged, and if you ask for an opinion, be prepared to accept it. You may not agree with it, but think about it. Was there some point that the Group judge found distasteful which you have been particularly lenient on? He may be wrong. You may be wrong. It is possible that, in context, both of you are right, but do think about the comments made on your winner. It is all part of the learning process.

WRITING YOUR CRITIQUE

You will probably have decided to write your critique after the show. Some judges, myself included, prefer to write them in full in the ring with the dogs in front of them, but this might be a little challenging for novice judges who are inexperienced at critique writing.

Put thought into your critique. It should reflect your opinion. It is not an opportunity to flatter or condemn. It should be straight and to the point, and I do not hold with the viewpoint that because a judge has given a dog a First Prize he should never criticise it. It may have been the best in a poor class, and if there is something you disliked about the dog, feel free to say so, albeit as tactfully as possible. Too many judges pussyfoot around their critiques, never saying what they actually felt about a dog. It is absolutely essential to have the Breed Standard to hand when writing your critique in order to check your facts. So many judges burst into print and make fools of themselves. For example, praising round bone in a breed which should have flat bone, complimenting a short back in a breed which should be fairly long, and so on. Always check your critique against the Standard.

The exhibitor paid for your opinion and critiques which say something to the effect of "Too well-known for comment" suggest that you are incapable of having an opinion, or are not sufficiently interested to form one. With the critique comes the job of describing the dogs which won and explaining the reasons why. All judges should be clear in their own mind that they are using the correct terminology for what they are attempting to describe.

TERMINOLOGY

The business of understanding and using the complex vocabulary of the dog world can be daunting. I remember once attending a breed seminar, a well-organised event, which aimed to acquaint those outside the breed – and some newcomers from within – more intimately with the subtleties of Breed Type. I would not profess to be an expert in the breed concerned, but I was familiar with the Breed Standard and had judged the breed several times, though not at Challenge Certificate awarding level. I was fairly happy with my own basic concept of the breed, but any help with honing the finer points had to be welcome.

Early on in the main speaker's presentation, he spoke in a very positive manner of the "correct roach back", using various illustrations of dogs which excelled or failed in this respect. I was, up to this point, wholly confident that the Standard for the breed called for "a slight rise over the loin" – quite different from a roach back which, in my understanding, starts from behind the withers as in the case of the Bulldog. Suddenly doubting my knowledge, I discreetly consulted the Breed Standard to check my facts. I was not mistaken. A slight rise over the loin was what was called for, and, furthermore, in a detailed and illustrated explanation of the Standard (which was included in the impressive brochure with which we had been presented) a roach back was clearly included as being a serious fault!

Not being one to suffer in silence, as tactfully as I could I asked the speaker to clarify the correct topline of his breed. It transpired that what he was looking for was exactly the same thing I was seeking, but his choice of terminology was incorrect. Had this point not been discussed at length, dozens of potential judges of that breed would have left the room with quite incorrect ideas, and have gone off searching for those wonderful roach backs when asked to evaluate the breed.

Driving home afterwards, it occurred to me that terminology is a terribly important aspect of our sport, as without a universal understanding of the words and expressions used, communication can never be wholly achieved. Mastering terminology should be one of the first priorities of would-be judges, for without a complete understanding of these "tools of the trade", it is impossible to converse, let alone write, knowledgeably about one's chosen subject.

There are hundreds of textbooks which to a lesser or greater degree deal with canine terminology. The best of these in my opinion is the late Harry Spira's book, which is so succinctly titled *Canine Terminology*. With the aid of excellent line drawings, this volume aims to explain what is what in the world of dogs. However, not everyone possesses a copy of this excellent book, sadly now out of print in the UK. The British Kennel Club publishes a *Glossary of Canine Terms* in similar format to its Breed Standards, but this is not illustrated and some of the explanations I find a little lacking.

It never ceases to surprise me how many people have totally different ideas as to what constitutes a wry mouth, and here I regret that our governing body's glossary is of little help. As the explanation of a wry mouth, it simply says "lower jaw does not line up with upper jaw". So, is any breed that requires an undershot mouth guilty of possessing a wry mouth? I am frequently asked by novice exhibitors to explain this not uncommon failing, and I attempt to do so by pointing out that there is a basic crookedness of the lower jaw which is such that the relative position of the left canines is different from that of the right canines. If you could imagine a vertical line drawn down the centre of the foreface, head on, the right half should, in theory, mirror the left. When the mouth is wry, it will not.

"Upright" is another adjective that seems to confuse, and I have heard this normally derogatory word used flatteringly to describe a dog whose overall demeanour would have been better described as "upstanding". There is a big difference. The word "upright" is commonly understood to refer to shoulder angulation. On a more elementary level, how many newcomers have you encountered who hear experts talking of a "beautifully short" dog, and assume that they are referring to height, rather than length of back? To the initiated this might sound ridiculous and stupid, but let us not forget that someone new to the dog game will be faced with an entirely new vocabulary in which words may not be what they seem.

There is a temptation to take a lot for granted when we reach a certain level in our learning curve, but it is always advisable to ascertain that whoever we might be talking to, or writing for, understands exactly what we mean by any given word or expression. Only the other day I was in the company of several experienced judges when it became apparent that one of the group thought that the second thigh was what is in reality the hock! This lady had been a top-level judge of her breed for some years, but it was obvious that she had never taken the trouble to acquaint herself with the most fundamental aspects of canine anatomy.

We can only contribute to the progress of dogs in general if we can communicate totally with one another, and be as articulate as possible. We should, therefore, be absolutely certain that we have a common language that we can each use, safe in the knowledge that we can avoid any misunderstanding. We should all endeavour to say what we mean, but sometimes we might not always mean what we say!

Chapter Seven

WHERE NEXT?

KEEPING RECORDS

After the show it is important that you document your judging. The prospect of judging at Championship level may never have occurred to you, but if you enjoy judging your breed, and are proved to be quite proficient, there is no reason why, in time, you should not award Challenge Certificates. It is essential that you keep accurate records of your judging, as when the time comes you will be asked to complete a detailed questionnaire for the scrutiny of the Kennel Club Judges Committee. You will need to list details of dogs which you have owned and bred, the names and numbers of those who have won their way into the Kennel Club Stud Book, and details of your inclusion on any Breed Club judging lists. It will also ask for full details of the shows you have judged.

You should, from your very first appointment, draw up a master-list containing essential information. A simple form, based on the actual questionnaire which you will eventually be asked to complete, would look something like this, with entries listed under the appropriate headings.

RECORD OF .... BREED CLASSES JUDGES

Name of Society	Type of Show	Date of Show	No. of Classes	No. of Dogs	No. of Entries

It is important that you transfer all the details of each judging appointment to this list after each show, and remember to deduct absentees from the relevant figures. You should also keep the actual catalogues, as occasionally the Kennel Club will ask you to provide these when they are carrying out spot-checks. In the past, well-established judges have been banned from judging for including inaccurate information on their questionnaires, so beware!

MOVING ON

After your first appointment you may well receive further invitations. There possibly have been officials or committee members from other societies watching you from ringside. If they were impressed, and heard favourable noises from the exhibitors who showed under you, they may make a note of your name for further reference. Try to avoid judging too frequently in the same catchment area. Most societies will put both a time and distance stipulation on any appointment they offer, which is quite justifiable. After all, you do not want a poor entry, and neither do you want to see the same set of dogs very soon after your previous appointment.

Judging out of your own area will also be a better test of your ability. You will not be sidetracked by knowing virtually all the dogs and owners, so your mind will be clearer to concentrate on the job in hand. It will also give you a broader outlook on your breed, as it could well be that your area is particularly weak, or strong, in that breed and seeing them at the opposite end of the country will make you realise how lucky, or unfortunate, you are.

For a judge to be successful, he must be genuinely interested in what he does. After that first appointment, make a note of your winners and spend Friday evening scouring the dog papers to see how the dogs you put up have fared under other, more experienced, judges. If they have won, read their critiques and see if they correspond with your own assessment of a particular dog. Over the coming months you will soon be able to work out for yourself if you were right or wrong when your winners go on to better things or sink without trace.

There seems to be, today, something of a stigma associated with the admitted desire to judge – which is a totally different thing to actually canvassing for appointments. Given that your background provides you with some substance as a potential judge, that you enjoy the process, and that you are genuinely interested in your breed, there is nothing wrong with wanting to judge – provided you want to do it the right way. You must remember that you have just begun to learn about your breed, through being asked to assess the dogs of others, and you should put that opportunity to good use to increase your knowledge of the breed and your understanding of all its subtleties and nuances. Apply yourself to the job with enthusiasm, and read as much as possible about not only your own breed, but dogs in general. Talk to the older judges and ask for their opinions. Take full advantage of the great experience and knowledge they have to offer, for some years hence they may not be around.

With each Open show you judge, you will encounter a new question, a new problem, and you have to deal with it yourself. There is no-one in the middle of the ring to help you out. If you come up against a difficult decision and are not happy with it, do not be afraid to discuss it with a more senior judge. They will, hopefully, give you their opinion, and will be impressed by the fact that you are genuine in your desire to learn, and do not assume that you already know it all. Remind yourself that it is an honour to be asked to judge other people's dogs, not a right, and do not abuse the privilege.

CLUB SHOWS

The normal progression within most breeds is that show officials invite enthusiasts who have been judging the breed at all-breeds Open shows for at least five years to officiate at a one-breed Club Open or Limited Show. These are highly prestigious events and are considered to be just one step away from a Championship appointment. At such breed club shows you will probably have your very first taste of large numbers, and you will usually discover that the quality of the dogs at this level will be much higher than you have previously encountered at the smaller shows.

This will mean that many of your classes may not be so easy to judge as those you have had to sort out before. You will find more dogs of better quality, calling for decisions which might not be so clear cut. Here you have to get "inside" the breed much more deeply, always remembering your clearly established priorities for breed type. You will also have more "high profile" exhibitors to deal with than you may have done at the smaller shows, and so it becomes even more important that you judge dogs, regardless of ownership. Although a lot of exhibitors who are used to winning may get a little steamed up in the heat of the moment, the more experienced of them will realise when a judge is doing his best and give you credit for that in the long run. They may not necessarily agree with what you have done, but if they can follow your reasoning and see what you are looking for, you will maintain their respect.

CHAMPIONSHIP SHOWS

After a Club show or two, you could receive an invitation to award Challenge Certificates. Your excitement will be boundless and the long wait until you hear whether or not you have been "passed" by the Kennel Club will be interminable. Provided you have fulfilled the basic criteria set down by the Kennel Club and the Breed Clubs, you may go through with flying colours, but if you have rubbed up a few breed club officials the wrong way, they may attempt to halt your progress. Happily this is not always the case, but it can and does happen. Even so I firmly believe that judges who always attempt to do their best will surface in the end.

When news comes of your being approved for the first Championship show, you will be thrilled, but as the day gets nearer you will become more and more aware of the responsibility entailed in helping to create Champions. Now, more than ever, you may find exhibitors being unusually friendly, asking to use your stud dogs, expressing interest in your next litter, and so on. Take it all with a pinch of salt and try to clear such things from your mind. When you are judging your own breed, it is hard to stay away from the ring when you are regularly exhibiting your own dogs, so you will just have to cope with being Mr Popularity for a few weeks.

Judging at a Championship show should be no different from judging at any other show, except for the pressures which you may imagine. Remember those little pearls of judging as if this were your last appointment, and you should not go far wrong. Britain is a comparatively small country. Exhibitors can drive from the southernmost show to the northernmost in ten hours. In the USA this would be considered a short drive! At most of our Championship shows the same hard-core of exhibitors will be showing a fairly consistent entry, with slight regional variations. The largest number of Championship show judges officiating will be breeder-judges – people who specialise in one breed which they show, breed, and in which they have dogs available at stud. Consequently, the British breed ring tends to be a rather incestuous place, where breeder-judges regularly meet to do battle. The established breeder-judge has one extra problem with which to contend, and that is judging stock which comes from his own bloodlines, or indeed which he has actually bred.

IN THE BLOOD

Nothing causes more comment than the apparent nepotism with which some judges seem to treat dogs which are connected to their breeding. It is a vicious circle of a problem, and one to which I believe there is no answer. Many breeders will have spent a lifetime developing their own particular kennel in an attempt to produce dogs which consistently produce their like. This will be done usually by a sustained programme of line-breeding; in other words mating bitches to dogs to which they are closely-related in order to emphasise their good points and establish a "family likeness". It can be assumed that most breeders like what they keep and what they show. If such breeders offer dogs at stud, the chances are that these dogs will produce puppies for other breeders which will develop into adults of the type admired by the stud dog's owner. When the owner of the stud dog comes to judge, it is therefore perfectly logical that he is likely to be drawn to the progeny of his own dogs – given that the offspring have overall merit, and that their major virtue is not merely their parentage!

Often established breeders will officiate overseas and find themselves putting up dogs which go back to their breeding. These will be dogs, handled by exhibitors, which the judge has probably never seen before, but if he has his eye in for a definite type, it will stand to reason that he can find that type – wherever he happens to be. A lot of nonsense is talked by dissatisfied exhibitors when a dog wins whose breeding has some connection with the judge of the day. How many times have you heard: "Well, of course, it's by her dog!" I have no difficulty in understanding why a breeder-

When Löwchen breeder and exhibitor Sally Gibbons turned up at the Welsh Kennel Club Championship show in 1990, she had never won a CC. At the end of the day she had won two! I awarded both CCs to her home-bred litter brother and sister, Ch. Tethall Damson Design and Ch. Tethall Daffodown Dilly who soon gained their titles. Interestingly, their sire, the record-holding Ch. Shirekhan Skean Dhu, had won his first CC and BOB from me when he was a puppy, while Skean Dhu's sire, Ch. Duncara Homespun, had been my Dog CC winner as a Veteran when I judged the Lowchen Club's Championship show in 1984.

judge should be drawn towards stock which is of his breeding, and it is to be hoped that when he gives such a dog top honours, its overall quality warrants the award. Where some judges come unstuck is that they are so hell-bent on making their own dog Top Sire in one of the many competitions which now exist, that they are seen to favour their own dog's progeny, whether the offspring concerned are good, bad or indifferent. This is totally another matter.

Just as some judges are seen to be unduly lenient on stock sired by their own dog, others are unusually hard and subconsciously penalise very worthy animals because of their breeding connections. This is not good judging. It is putting good dogs down in a misguided attempt to appease the ringside and create an aura of respectability and fairness. If, in your opinion, the best dog on the day happens to be sired by your dog, it should win. If others cannot see its obvious merit but only its breeding, that is their problem, not yours.

JUDGING HOME-BRED STOCK

A still more sensitive area, and one which causes much more adverse comment, is the practice of showing a dog under a judge who is actually its breeder. Here we enter a minefield. The Kennel Club rules state quite clearly that a judge can judge any dog, unless it has been in his ownership within the twelve months previous to the show, or it has been handled in the show ring by the judge during the same period. It has been suggested that a rule should be brought in which would prevent dogs ever being shown under their breeder. That, I feel, would be a retrograde step.

To begin with, there are some numerically weak breeds where most of the top winners stem from one major breeder, who is happy to sell good stock for others to win with. When that judge comes to officiate, if the top-quality dogs which have dominated the breed under other judges are denied the chance to show, would that not weaken his entry considerably as far as quality and type is concerned? Furthermore, given that a dog has enjoyed a great run of success under all sorts of judges, and is a current contender at Group level, should that exhibitor be robbed of the chance of furthering its career at top level, simply because its breeder happens to be judging the breed at a major show?

I don't think that the majority of sensible exhibitors have a problem with exhibitors showing under their dog's breeder, if the dog already has an established career. I feel that tempers run high when a dog which has had a fairly indifferent record manages to win its title through gaining CCs under its breeder, her husband, and the exhibitor's best friend! That will encourage onlookers to jump to their own conclusions. Just because a dog carries the judge's affix, he does not necessarily have to like that dog. If he does, all well and good. In situations like this, the problem usually lies not with the judge or the exhibitor, but the mischief-makers!

If the Kennel Club was to introduce a preventive rule on this matter, where would it end? Outlaw dogs sired by the judge's dog, dogs owned by exhibitors who sit on the same committee as the judge, or by exhibitors from the same area? There is no limit. I feel it is a matter for exhibitors and their own conscience. I know some breeders prefer not to have dogs they have bred shown under them. They are entitled to that viewpoint. Others actively encourage the practice. We each have our own code of ethics. What would appear unfair to one judge will seem quite acceptable to another. I well remember the outcry when a judge awarded a CC to a dog owned by his daughter and son-in-law. The reason for their showing was that they "wanted his opinion". Personally, I would have thought that they could have asked for, and got, that over Sunday lunch, rather than paying to enter a dog show!

While it may not be easy, breeder-judges should aim to evaluate dogs whose breeding is connected to them in any way as objectively as possible. They should not favour them, but neither

Some breeders seem to establish such a definite type that it is easy to find dogs of their bloodlines, regardless of where they are judging. Molly Coaker of the Homerbrent Cavaliers is such a breeder. At the 1992 Adelaide Royal show in Australia I awarded BOB and the Toy Group to the British export, Aust. & N.Z. Ch. Homerbrent Cartoon, owned by Jenny Egan (handling) and Bronwyn Murdoch.

C.S. Photography

should they penalise them. Faced with such dogs, the judge will be damned if they do and damned if they don't put them up. If you put them up, it will be said that you are leaning towards your own stock. If you put them down, it will be swiftly suggested that you do not have a very high opinion of what your breeding produces. In the long run, it is a no-win situation.

Chapter Eight

BRANCHING OUT

It is often presumed that once a judge has been approved by the Kennel Club to award Challenge Certificates in a breed, they are approved for life. This is not the case. The approval is given for one appointment, and one appointment only. Should breed clubs express written disapproval of a judge's first Championship show appointment in their breed, the Kennel Club may choose to turn down the judge concerned should he receive a subsequent invitation to award CCs in the same breed. Overseas judges find it difficult to understand our system, as foreign Kennel Clubs tend to license judges, and once they have been given breeds, they have them permanently, unless found guilty of some heinous crime.

TAKING ON NEW BREEDS
Although judges begin working with their own breed, there is a strong possibility that, long before they award their first set of Challenge Certificates, they will have been asked to judge other breeds at Open show level. Unfortunately, this usually stems from economics, as many Open shows are reluctant to employ individual judges for every single breed they classify. It is flattering to be asked to judge another breed, but it is not to be recommended, unless a judge is really interested in that breed and prepared to learn about it.

In the event of your being asked to judge a different breed, the chances are that it will be a similar, or related, breed to your own. For example, if you are a Boxer person you may be asked to judge Dobermanns. If you have Lhasa Apsos, you could be invited for Shih Tzus as well. It is important to recognise that while another breed may be considered akin to yours, there will be very basic differences which make that breed just as individual as yours. It is essential that you make it your business to find out about the type-basics in other breeds, before you contemplate accepting an invitation to judge them. Judges within the dog world are fanciers to a greater or lesser degree. Some will simply "play at" dogs at weekends, and for the most part of their lives, dogs will not figure too largely. Others will find that keeping dogs eventually takes over their life, and the dogs tend to dictate their lifestyle. Relative to your degree of involvement in the dog sport, will be your capacity and opportunity to learn. I consider myself very fortunate in that, for ten years, my sole occupation was publishing and editing a glossy monthly magazine which was devoted to dogs. Working in that environment gave me the opportunity to read millions of words which had been written about various breeds, and that was extremely beneficial in getting to understand many breeds which I had never owned. Few people in the sport are lucky enough to be able to earn a living from a dog-related activity, but those who are will find themselves absorbing considerably more knowledge than "part-time" enthusiasts.

The first time I awarded CCs in Dobermanns, I gave the Dog CC to the fourteen-month-old Sallates Ferris. He was the first home-bred Sallate Dobermann CC winner for young Graham Hunt, though many more were to follow. Ferris subsequently went on to become the youngest and most quickly titled Dobermann ever. He currently holds the Breed Record with forty-two CCs, he has won nine Working Groups (including two at Crufts) and was four times Best in Show at general Championship shows. He also won a rare double with the Pedigree Chum Champions Stakes Finals and the PRO-Dogs Stakes Final. Jordan

It is true that there is only one way to really understand a breed, and that is to live with it. Only when you have reared a puppy, trained it, shared your home with it, and shown it, can you begin to fully appreciate the breed with all its characteristics. Judges who have not owned a breed are greatly disadvantaged when they come to judge it, particularly in the case of puppies and youngsters, who are at varying stages of development. It is, in my opinion, impossible for a judge who has never bred Great Danes, or Yorkshire Terriers, for example, to knowledgeably assess a class of six to nine-month-old puppies in those breeds. The picture with which he would be presented is so different from the mature, finished article that the Breed Standard would seem almost irrelevant, due to the immaturity and disproportion of the albeit promising fledgling.

BREED PECULIARITIES
Living with a breed gives a judge an insight which can never be achieved by someone "outside" that breed. It also acquaints judges with a breed's peculiarities which may never be referred to in the Breed Standard. As an example, when I first began judging Cavalier King Charles Spaniels, I was horrified to find so many puppies whose mouths were slightly undershot, and I penalised them accordingly. I discussed this with some successful Cavalier breeders, and they assured me that many such mouths would finish up as perfect scissor bites. I viewed that advice with a little suspicion, but, in time, I encountered several adult Cavaliers who had perfect bites, yet who had been slightly undershot as puppies. Consequently, I am now less alarmed at puppies in that breed

who are a little "under", and have become more tolerant of that failing in a youngster. Reading a Breed Standard does nothing to help you understand how that Standard is generally perceived and interpreted by most of the people within the breed. I recall vividly the very first time I judged Boston Terriers at an Open show. It was in East Anglia, which was at the time something of a hot-bed of the breed. Having studied the Standard religiously, and read as many articles and books on the breed as I could find, the message was coming across loud and clear that correct markings were essential, and this obviously influenced my decisions. I particularly remember one class in which I placed Second a dog I admired greatly, but whose markings seemed to be very lacking. The dog I placed First was beautifully marked, but not of the overall constructional merit of the Second dog. After judging, I spoke to the exhibitors and asked their opinion of how I had done. One lady assured me that it was quite an acceptable job: "But you paid too much attention to markings". From then on I had a slightly different perspective on that aspect of the breed, and now I tend to be a little more forgiving of less-than-ideal markings in an otherwise excellent Boston than I was on my debut.

It is impossible for any would-be multi-breed judge to actually own all the breeds he will at some time be called on to evaluate. The next best thing, however, is to have a friend in another breed who is happy to let you visit, in order to watch puppies at different stages of growth. This can be a very rewarding exercise, provided that the particular friend does not brainwash you into believing that they have the best dogs in the world, and everyone else is breeding untypical rubbish! Breeders can become a little biased in their assessment of their own stock, but when you gain the individual's confidence, most will discuss their dogs as objectively as possible.

ALL-ROUNDERS

In past generations, the progression of judges' careers tended to be slower than it is today. Usually they judged their own breed first, then took on another similar breed after some years, and gradually began to cover a sub-group and later a whole Group. Such people were also being exposed to good dogs outside their own Group, but never presumed to judge them. I can think of several people who have only recently been recognised as "All-Rounder" judges, who suffered through being labelled as Group specialists. I have frequently heard a particular judge's name being discussed as a possible outside opinion for a certain breed, which is not within their Group, only to hear: "But he's a Toy man", or "She's a Gundog woman!" The new generation of multi-breed judges are well aware of this fact and tend to try to gain a foothold in as many of the six Groups as possible very early on in their careers. Often this involves "targeting" one of the minority breeds in a Group where the owners are frequently so flattered that a well-known judge is taking an interest in their breed, that they are welcomed into the fold and soon realise their ambitions. This is not always the case. I know full well that you only have to turn up at a breed club Championship show out of genuine interest, and some people will become very suspicious indeed! Judges will vary in the level of competence which they will demand of themselves, and the opinion as to how many breeds they can judge will also differ from judge to judge.

Personally, I feel that most of the really experienced and knowledgeable judges are capable of doing an acceptable job in all breeds. Armed with a Breed Standard and their basic eye for quality and balance, honed over many years of practice, they could probably make a reasonable job of any breed. To many judges, that is all they would require of themselves. However, is it good enough to be able to make acceptable decisions, based on what is fundamentally instinct, but at the same time be incapable of explaining in detail why some of those decisions were made? I know that some judges have the "I know what I like" frame of mind, and they feel that is sufficient. That is their privilege, but I feel that the really serious judge is not happy until he knows that he could justify the most minor placing to a far more experienced breed specialist (and I mean "specialist" in the truest sense of the word), if challenged. Someone once told me that in a lifetime it was impossible to fully understand more than a dozen breeds. In some ways, he may have been right.

SOUNDNESS VERSUS TYPE

An old theory, which seems to be quoted less frequently these days, is that All-Rounders judged for soundness, and Breed Specialists for type. That is a very simplistic view of the whole question of judging, which presupposes several beliefs. Firstly, it assumes that All-Rounders are incapable of appreciating type, and it also suggests that Specialists have little regard for soundness. In my experience, it is a sweeping statement which does not hold water. I have seen many All-Rounders putting up very typical dogs whose soundness has been questionable, and similarly, I have watched many Specialists rewarding rather untypical dogs who have been well constructed.

Judging is all about balance and perspective, and I think in both categories of judge – Specialist and Non-Specialist – you will find judges whose aim is to place dogs which have a high degree of typicality coupled with correct movement. Many times I have been faced with a class of dogs, and I soon realised that if I judged solely on type, I would end up with some rather unsound dogs at the head of the line. However, if I judged on movement alone, I would have a distinct lack of type in my winners. So what can you do? You have to compromise and go for the dogs which possess an above-average level of both type and soundness. No dog is perfect and, as I have said before, judging is all about putting them up because of their virtues and not down because of their faults. At the end of the day you have to trust your eye, and remember to always be guided by your basic instinct and gut feeling. If a dog really "turns you on", it is a big mistake to analyse it too critically, as you may well end up talking yourself out of putting it up.

NEW PERSPECTIVES

You will find as you begin to judge other breeds, they may help to give you a slightly different perspective on your own. You may discover that, having judged many dogs in various breeds, an aspect of your breed, which you had previously considered extremely important, is perhaps not quite so vital in the whole scheme of things. Judging other breeds also helps in your attitude as a breeder. For example, if you are involved with a breed where fronts are generally bad, the fact that you have got accustomed to bad fronts will result in your finding them less offensive. When you start judging other breeds similar to your own, and discover lots of dogs with really good fronts, you will come back to your own breed and realise just how bad fronts have become. You will then, hopefully, resolve to do something about improving them.

So, you see, the judging process can have far-reaching effects on your ability as a breeder as well as judge. You may also find, with your change in perspective, you approach your own breed rather differently as a judge.

Judging breeds other than your own is a great challenge, and it can, in many ways, be far more satisfying. Unless you are the sort of judge (hopefully not) who spends a few weeks studying form before you judge another breed, you should know very few of the dogs and very few of the exhibitors. You will not know who has won what, and that means there are far fewer extraneous factors to be blotted out from your mind when you are judging. Some judges seem to have a remarkable capacity for recognising big winners in breeds with which they are not involved. If you are to take your judging seriously, this is quite unnecessary, as long as you have the courage of your convictions and faith in your own judgement.

Chapter Nine

GROUP CLASSIFICATIONS

Since the advent of the World Congress of Kennel Clubs, it has been hoped that the international aspect of dog breeding and exhibiting would become more streamlined, with fewer irregularities from country to country than have been seen in the past. While it would be extremely cynical to suggest that nothing of value has resulted from these indifferently-supported gatherings, the systems in several countries remain considerably at odds to those of others. If we look at one aspect of dog shows – that of Group classification – we will find many incongruities. The UK still divides its breeds into six Groups, while the United States and Australasia have for some years implemented a seventh Herding Group (the UK still classifies these breeds in its unmanageably large Working Group, though at the time of writing a totally different Group classification is under consideration). In Europe there are more Groups categorised – ten in the majority of countries under the FCI umbrella.

It would be a cumbersome task to attempt to compare the European Groups with those of the countries who still favour six or seven, but even within those the differences can cause problems for judges who are invited to officiate overseas. In the UK we presently classify the Japanese Akita and Schnauzer as Utility breeds, yet in the US they appear in the Working Group. In the US Miniature Schnauzers are regarded as Terriers, yet in the UK they are Utility. Toy Poodles and Shih Tzus appear in the British Utility Group, whereas their American cousins compete with the Toys. These groupings are essentially based on tradition, and on the surface they may appear to be of little consequence, although one must be tempted to ponder whether the appearance of the Schnauzer in the American Terrier Group may encourage a slightly different topline and tail-set from that advocated by the Europeans. Similarly, does putting the Shih Tzu in the US Toy Group result in a smaller, more refined animal than the British dog who appears in Utility? There can be conceptual differences which are not governed by Breed Standards.

GROUP AND BEST IN SHOW JUDGING
The fact that so many countries cannot agree on what Group contains which breeds suggests to me a quite fundamental statement, and that is that Group and Best in Show judging is quite far removed from the bricks-and-mortar of the sport – namely, the *breed*. Judging of variety competitions of any degree will always remain an inexact form of assessment. It is impossible to compare a Chihuahua with a Dobermann. We can only compare a given Chihuahua to our mental ideal of that breed, and the Dobermann to its corresponding blueprint. When we run the two evaluations through our psychological computer, we conclude that one is better than the other. However, we can compare six Dobermanns against each other directly, simply because we are

using the same yardstick for each. It is at breed level where judging is of prime importance. What happens beyond does not have quite the same impact. Educated judging of a breed entry ensures that type is maintained, and, hopefully, quality and conformation is improved. The inexactness of variety judging is proved conclusively by the fact that certain breeds account for many Groups; other breeds for hardly any. This does not mean that some breeds are awash with great ones, while others have none. It simply indicates that, in the eyes of many judges, particular breeds make good "Group dogs" while others tend to be overlooked.

The late Raymond Oppenheimer was a fascinating man. An outstanding breeder of Bull Terriers (on which breed his books are considered masterpieces) with forthright opinions on all matters canine, he had a theory which, on the surface, sounds ludicrous but the logic behind his thinking bears close scrutiny. With regard to judging, he said that the entire system was upside-down. He maintained that when a fancier expressed the desire to judge, he should be invited to award Best in Show. There, in theory, he would be presented with a handful of quality dogs which he would be required to evaluate, and his decision – no matter how unacceptable – would do little harm. Having judged several Bests, Mr Oppenheimer advocated that the aspirant judge should try his hand at judging Groups. This would entail more knowledge and application, and would be a greater test of his ability than his prior assignments. Then, having acquitted himself well with his Group judging, and only then, should a judge be entrusted with a Breed, because this was by far the most important aspect of judging, and the area in which most damage could be perpetrated by a judge's shortcomings. As I said, ludicrous it may be in practice ... but worthy of thought.

We may not agree on how we should group our various breeds, and I doubt that we ever will, but this fact should merely serve to remind us – contrary to popular opinion – that variety judging is not really what dog showing is all about. What matters is the Breed. Remember the old saying: Look after the pennies, and the pounds will look after themselves?

In the next chapters it is my intention to look at the different breeds, within the context of their Groups and sub-groups, and try to establish some breed essentials. It would be impossible in a book of this size to go into great detail about each and every breed, but there are fundamental aspects of all the breeds which should be uppermost in any judge's mind if he is keen to preserve breed type and not damage the breed through ignorant judging. I have restricted this section to the more popular breeds which currently enjoy Challenge Certificate status. I should also stress that this book is not written for the complete novice. By definition, no complete novice would be contemplating judging without some extent of basic grounding (or would they?). Therefore, you will note that in my summary of breed essentials there are a lot of points which have been left out, as I have assumed that their mention would be unnecessary.

For example, I have only mentioned mouths in breeds which require other than the "normal" scissor bite. Similarly, I have made little mention of shoulders, as in the vast majority of breeds it is assumed that the shoulder will be well laid back and make an angle of 90 degrees with the upper arm. I have also taken it as understood that readers of this book will be aware that the majority of breeds will move true fore and aft. In other words, with the forelegs remaining parallel, or slightly converging with speed, and the hindlegs doing likewise. Consequently, I have chosen to elaborate on movement only in the breeds where a specific or rather unusual gait is called for. As regards size, I have mentioned this only in breeds where it can create some kind of problem, and I have refrained from automatically listing height or weight, as I assume that readers of this book will have a sufficiently educated eye to already know what is, and looks, correct.

Understanding the various breeds, however, involves more than simply knowing the salient breed features, and no matter how word-perfect a judge may be in this respect, appreciation of correct type and structure can only be achieved when you understand how the component parts fit together and complement each other. The art of skilled judging is to develop a picture of perfection in your mind's eye, based on actual dogs you have seen, and hone that picture with every improvement you encounter. It is a long process, but one where practice really does make perfect – or almost!

Chapter Ten

THE HOUND GROUP

If we start with the Hound Group, we can basically split most of its member breeds into two sub-groups – Sight (or Gaze) Hounds and Scent Hounds. In addition, there are the hunters of Spitz-type, the Elkhound and Finnish Spitz, and the "odd man out", the Rhodesian Ridgeback who is not strictly speaking a clear-cut Sight or Scent Hound. Indeed, in some countries he is not classified as a Hound at all.

SIGHT HOUNDS

THE AFGHAN HOUND
The first of the Sight Hounds I will discuss is the Afghan, quite the most numerically popular of its sub-group in the UK, though the breed has happily put the popularity boom of the seventies behind it. The Afghan is a hound of great dignity, it is naturally aloof, and the breed should look through,

The world-famous Grandeur kennel of Afghan Hounds was originally established by the legendary character, Sunny Shay, and subsequently taken over by Roger Rechler with unrivalled success. The Grandeur kennel, based on Long Island, New York, USA, is indeed well-named and has produced many outstanding winners. Ch. Tryst of Grandeur, pictured left, is an in-bred daughter of the record-breaking Ch. Triumph of Grandeur. She is owned by Gregg, Scott and Todd Rechler and was handled by Michael Canalizo, to win BOB under me.

Bernard Kernan.

rather than at, a judge. Its eastern expression is created by the upwardly slanting eye, which should be almost triangular in shape. The long foreface, with punishing jaws and only slight stop, is essential to the typical Afghan head. The true Afghan outline will only be achieved when the dog is correctly constructed, displaying prominent and wide-apart hip bones, and the low-set, ringed tail.

The Afghan's movement is one of its greatest assets, being smooth and springing "with a style of high order". To me, the very essence of this breed is its nobility and natural arrogance, and Afghans which do not move with spring and style, with their tails raised, cannot be considered typical. Remember that the Afghan's pasterns should be long and springy, with pads well down on the ground. Judges who look for Afghans well up on their feet, do not understand the breed. When judging Afghans, undue emphasis on lavish coats and stacked outlines can lead to questionable decisions. Correct construction, temperament, and movement are all-important.

Remember that the breed should have a natural saddle (short hair from the shoulder to the tail-set), yet many present-day dogs seem to have lost this important breed characteristic, with coats being parted and groomed Yorkie-style. Underneath the coat (which can be any colour) there should be fair spring of rib, more so than in some Sight Hounds.

THE BASENJI
The Basenji, with its distinctive chortle, is one of the most elegant of the Sight Hounds, and I find it best to judge them on the move. The typical long, tireless, swinging stride is unique to this breed, yet many Basenjis which look splendid going around have a habit of stiffening up and not looking their best when standing. The head should display distinct wrinkle when the dog is alert, and its ears should be small, pointed, erect and slightly hooded. The well-crested neck is vital to the perfect Basenji outline, as is the high-set, tightly curled tail. Note that the posterior curve of the

Red-and-white is by far the strongest colour numerically in Basenjis, but black-and-whites and tricolours are equally acceptable, and brindle specimens are proving increasingly popular in the USA, though currently the British breed standard does not embrace this colour. I awarded the tricolour, Ch. Azenda Midnight Caller, owned by Ken Richardson, his first CC and BOB when he was a puppy.

David Dalton.

buttock extends well beyond the root of the tail, creating a "shelf", without which a Basenji will lose type in its outline.

The Basenji coat should always be short, sleek and close. Harsh, coarse coats are not typical. When judging this breed, you should be aware of its sometimes aloof disposition. They can shy off heavy-handed judges, so approach them with understanding.

THE BORZOI

The Borzoi is another of the aristocratic Sight Hounds which is elegance personified. Its outline is curvaceous, and remember that its ribs are narrow and oval, rather than being well-sprung. The bone of the Borzoi is blade-like, rather than round and well-finished. The head is long and lean, well filled in below the eyes, and with no perceptible stop and something of a "Roman nose". The breed should have a prominent occiput, and small, delicate ears which, when relaxed, should be

Rose-Marie Downes' Borzoi, Ch. Vronsky Zapata, qualified for the Pedigree Chum Champions Stakes Finals under me at a Southern Counties show. He won twenty-one CCs in all and a Hound Group before his tragic death at seven years of age. He has, however, made a great impact on the breed by siring thirteen different CC winners, at least eight of which are Champions.

Trevor Sharp.

folded back. The hindquarters must be wider than the shoulders, and while the forefeet are oval, with toes close together and well-arched over thick strong pads, the hind feet are longer and less arched. Check the length of the tail by bringing it down between the hind legs and up to the top of the nearest hip bone. It should be at least this length. In action, the tail should not rise above the level of the back. The Borzoi, for all its elegance, should convey great power, and while there is a spring in the gait, the breed tends to exhibit more forehand reach and lower head carriage than its cousin, the Afghan. Avoid woolly coats, and remember that any colour is acceptable. Some judges seem to assume that Borzois can only be flashy red and white, or tricolour . Not so!

THE DEERHOUND

Of all the breeds of dog, it is often said that none has remained as unspoiled and unchanged as the Deerhound. Its disposition is friendly and gentle, never aloof like some of the Sight Hounds. The breed should be built for speed and power, and the effortless strength seen in a beautiful Deerhound is, indeed, a sight to behold. The long head should show a flat rather than rounded skull, with a slight rise over the eyes. Avoid large pendulous ears, and also prick ears. The ears should be small, high-set and folded back when the dog is relaxed.

The Deerhound must have a strong, reachy neck and the chest is deep rather than broad, but never too narrow or slab-sided. The loin must be well-arched and droop to the tail. A flat topline which creates a "boxy" looking Deerhound is quite wrong. There should be great length from hip to hock, with good angulation and the bone is broad and flat, not round. The tail is curved when moving, but not carried over the level of the back. Ring tails are undesirable, but the tail should be well-covered with hair, thicker and more wiry on the upper side. The Deerhound should move with a long stride, and the gait should be effortless. White blazes or collars are unacceptable, but a small amount of white on the chest, toes and tail-tip are tolerable. The vast majority of Deerhounds are blue-grey or dark brindle, but judges sometimes forget that reds and fawns with black points are quite acceptable.

I awarded Dr Seumas Caine's Deerhound, Ch. Rosslyn Carric, her first Hound Group at the Scottish Kennel Club Show in August 1992. She subsequently won the title of Top Scottish Show Dog for that year. Like all her owner's hounds, Carric is regularly coursed, which fact is reflected in her marvellous fitness and condition.
David Lindsay.

THE GREYHOUND

The Greyhound is a running machine, its construction showing great muscular power, a long head and neck, deep chest, well-laid shoulders, arched loin and powerful well-angulated hindquarters. It is a very basic breed to judge, with nothing to hide. A long neck, elegantly arched, is essential, and the pasterns should be slightly springy. The flanks are well cut-up. and the back rather long and

The brindle Greyhound dog, Ch. Solstrand Double Diamond, owned and bred by Dagmar Kenis, won "only" fourteen CCs, yet went on to win twelve Hound Groups and five Best in Show awards at All Breeds Championship shows during the 1978/9 show season, finishing up as Top Male of All Breeds in 1978 and Top Sighthound in 1979.

broad. It used to be said that the Greyhound's back should be flat enough for a dinner-plate to be placed on it. Short-backed, "neat" Greyhounds lacking scope are not typical.

The gait of the Greyhound is quite different from the Afghan in that it is low-reaching rather than high-stationed. The whole carriage of the dog differs, and when the Greyhound moves, its hindlegs come well under the body, giving great propulsion.

THE IBIZAN HOUND

The Ibizan has several unique breed characteristics, which can cause problems for judges who do not fully understand the breed, not least of which is its movement. It has a long, far-reaching stride, yet there is a distinctive hovering before the foot is placed on the ground. This, apparently, reluctant gait may perplex judges, but it is a characteristic of the breed. The Ibizan is one of the few breeds to require a rather steep, short shoulder blade and erect pasterns; it also requires the ribcage to be approximately two to three inches above the level of the elbow, and the hindquarters to show no great angulation, so you see this is no "average" hound.

The amber, almond-shaped eyes coupled with the large, stiff, but highly mobile ears, which form a continuous line with the long, well arched neck, all help to create the unique Ibizan expression.

The Ibizan Hound is not an easy breed to judge, with several of its breed characteristics being rather unusual, and quite far removed from the "norm". For example, the breed should have a rather steep, short shoulder blade, long, erect pasterns and the ribcage should be no deeper than about 2.5 inches above the elbow. The breed also has a unique hovering gait. Illustrating the breed so beautifully is Jenny Startup's Ch. Paran Christmas Ivy who became only the second Ibizan to win a Hound Group at a U.K., Championship show when I gave her that award at Leeds Championship show in 1993. *John Hartley.*

The ribcage is long and flat, and the Ibizan is short-coupled with noticeable tuck-up. The breastbone is very prominent, and it is worth remembering that the front feet are allowed to turn slightly outwards. The Ibizan has a long, thin, low-set tail, which can be carried high but should not curl or be carried low over the back. Remember too, that there are two coat types, rough and smooth. The Ibizan allows for considerable size variation (22-29 inches), but balance should be more important than actual height.

THE IRISH WOLFHOUND
This is the gentle giant of the Hound Group – a classic combination of substance and grace. Its temperament is gentlemanly and friendly, and its movement should be easy and active, always true from all angles. Both the head and neck of the Wolfhound should be comparatively long, the eyes dark and oval, and the ears small, rose-shaped and velvety to the touch. They should, ideally, be

An outstanding example of an Irish Wolfhound is Zena Thorn-Andrews' Ch. Drakesleat Kyak, the top winner of all time in his breed with forty-one CCs. The previous record of twenty-six CCs had stood since 1908! He won three Best in Show awards at All Breeds Championship level, ten Hound Groups and ten Reserve Groups. He sired at least one Champion in every litter he produced, including Ch. Drakesleat Sovryn, the breed's top sire. He has been named by several leading all-rounders as their favourite dog of all time.

David Dalton.

dark and not hang close to the head. The breed seems to have something of a problem with mouths, and while the Standard tolerates a level bite, it is not desirable. The ideal is a perfect scissor bite, though often in this breed, mouths will be found where the two central lower incisors are slightly dropped, a failing found in several large breeds. It is the judge's job to decide on his own priorities, and whether or not he is prepared to dismiss an otherwise excellent dog on the strength of less than perfect dentition. (Personally, I tend to be a little forgiving of slightly irregular dentition in an exceptional dog if the jaws are correctly set.)

The Irish Wolfhound is a much broader dog than its close relative, the Deerhound, and when judging the two breeds, I feel it is important that Deerhound traits should be penalised in the Wolfhound and vice versa. If you have to think twice whether a dog is a Wolfhound or a Deerhound, the one thing you should know immediately is that it is not a good specimen of either breed! Look for good bone, no loose skin about the throat, with the elbows well under the dog.

The Wolfhound is a series of graceful curves, the back being long rather than short, the loins arched, and the underline well drawn up.

The Standard specifies that great size should be aimed at and asks for an average of 32-34 inches in dogs. Although it is unlikely that many judges will ever encounter one, it is worth bearing in mind that black and pure white are both acceptable colours, in addition to the more numerous grey, brindle, red, fawn, wheaten and steel-grey hounds.

THE PHARAOH HOUND

This breed is often confused with the Ibizan Hound by the layman, yet there are several basic differences between the two breeds. The Pharaoh is generally a smaller dog (21-25 inches), and its only acceptable colour is tan or rich-tan with a white tail-tip being highly prized. The only other white markings allowed are a star on the chest, white on toes, and a thin white blaze on the head (though this is, in reality, rarely seen). The movement of the Pharaoh is much more "normal" than that of the Ibizan, with it simply covering the ground well and seemingly effortlessly. The Pharaoh's brisket drops to the elbow. Unlike the Ibizan, its shoulders are long and well-laid, and its hind angulation is moderate.

THE SALUKI

This is a breed which has always struck me as being like precious porcelain in its grace and harmony, yet as a functional Sight Hound it is built for strength and speed. One of its major breed characteristics is the foot, which is moderately long with slightly webbed toes, the two innermost toes being considerably longer than the outer on all four feet. The front feet point forward at a very slight angle when standing. The Saluki is naturally reserved with strangers, and this is a point which judges should remember when approaching the breed. The long and narrow head should show great quality, but is relatively wide between the ears. The large oval eyes should be dark or hazel in colour and sparkle with expression. The ears should reach to the corner of the mouth when pulled forward. The Saluki's chest is deep and moderately narrow, the pasterns slightly sloping, and the bone is more oval than round. Sufficient length of loin is important, and there should be the typical Sight Hound's gentle arch, but never a roach back. The tail-tip should reach to the hock and not be carried over the back line. The gait of the breed is most important for it is light and effortless, yet has reach and drive, the body lifting off the ground with long, even strides. It is a dignified and unhurried action. Judges should remember that the breed has a smooth-coated variety which is equally as acceptable as the feathered.

THE WHIPPET

This breed poses a problem for some judges who seem to have difficulty assessing the correct Whippet topline which is not flat-backed, but is definitely not roached. The arch is specifically over the loin, and the back should be firm, broad, and somewhat long in its entirety. It is important that the outline is maintained on the move and that the Whippet does not flatten out completely as some tend to. The ribs should be well sprung and the brisket deep with a definite underline. The Whippet head is long and lean with very expressive oval eyes. The ears should be rose-shaped and fine, and it is worth remembering that the nose should be black, but that in blues a bluish tinge is permitted, a liver nose is acceptable in livers, and a butterfly nose is allowed in particolours or whites. The Whippet's feet should be very neat, yet well split up between the toes, and the pasterns should be strong with slight spring. An elegantly arched neck is essential for a balanced outline, and the movement should be free with what used to be called a "daisy cutting" action. Avoid high-stepping or mincing Whippets. There should be great propulsion in the hind movement. Size is sometimes a problem in the breed. The British Standard still has a recommended maximum of 20 inches, whereas the Americans have a ten per cent difference with a maximum of 22 inches for males.

SUMMARY

When judging Sight Hounds, I feel it is important to remember their original purpose and the attributes which would have helped them excel at their job. With some of the breeds, their temperament and character is rather different from what is perceived as that of the ideal "show dog", but judges should appreciate this when confronted with a Saluki or Afghan, who may seem a little apprehensive at first. Carriage and effortlessness of movement is vital in these breeds, as should be hardness of condition and musculation. Far too many hounds are soft and lacking muscular fitness, yet these should be essential in breeds where stamina was all important.

Remember that running hounds should possess a degree of length. Ultra-short backs and dead-level toplines would render a Sight Hound virtually useless. Generally, they should all be true up and down, although the Ibizan's highly individual gait may throw some judges. The difference in profile action between the Afghan and the Greyhound, for example, should be studied and assessed as they are quite different, if wholly typical. The Afghan who holds itself and moves like a Greyhound is not a typical Afghan, even though it is a fellow Sight Hound. Judges must be able to appreciate these subtle differences.

SCENT HOUNDS

Just as the Sight Hounds were developed to spot their prey visually, so the Scent Hounds were selectively bred for their excellent noses.

THE BASSET HOUND

The Basset may be short-legged, but he should possess great substance along with an amount of loose skin. The head of the Basset is domed with moderate stop and a prominent occiput. The skull and muzzle are almost equal in length, the muzzle, if anything, is slightly longer. There should be

Bill O'Loughlin's Basset Hound dog, Ch. Bassbarr O'Sullivan, has proved to be one of the outstanding British dogs of the 1990s. In 1993 he was the Top Winning Dog of All Breeds.

Abbey Marketing.

noticeable wrinkle at the brow, and the the flews of the upper lip are well-developed. Large and open nostrils may protrude slightly beyond the lips. In light-coloured hounds, the nose may be brown or liver, otherwise it should be black. Eye colour should be dark to mid-brown, and the eyes are neither prominent nor deep-set. The ears are low-set below the eyeline and should be long, reaching well beyond the end of the muzzle. They tend to be narrow rather than wide, and should have a noticeable inward curl.

The neck is muscular and well-arched, fairly long and has some dewlap. The Basset possesses great bone and its front should be firm at the shoulder with the upper forearm slightly inclined inwards, but this should never be exaggerated to such an extent that the forelegs actually touch. The forechest fits snugly into this "crook" and the breast bone is prominent. The ribs should be well rounded and carried well back. Though the withers and quarters should be approximately the same height, the loins may arch slightly, and judges should note that the Standard is specific in describing the back from the withers to the onset of the quarters as "not unduly long". The hindquarters should display that lovely "apple bottom" when viewed from behind. The tail should be rather long with a strong root, and carried sabre-style. The action of the Basset is smooth and free, with plenty of forward reach and great drive from behind.

THE BEAGLE

A very compact, smart little hound, it should always be remembered that this breed was developed to be followed by huntsmen on foot. The size of some specimens suggests that they could only be kept up with by a marathon runner! The British Standard has a minimum of 13 inches and a maximum of 16 inches, whereas in the USA Beagles are shown as two separate varieties – up to 13 inches and up to 15 inches.

The breed is, in all respects, a very "moderate" one, free of exaggeration. Avoid hard expressions, frown and wrinkle, and at the other end of the scale, gay sterns which are carried over the back. The expression of the Beagle is one of its greatest assets, and that mild, pleading look is essential to the breed. Good round bone of quality – right down to very tight feet – should be

In the USA Beagles are judged as two separate varieties, unlike Britain where only one size is classified. I awarded Best of Breed to 13-inch Beagle, Am. Ch. Lanbur Fancy Pants, at Monmouth County Kennel Club.

John Ashbey.

While constructional qualities and correct movement are essential aspects of any hound breed, the Beagle Breed Standard also draws attention to the importance of a mild, appealing expression. This will only be achieved with an eye which is the correct dark brown or hazel colour, with too light an eye – or equally, yet surprisingly, too dark – creating a rather hard and untypical expression. The ideal Beagle expression is illustrated by Danish Ch. Tragband In Hot Water, which I bred out of the breed record holder, Ch. Too Darn Hot for Tragband.

Jesper Pedersen.

evident as sometimes the breed produces bone which is rather "fluted" in appearance. This detracts from the overall quality of the dog. The body should be short-coupled with well-sprung ribs, level topline, and the chest should extend to below the elbows. There is no excessive tuck-up. The breed has a tendency towards rather wide front movement. Personally, in view of its purpose of following scents with head down, I find this less objectionable than too-narrow "terrier" fronts, which are not at all typical. Remember that all hound colours are acceptable – not just blanketed tricolours as some judges seem to think!

THE BLOODHOUND

This is the definitive Scent Hound and should have a dignified and solemn expression. It should stand over a lot of ground, and the skin must be thick and loose if the hound is to be capable of work. The head is quite narrow and long, with little stop and noticeable occiput. The breed's nostrils are, obviously, large and open and the lips fall squarely. Due to the loose skin, the breed can have eye problems and inturning eyelashes should be penalised. The long ears are thin and, like the Basset's, curl inwards. The round bone should be strong and the chest well let down. The thigh and second thigh should be very muscular, and the movement of the breed is elastic, and swinging, with the tail carried in scimitar-fashion. It is important that the Bloodhound coat should be weatherproof. In assessing the breed, excessive wrinkle should be avoided, yet those specimens with insufficient loose skin will appear plain and untypical.

THE OTTERHOUND

This breed is closely linked with the Bloodhound. It is considered similar to it in many ways, yet it has individual traits with which judges should be familiar. The head is clean, and deep rather than wide. The skull is moderately domed, and has a slight occipital peak. The skull is slightly longer than the muzzle, and the Otterhound should have plenty of lip and flew. Yellow eyes are undesirable, and a valued breed characteristic is the ears which are long, set on level with the eyeline and having a characteristic fold, the frontal edge folding inwards giving a "draped" appearance. The ears should always be well covered with hair.

The Otterhound is a strongly-boned dog with slightly sprung pasterns, and a deep oval ribcage. Its body should not appear too wide or too narrow. The topline is level and the back broad, with a short, strong loin. The large, round, well-knuckled feet must be thick-padded, and although compact, they should be capable of spreading, and webbing should be detectable. The tail is carried straight or in a slight curve, and the coat should be dense, rough, harsh and waterproof, yet should never appear wiry or broken. There is an obvious undercoat and the coat texture is often oily. The Standard stresses the need for natural presentation and no trimming, so judges beware!

On the move, the Otterhound appears loose and shambling at a slow pace, but springs into a loose, long-striding and active trot. A slight butterfly nose is permissible, and the Otter can come in all recognised hound colours as well as the whole-coloured grizzle, sandy, red, wheaten and blue, which may carry slight white markings on the head, chest, feet and tail-tip. Colours which are not allowed are liver and white, and white hounds with black-and-tan patches which are distinctly separate.

THE PETIT BASSET GRIFFON VENDEEN

When this breed first appeared in the British show ring, there was the tendency for many judges to assess them simply as rough-coated Bassets, which they definitely are not. The breed is altogether more compact than the Basset, and rather lighter in general build. The PBGV has a well-defined stop, and is well cut away under the eyes. The muzzle is a little shorter than the skull, and the large eyes should show no haw. The ears are low-set and fold inwards, and should reach to the end of the nose. There is no dewlap and a level bite may be accepted.

The forelegs should be straight, yet a slight crook is acceptable. The pasterns slope slightly, and the chest is deep with a prominent breastbone, the ribs moderately rounded, and the back of only medium length. The feet should be not too long, and they should be tightly padded. The tail is high-set and carried sabre-style. The movement is free and driving, and the coat rough, long and harsh to the touch, showing a definite thick undercoat. Silky or woolly coats are untypical, and the breed should be shown untrimmed. Its colours are white with any combination of lemon, orange, tricolour or grizzle markings.

THE DACHSHUNDS

The Dachshunds are not, strictly speaking, Scent Hounds as they were bred to go to ground, though considering the size of some Standards (ideal weight 20-26lbs), one wonders how large a hole they would need to manoeuvre! In the UK they are shown as six distinct varieties: Miniatures and Standards in Smooth, Long, and Wire Haired. Miniatures must be under 11lbs in weight, and they are weighed in traditionally prior to competing. The Dachshund must be long and low, but with a compact, well-muscled body.

Head carriage is typically "defiant" and proud. The head should appear conical in shape when seen from above and is fairly long. The eyes should be almond-shaped and dark, except for the

The Longhaired Dachshund bitch, Ch. Frankanwen Gold Braid, was my winner when I judged my first Hound Group. Owned by Wendy Barrow, she is the top-winning Longhaired bitch with forty CCs, and she won thirteen Groups in all as well as Best in Show at Group and All Breeds Championship shows. She was one of three Champions in one litter, as was her dam, Ch. Frankanwen Gold Bangle.   *Gerwyn Gibbs.*

Zena Thorn-Andrews' Miniature Wire-Haired Dachshund, Ch. Drakesleat Ai Jail, was the top-winning Hound bitch for 1979/80/81 and the top-winning Miniature Wire for four years. She won thirty-one CCs in all, four of them at Crufts and three of those with Best of Breed. She produced two Champions in her first litter and the record-holding Ch. Drakesleat Ai Jinks in her second.   *Kasper McFarlane.*

chocolates who may have lighter eyes. Wall eyes are allowed in dapples, one or both. In my experience, many Dachshunds can be stacked to look impressive, but when they move their toplines tell a different story, so judges should spend time assessing profile movement.

A long and muscular neck helps create the typical Dachshund outline, along with the very prominent breastbone. From the front, the chest should appear full and oval. Remember that the Standard requires the Dachshund body to be sufficiently clear of the ground to facilitate free movement. The Dachshund moves with a long stride, with driving hindquarters. It does not high-step. The front feet (which are larger and fuller than the hind feet) may turn out slightly. All colours except chocolate variants should have black nose and nails.

SPITZ BREEDS

THE ELKHOUND

This is a typical Spitz breed whose workmanlike qualities should always be evident. The Spitz characteristics of high-set, small, firm and erect pointed ears, and a high-set, tightly curled tail should be obvious. The Elkhound head is wedge-shaped, and fairly broad between the ears, never narrow and mean-looking. Furthermore, the foreface should be broad at its base, never pinched, and the gentle tapering should be such that the head never appears pointed or too sharp. The head should be completely dry with no loose skin or wrinkles. The eyes are medium size, oval rather than round, and of a dark brown colour. The expression is open and friendly.

The Elkhound must have a powerful neck of medium length, and it usually carries a rich ruff but should be free of dewlap. A powerful, short body is a breed essential. Long, weak-backed specimens are just not typical. There should be plenty of depth and breadth of chest with good spring of rib, but the correct proportions of the breed are such that it should have an amount of daylight underneath it and never appear "dumpy". The hind angulation is moderate, and the feet small, slightly oval and tight. The tail should, ideally, be curved over the centre of the back. The Elkhound's movement should be impressive and effortless, and at speed the legs will converge equally towards the centre line of the body.

The coat is important. It should be close, plentiful and weather resistant with a dense woolly undercoat and coarser, straight top coat. Colour too is important, the breed always being a shade of grey, with black tips to the outer coat, yet lighter on the chest, stomach, legs, the underside of the tail and buttocks. The ears and foreface should be dark, with a dark line from the eye to ear being desirable. Avoid sooty or rusty colours, white markings and "spectacles", which are essential in the Elkhound's distant cousin, the Keeshond.

THE FINNISH SPITZ

The other Spitz breed to be found in Britain's Hound Group is the Finnish Spitz, that very vocal, bright-red dog. Judges should remember that this breed is a rather lightly-built dog with only medium bone, and coarseness or the impression of a low, thick-set dog is quite wrong. The head has a foxy expression, with small and sharply pointed ears, almond-shaped dark eyes with black eye-rims, set slightly aslant, and a slightly arched forehead with moderate stop and relatively narrow muzzle. The nose and lips should be black.

The outline should be almost square, with deep chest, slight tuck-up and only moderate hind angulation. The tail should be plumed and curve from the root forward and downward, pressing against the thigh. Judges should check tail length which, extended, should reach to the hock. The Finnish Spitz is light on its feet and should have a spring in its step, moving with drive. There should be a soft dense undercoat, lighter in colour than the top coat, which should be longer and coarser and of a bright red-brown or red-gold colour. There is lighter hair on the inner ears, the cheeks, under the muzzle, on the chest, behind the shoulders, inside the legs, on the back thighs and the underside of the tail. A narrow white stripe on the chest is permitted but not desirable, and the occasional black hairs on lips, and, if sparse and separate, on the back and tail can also be forgiven. Puppies sometimes have black hairs which disperse with age.

THE RHODESIAN RIDGEBACK

The "odd man out" in the British Hound Group is the Rhodesian Ridgeback, which may have been developed as a hunter's dog, but is equally well-known as a guard. The most obvious of its breed characteristics is the ridge which should be clearly defined, tapering from the crowns, and symmetrical. It starts behind the shoulders with two crowns which should be identical and no deeper than one-third of the length of the entire ridge.

Temperament is important in the breed and aggression or shyness should be penalised. The Ridgeback head is fairly long but is still rather broad between the ears. It should be wrinkle-free when relaxed and has a moderate stop, with deep and powerful muzzle of fair length and the lips should be clean and close-fitting. The eyes should be round and sparkle with intelligence. The ears are high-set and rather wide at the base and should be carried close to the head. The neck should be fairly long, strong and free of throatiness, the bone should be heavy and the chest not too wide and "bully", rather deep and capacious. There should be good rib spring without being barrel-ribbed, and the loins must be strong and muscular with a slight arch. There is good turn of stifle and the feet should be well-knit. The Ridgeback should carry its tail with a slight curve but never a curl. The movement is true, free and active.

The colour is light to red wheaten, and while a little white on chest and toes can be forgiven, excessive white here, on the belly or above the paws is undesirable. A dark muzzle and ears are permissible.

SUMMARY

As with the Sight Hounds, I feel that in evaluating the Scent Hounds and the other members of this Group, it is important that judges should be acquainted with the original purpose of the breeds and try to place great emphasis on these aspects of the dogs which would be essential to their fulfilling their original duties, rather than getting carried away with more superficial aspects.

Chapter Eleven

THE GUNDOG GROUP

The Gundog Group, or the Sporting Group as the Americans and Canadians prefer to call it, consists of various Sub-Groups which can be broken down into Setters, Pointers, Retrievers, Spaniels and the versatile HPR (Hunt, Point and Retrieve) breeds. Gundogs were bred to work, and their physical soundness and mental stability should be of paramount importance. Sadly, today, few gundogs seen in the show ring are ever required to acquit themselves in the field, and as a result in some breeds the aesthetics tend to have overtaken the fundamentals in judges' priorities. There was a time when the Gundog Group at Championship shows could be relied upon to produce some of the soundest moving dogs. Today, I feel this is no longer the case.

SETTERS

THE ENGLISH SETTER
This is a clean-outlined and elegant breed which can be blue belton, orange belton, lemon belton, liver belton or tricolour in colour, and in markings even flecking is preferable to dogs with heavy colour patches. The English Setter's head is oval from ear to ear and should indicate plenty of brain room with a well-defined occiput. The muzzle is quite deep and square in appearance, and the nose-stop length should equal stop-occiput. The nose will be black or liver depending on coat colour. The eyes should be bright and expressive, oval and dark-brown, though liver beltons may have lighter eyes.

The neck of the English Setter is distinctive, being muscular and lean, slightly arched at the crest and it should be free of throatiness. The body should be well ribbed up, the forelegs muscular and round-boned, and feet should be well-padded and tight, the pasterns being straight and strong. The back should be level, though loins are wide and slightly arched. The stifles are well bent and thighs long from hip to hock.

On the move, the English will hold its head high and the action should be free and graceful, showing great flexibility of the hock and powerful drive from behind. The tail should follow the line of the back and should not be longer than the distance to the hock. It is carried slightly curved and slashes when the dog is gaiting, but should not be carried higher than the level of the back. The English is not as racy as the Irish Setter, but neither is it as bulky as the Gordon. Extreme examples which suggest either of these cannot be considered really typical.

THE GORDON SETTER
The Gordon has a shining coal-black coat and chestnut red markings (two clear spots over the

eyes, on the muzzle not reaching above the base of the nose, on the throat, two clear spots on the chest, on the inside of the hindlegs and thighs, from the hock to toes, and on the foreleg up to the elbows behind and to the knees or thereabouts in front, and around the anus). This Setter should be built like a "weight-carrying hunter". The head is deep rather than broad, but the skull is broader than the muzzle indicating brain room. There is a clearly defined stop, and the occiput-stop length should be greater than that of the muzzle. The cheeks should be clean, and while the flews are not pendulous, the lips should be clearly defined.

The muzzle should be not quite as deep as it is long. The nose is large with open nostrils and always black. Eyes should be dark-brown and set sufficiently under the brows. The neck should be long and lean with no dewlap. The bone of the Gordon is flat rather than round (as is the case with the English), and the pasterns are upright. The Gordon has a deep brisket with well-sprung ribs, but the chest should not be too wide. Loins are wide and slightly arched, the stifles are well-bent and the hocks short. The feet should be oval and close-knit, the coat as free from curl or wave as possible. The tail should reach no further than the hocks, and should be carried horizontally or below the back line. The Gordon should move straight and true with great drive behind.

THE IRISH RED AND WHITE SETTER

This is a relatively recent addition to the British show rings, and when it first arrived some judges felt it was simply an Irish Setter with white markings. In actuality, it is a heavier breed than the Irish and the Standard requires it to be athletic rather than racy. The head is broad in proportion to the body with good stop. While the skull is domed, it does not have the pronounced occiput of the Irish Setter. The muzzle should be fairly square and clean. The eyes are round and fairly full, dark-brown, and should not show any haw.

The neck should not be too thick, is slightly arched and free from throatiness. The bone should be oval, the pasterns slope slightly, and like all working gundogs, the shoulders should be well laid. The hindquarters are wide and powerful and musculation is repeatedly referred to in the Red and White's Standard. The movement of the breed should be free striding and effortless with great drive. Like the other Setters, the tail should not be too long and should be carried level with, or below the back line. The coat allows for a slight wave but never a curl, and it should be finely textured. The colour of the Red and White is one of its great assets – a clear pearly-white background with solid red patches. Mottling or flecking is allowed around the face and feet and up the foreleg to the elbow, and up the hindleg to the hock.

THE IRISH SETTER

This is a much more racy breed, and should always appear full of quality and refinement. Once an Irish looks cloddy or bulky, you know it is not an excellent example of its breed. While the Irish head should be long and lean, it should not be narrow or snipey. The skull is oval and the occiput well defined. The head is beautifully balanced, and, in profile, it should be parallel and equi-distant from occiput to stop as stop to nose. The head should also display slightly raised brows. The muzzle is moderately deep without ever appearing "lippy", and the nose may be black, dark-mahogany or dark-walnut! The Irish eyes are described as an unshelled almond in shape, and the expression is always kindly.

The neck is clean and long with no dewlap, and the body as deep as possible in chest, and rather narrow in front. The ribs are still well sprung, and where the Irish differs slightly from the other Setters is that its topline slopes gently downwards from the withers. Despite its raciness, the Irish should have wide and powerful quarters with good sweep from hip to hock, and its feet should be

For Jackie Lorrimer's Irish Setter dog, Sh. Ch. Danaway Debonair, 1993 was a year to remember. Not only did he begin the year by winning Best in Show at Crufts, but later in the year he added to his score of All Breeds Bests in Show and also created a new record for CCs won in the breed. He is a multiple Group winner and one of many Show Champions sired by the history-making stud dog, Sh. Ch. Kerryfair Night Fever.

Anne Roslin-Williams.

small and toes well-arched. The free flowing action of the Irish should show perfect coordination, the tail is carried as nearly as possible to the level of the backline. The well-fringed coat should always be a rich chestnut colour with no trace of black. White on the chest, throat, chin or toes, a small star on the forehead, or a narrow blaze on the nose should be tolerated in an otherwise exceptional dog.

The four Setter breeds are very similar in many ways, but judges should be acquainted with the subtle differences, such as head shape, bone type and topline, if they are to understand type in each.

THE POINTER

The Pointer is a most handsome and curvaceous dog with an aristocratic look. In Britain, two quite distinctive types were frequently seen until recently, one with alleged Foxhound ancestry, and one with a very distinctive head typified by a very definite dish-face. The Pointer's head should have a well defined stop and pronounced occiput. The nostrils should be wide, soft and moist, and the muzzle somewhat concave, giving a *slightly* dish-faced appearance. There is a slight depression under the eyes, and the soft lips are well developed. The eyes should be bright and kindly, the ear leathers thin and set fairly high, being slightly pointed at the tips.

The neck is long and muscular, the chest just wide enough for plenty of heart room. The bone should be oval with visible back sinews on the forelegs. The knee joint should be flat with the front leg and the pasterns lengthy and slightly sloping. The Pointer is short-coupled, with prominent haunch bones well-spaced. Hindquarters should be very muscular, and feet well knit and oval. The tail should not be over-long, thick at the root, and in action it should lash from side to side. The movement of the Pointer is smooth and covers plenty of ground, and judges should remember that hackney action is definitely out – some in the breed fail in this respect.

It is also worth remembering that self-colours and tricolours are acceptable. I have been in the company of British judges in Europe who were appalled to see a black Pointer winning, yet under our own Standard such a dog would be perfectly permissible.

THE RETRIEVERS
Some may believe that our Retriever breeds differ only in coat and colour, but size and head type will reveal other fundamental differences.

THE CURLY COATED RETRIEVER
This is the largest Retriever with a maximum height of 27 inches. Its skull is flat, and its muzzle is neither snipey nor coarse. It has rather small ears lying close to the head and covered with short curls. The ribs are well sprung, the brisket should be deep, and the Curly should have no obvious tuck-up. It should have round, compact feet, and a moderately short tail, which is covered in curls, and is never carried gaily or curled. The Curly's movement is driving and covers a lot of ground, but it is its coat, either liver or black, which is its most distinctive feature. The coat is a mass of crisp, small curls, which should cover the body of the dog evenly.

THE FLAT COATED RETRIEVER
This Retriever may also be black or liver, yet has a maximum size of 24 inches. Its head is long and nicely moulded, with just a slight stop and a moderately broad skull. The eyes are dark-brown and the expression highly intelligent. Overdone Flatcoat heads, which tend towards the Labrador, are quite untypical. The chest is deep and fairly broad, but it should be remembered that the foreribs are rather flat, the ribcage springing out towards the centre, then becoming lighter towards the hindquarters. Only moderate bend of stifle is called for, and the hocks are well let down. The feet should be round and strong, and have thick soles. The Flatcoat's tail is short, straight and carried gaily if never much above the level of the back. The movement is free and flowing, straight and true.

THE GOLDEN RETRIEVER
The Golden has the same height maximum as the Flatcoat (24 inches) and its coat can be flat or wavy, and any shade of gold or cream. Neither red nor mahogany are allowed, but some of the shades of cream seen in the show ring in recent years have been closer to white, in my estimation. The Golden's head has a broad but not coarse skull, and a muzzle which is wide and deep. The skull and muzzle should be of equal length, and the nose should, ideally, be black. The eyes are dark-brown with black rims, and the expression is totally benign.

The construction of the Golden is very basic with good bone, deep, well-sprung ribs and a level topline. It should be short-coupled with well-bent stifles, and the forelegs placed well under the body. The feet should be round and cat-like, and the tail reaching to the hocks, should be carried level with the back and free from a curl at the tip. The Golden should move with power and drive, showing a long and free stride with no hackney action.

David and Marion Hopkinson's Sh. Ch. Rocheby Royal Oak illustrates splendid Labrador Retriever type. After becoming Top Sire in the breed for 1992 he was exported to France, leaving behind him many winning children as well as his highly successful litter sister, Sh. Ch. Rocheby Popcorn, who was Best of Breed at Crufts 1992.   *John Hartley.*

THE LABRADOR RETRIEVER

The Labrador is the smallest Retriever in height with a maximum of 22.5 inches for males. It can be black, yellow or liver (more popularly called chocolate). The yellow can range from light-cream to red-fox – sometimes a controversial colour. A small white spot on the chest is tolerated, but no other markings. The impression of the Labrador is of a rather broad dog, but broad due to his construction rather than obesity. Some Labradors being shown have difficulty in waddling across the ring, much less going out for a day in the field!

The Labrador's skull is broad with a definite stop. The head should not be "cheeky", and the muzzle should indicate power and strength. The nose is wide and nostrils well-developed, and the brown or hazel eyes indicate intelligence and a friendly disposition. The neck is clean, strong and powerful and neither unduly long nor short. The forelegs are well boned and straight, the feet round and compact with well-arched toes and well-developed pads. The chest is wide and deep, the ribs well-sprung and barrel-like. The topline should be level and the hindquarters well-developed with no fall-away to the tail. The stifles are well bent and hocks well let down.

The tail is a major breed characteristic of the Labrador, being very thick at the base, gradually tapering towards the tip. It is of medium length and free from feathering, but is covered in short, thick, dense hair, which gives it a rounded appearance. This is referred to as the "otter" tail, and it may be carried gaily but should not curl over the back. The Labrador's coat is also one of its trademarks. There is a weather resistant undercoat with a harsh-feeling top coat, which is short and dense and free from wave. The movement of the breed is free, straight and true.

SPANIELS

THE AMERICAN COCKER SPANIEL

Of the Spaniels being shown in Britain, none has proved more controversial than the American Cocker, with the breed narrowly escaping, on one occasion, being transferred from the Gundog Group to the Utility, so incensed were purist Gundog fanciers by its lavish coat and great glamour. Ironically, it is a breed which has provided many top-winning Gundogs over the years. While the American has obvious glamour, it should always be remembered that it is, in theory at least, a working gundog. Indeed, its own Standard requires, above all, that it should be a "serviceable looking dog".

It is a square-outlined dog, well up at the shoulders, with a head which should be soft and plushy-looking with full round eyes. The skull is rounded but not domed, and the stop and eyebrows well defined. The muzzle is broad and deep, and in no way long. The ears are set no higher than the eyeline, and should extend to the nostrils. The neck is long and muscular and free

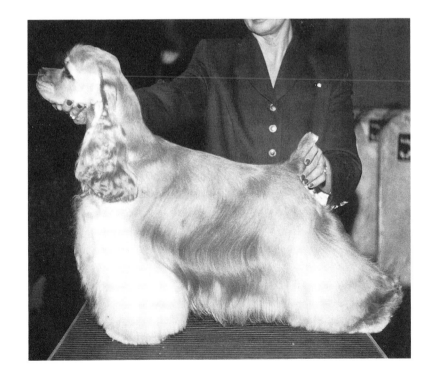

I awarded Yvonne Knapper's buff American Cocker bitch, Sh. Ch. Sundust Thumbelina, one of her several CCs and also Best of Breed, and she illustrates excellent American Cocker type. Royally bred from two Show Champions, she herself produced CC winning puppies.

from dewlap, it rises acutely and is slightly arched. The American has deep and well-sprung ribs, and the chest must reach to the elbows. It is short-coupled, and the back slopes slightly and evenly from the withers to the high tail-set. The strongly-boned hindquarters should display good angulation, but not so much so that the dog appears to be kneeling! The feet are compact with deep, strong pads, and the hindlegs should appear parallel when moving or standing. The tail is carried with the level of the back or slightly above, but never vertically, terrier-style. The movement of the American should cover the ground well and be smooth and effortless, never jarred. The coat should not be so excessive as to hide the natural outline of the dog, and the texture should be silky, flat or slightly wavy. Penalise excessive coats as well as woolly or curly texture. In addition to the solid colours, there are black-and-tans where the location of tan markings is important. There should be a clear spot over each eye, on the sides of the muzzle and under the cheeks, on the underside of the ears, on all feet and legs, under the tail, and optionally on the chest. Particolours should have the colours well broken up and clearly defined.

THE CLUMBER SPANIEL

The Clumber is the most heavily-boned of the Spaniels, and while it has considerably more substance than its distant cousins, it should still maintain a look of activity and move with great drive. Having said that, the movement of the Clumber (and Sussex) is quite distinctive from the other Spaniels, as their body shape is such that there is a definite roll in the gait. The Clumber is also more reserved in character than the other rather out-going Spaniels.

The head should appear square and massive with a broad top-skull and definite occiput. The brows are heavy, the stop deep, and the muzzle has well developed flews. Despite there being much work in the head, it should be free from exaggeration, and if judges remember "square" when judging the Clumber head, they won't go far wrong. The eyes are dark-amber, light by comparison to other Spaniels, and are rather deep-set. There is some visible haw, but this should never be excessive. The ears are large and the shape of a vine leaf, and they hang slightly forward (unlike the other Spaniels). The neck should be fairly long and powerful, the forelegs short, straight and well-boned (not bow-legged as some people seem to think).

The Clumber body is long and heavy, and near to the ground, the ribs are well sprung, and the back should be straight and broad. The depth of flank is such that the Clumber should show no visible tuck-up. The hindquarters are well angulated, and feet should be large and round. The tail is set low, well feathered, and carried level with the back. A plain white body is preferred with lemon markings, but orange markings are permissible.

THE COCKER SPANIEL

The Cocker should be compact, sturdy and be merry in character, its tail constantly wagging when on the move (an increasingly rare sight, I regret to say). The Cocker head is well balanced and not coarse in any way, with cleanly chiselled skull and square muzzle, with a distinct stop mid-way between. The eyes are full and expressive, never light or loose; the ears are set on level with the eyes, and they should be long enough to reach the end of the nose. You want clean throat and moderate length of neck in a Cocker, and while the breed should not appear "dumpy" in any way, the Cocker should not be a "leggy", or tall breed. The body is compact with well-sprung ribs, and the topline slopes gently down from the end of the loin to the tail. The hindquarters should be well-rounded, with well-turned stifles and short hocks, the cat-feet being firm and thickly padded. The action of the Cocker should cover a lot of ground. The coat is flat and silky, never curly, and remember that self-coloured dogs may only have a little white on the chest.

Denise Barney's Cocker Spaniel dog, Sh. Ch. Cilleine Echelon, won thirty-six CCs and four Gundog Groups during his show career as well as six Best in Show awards at Club Championship shows. He also sired nine British Champions, equalling the post-war record for a blue stud dog. John Hartley.

THE ENGLISH SPRINGER SPANIEL

The English Springer is the most racy of the Spaniels. The skull is broader and more rounded than the Cocker, and there is a distinct brow, divided by fluting between the eyes, which gradually disappears on the forehead, The cheeks should be flat, the foreface should be broad and deep, and well chiselled below the eyes, with a fairly deep and square flew. The almond-shaped eyes should be dark-hazel and very kind in expression. The ears are long and wide, set on line with the eye, and they should lie close to the head. Again, there should be no throat, and the lengthy, muscular neck should be slightly arched and taper towards the head.

The body should be neither short nor long, with deep chest, well-sprung ribs, and a slight arch over the muscular loin. The hindquarters should be moderately well-angulated, and feet tight and well-rounded with strong pads. The tail, like the Cocker's, is set on slightly lower than the back,

Angela Adams' Sh. Ch. Feorlig Country Classic went on to win Reserve Best Gundog at Crufts 1987 following his very first CC and BOB. He was Angela's first show dog and bought primarily as a pet. His first major win was at Blackpool Championship show in 1985 where he won Best Puppy in the breed under the late Joe Braddon, Best Puppy in the Group under Jean Waring, and Reserve Best Puppy in Show under Leonard Pagliero, whose winner that day was the Afghan Hound, Ch. Viscount Grant – later to win Best in Show at Crufts. In 1987 he was also the overall winner of the "New Faces" competition, run by Dogs Monthly magazine in conjunction with Pedigree Petfoods and aimed at first-time CC winners.

David Dalton.

Some British English Springer Spaniel breeders feel so strongly that the American version of the breed has developed differently from that in the breed's homeland, that they have formally suggested that the breed there should be re-named "American Springer". Certainly the breed in America is more glamorous than its British counterpart, as illustrated here by Ch. Salilyn's Condor, handled by Mark Threlfall for Julia Gasow and Donna and Roger Herzig, pictured winning a Sporting Group at the famous Westminster Kennel Club show.

John Ashbey.

and the English Springer Standard actually calls for a well feathered tail, though few will be found in the show ring. The English Springer's action is quite individual, as the forelegs seem to swing forward straight from the shoulder, throwing the feet very far forward, apparently effortlessly. The hocks drive well under the body, and at a slow speed the breed may pace. Look for a straight and close but weather resisting coat, and remember that black-and-white is just as correct as liver-and-white, and either colour may also have tan markings.

THE FIELD SPANIEL

This Spaniel is closely related to the Cocker, yet their heads are really quite different. The Field has a well-chiselled head, which has a well defined occiput and is lean below the eyes. The eyebrows appear to be slightly raised, the eyes are almond-shaped but still wide open, and the stop is moderate. The muzzle is long and lean, if not snipey, and is not squarely cut – it curves from the nose to the throat. It is the relative balance of the skull to muzzle, and also the head profile, which most immediately distinguishes the two breeds.

Also, of course, the Field is larger, being 18 inches at the shoulder, whereas the Cocker should be 15-16 inches. Furthermore, the length of the Field's ribcage is two-thirds of the body length, so it is not really as compact a dog as the Cocker. Otherwise the breeds remain basically similar in coat and movement. In colouring, the Field can be black, liver or roan, or any of these with tan markings. It should also be remembered that clear black-and-white or liver-and-white are unacceptable, so roaning should be obvious in those colours.

THE IRISH WATER SPANIEL

Some enthusiasts argue that this breed should not be regarded as a Spaniel at all, but should be considered to be an HPR breed. I do not propose to enter into that argument in this book. The Irish

Gregory M. Siner's owner-handled Irish Water Spaniel bitch, American Ch. Pool's Ide Oprah O'Reilly, is seen winning Best of Breed under me some weeks after she won the national Specialty for the breed in the USA. At this Long Island show her son was Best Opposite Sex and Best of Winners. Her rather extreme presentation may be frowned upon in Britain.

Bernard Kernan.

On the first occasion I awarded Challenge Certificates in Irish Water Spaniels I gave a first CC to Nick Waters' home-bred bitch, Sh. Ch. Zanfi Calamity (pictured here). Two years later I awarded a third CC to her granddaughter, Sh. Ch. Zanfi Saffron. Saffron's brother, Zanfi Sphinx, created history by becoming the first Irish Water from whom semen was taken to be used on a bitch in the USA. Liz Waters.

Water's coat is its distinguishing feature, being oily and a mass of curls or ringlets. On the body, the coat is dense, crisp ringlets (not as tight as the Curly Coated Retriever), which should not be woolly. The head has a pronounced top-knot of long curls, but the muzzle is smooth as is the throat. The skull is of good length and width with plenty of brain room, the muzzle long and rather square with gradual stop. Eyes should be almond-shaped, fairly small, mid to dark-brown and alert in expression.

The long oval-shaped ears hang close to the cheeks, and the neck should be arched and fairly long. The ribs should be carried well back and so well-sprung as to appear barrel-ribbed (considered a fault in many breeds). The back is short and level, the hindquarters well-angulated and short in hock. The tail should not reach as far as the hock, is thick at the root and tapers to a fine point. It is low set and straight, and the first three to four inches should be covered with close curls which stop abruptly. While the Irish Water should move freely, with reach and drive, a characteristic roll is accentuated by the barrel ribs. The colour is a rich dark-liver with an almost purplish tint.

THE SUSSEX SPANIEL

Like the Clumber, the Sussex is a massive and low-built Spaniel. It has an even more definite rolling gait than the Clumber. It has a wide skull, with moderate curve from ear to ear, with a central indentation and pronounced stop. The brows frown, and the liver nose should show well developed nostrils. The eyes are hazel, fairly large but not prominent, and they create a soft expression, with little haw showing. The ears must be thick, fairly low-set and lie close to the skull (unlike the Clumber).

The neck should be fairly long and arched, but the head carriage is not much above the level of the back. There can be slight throatiness. The forelegs are well boned and short, and the hindlegs should not be noticeably shorter than the fore, or over-angulated in any way. Furthermore, the body must be deep, strong and level with no sign of a waistline. Criticise a Sussex for lack of body shape and you can be in deep trouble! Feet should be well feathered between the toes, round and well padded. There must be ample undercoat, but the top coat is abundant and flat with no curl. The unique colour of the Sussex is rich golden liver, the hair shading to golden at the tip, with the gold predominating. Dark dull livers are not encouraged.

THE WELSH SPRINGER SPANIEL

The Welsh Springer is not as leggy as its English cousin, it is smaller (18-19 inches) and that wonderful rich red-and-white colour. The head is slightly domed in skull, with a definite stop, well chiselled below the eyes. The ears are much smaller than the English and vine-leaf shaped, and the muzzle is not quite as full and deep as the English. Ears should be hazel or dark-brown. The body should not be long, but balanced in relation to the length of leg, with good depth and spring of rib. The loin should be muscular and slightly arched, and the whole body well coupled.

The Welsh is a very basic breed with no exaggerations. It has powerful movement, with great drive from the rear coming from well-developed hindquarters. Judges should remember the Standard's requirements regarding height, and sometimes front movement can pose problems, often being rather wide and loose.

Tom Graham's Welsh Springer Spaniel, Sh. Ch. Russethill Royal Salute over Nyliram, became the first of his breed to qualify for the Dog World/Spillers Pup of the Year finals and subsequently the Pedigree Chum Champions Stakes. He was the top winner in his breed for 1992/93, won Reserve in the Gundog Group at Crufts in 1993 and later distinguished himself by becoming a multiple CC and Group winner.
Andrew Brace.

THE HPR BREEDS

THE GERMAN SHORTHAIRED POINTER

A versatile HPR breed of medium size, which stands over a lot of ground but is short-backed and graceful in outline. It can be solid black or solid liver, or either of these colours in a spotted or ticked coat pattern. The head is clean-cut and neither too heavy or fine. The skull is fairly broad and rounded, and the nasal bone rises gradually from the nose to the forehead without a well-defined stop as such, yet in profile there appears to be definite stop, due to the position of the eyebrows. The lips fall almost vertically from the nose which protrudes slightly, the lips curving slightly to the corner of the mouth. While the lips are well-developed, they should not be pendulous so the impression should be clean rather than "lippy". Dish-faces and snipey forefaces are undesirable.

The eyes should be medium size, soft and intelligent, and they should neither protrude nor appear deep-set. The shade of brown should tone in with the coat. Light eyes should be penalised. Ears are broad and high-set, hanging close to the head. There should be no noticeable fold and they are rounded at the tip, reaching almost to the corner of the mouth when brought forward. The neck is fairly long, muscular and slightly arched, thickening towards the shoulders. There should be no loose skin and the coat is short, flat and coarse to the touch, fitting tautly.

The forelegs are straight, lean and muscular but not coarse-boned, pasterns slope slightly, and the shoulder blades should be close at the top with long upper arms, and the elbows well under the dog. The chest is deep rather than wide, with ribs well-sprung, the ribs reaching well back to the tuck-up. The back is short and firm, the croup wide and sloping slightly to the tail. The hocks should be square with the body and stifles well bent. The tail should be carried horizontally. The GSP's gait is lithe, and at speed the dog will single-track. The breed should cover plenty of ground and show reach and drive, with great propulsion from the hindquarters.

THE GERMAN WIREHAIRED POINTER

This breed is slightly larger and fractionally longer than the Shorthaired, and its head has a moderate stop. Otherwise the breeds are very similar in most respects. The Wire coat should consist of a thicker and harsh top coat, no longer than 1.5 inches, with a dense undercoat. The coat should lie close and not mask the body shape, but it should be sufficiently profuse to provide protection. On the head and ears the hair is thick and short, but never soft, and there should be bushy eyebrows and a full, but not over-long beard. The German Wire can be liver-and-white, solid liver, or black-and-white.

THE HUNGARIAN VIZSLA

The Vizsla, with its distinctive russet-gold jacket, is a medium-sized and medium-boned HPR breed, and coarseness and bulk should always be avoided. The head is lean and aristocratic, with a moderately wide skull and moderate stop. The muzzle should be slightly shorter than the skull, and although it tapers, the muzzle should appear squared-off. The lips should cover the jaws well but not appear pendulous. The nose is brown. Eye colour should be slightly darker than the coat, oval in shape, and neither deep nor prominent. Black or yellow eyes are undesirable. The ears are fairly low set and relatively long, but of a rounded 'V' shape. They are thin rather than fleshy and should hang close to the cheek.

The neck is moderately long, arched and free of throatiness. Pasterns should be upright, and the back level, short, and with high withers. The chest is fairly broad and deep with a prominent breast

*I first met Peter and Liz Harper's Hungarian Vizsla, Sh. Ch. Pitswarren Levi,
as a minor puppy when I judged stakes classes at the 1989 Bath Championship
show and made him Best Puppy on the day. He created a breed record for
puppy wins in 1989, won his Junior Warrant at nine months, gaining his Show
Championship at nineteen months of age. To date, he has won twenty-five CCs
with seventeen BOBs, including Crufts 1993, and has three times taken Best in
Show at breed club Championship events. He is now the top-winning Vizsla of
all time in the UK and the first of his breed to win Reserve BIS at an All Breeds
Championship Show.*

bone. The distance from withers to the base of the chest should be equal to that between the chest
and ground. Ribs should be well sprung, and there is a slight, but not too pronounced, tuck-up. The
croup and back should be well muscled. Moderate angulation is called for with well-developed
thighs. The feet are rounded, arched and tight, and the nails should be a shade darker than the coat.

The tail is fairly thick and, ideally, it should be carried horizontally. The Vizsla has an elegant
gait and should cover the ground with grace. Small white marks on the chest and feet can be
tolerated, but not encouraged. Front movement has been a problem with the breed, but the breeders
seem to have made great strides of late in this direction.

THE ITALIAN SPINONE

The most recent breed to be allocated Challenge Certificate status by the Kennel Club is the Italian
Spinone, an ancient Italian all-purpose gundog which in recent years has found great popularity in
the UK. A very solid dog, the Spinone is dissimilar from most other gundog breeds recognised in
Britain, though in Italy it is very much akin to that country's smoother-coated Bracco. It has a

distinctive head, which should show a pronounced occiput, a lean and flat skull, and be equal in length from nose to stop and stop to occiput. The stop slopes gently and there is a noticeable median furrow. The nose should appear "spongey" and rather large, and it protrudes beyond the rather fine lips, which are not unduly loose.

The Spinone's eyes should be large, quite round and open, with tight lids. In colour, the eyes will be deep-yellow in white dogs and ochre in brown roans. The ears are set level with the eyes and, while fairly long, they should not drop to below about two inches beyond the jaw line. They are triangular in shape, with slightly rounded tips, and the inner edge should hang close to the cheek.

The neck is fairly short but strong and muscular, and there tends to be noticeable dewlap. The Spinone has strong, oval bone, straight forelegs, but with slightly sloping pasterns. The forefeet are round and compact whereas the hind tend to be more oval. Interestingly, the Breed Standard calls for dewclaws on all four feet. A major breed characteristic, not always fully understood by judges, is the Spinone's topline. The withers are rather high and the topline slopes slightly downward to the strong loins, then proceeds to rise upward from the loin to the broad and muscular croup. The croup slopes gently downward to the thick tail – the set of which should be seen as a continuation of the croup.

In proportions, the Spinone should appear equal in body length and wither-height. Its chest is broad, its ribs well-sprung, and the prosternum is quite pronounced. The brisket should reach at least to the level of the elbows. The hindquarters should be broad, muscular and strong, with long thighs and well let down hocks. Movement should be free and true. The Spinone's skin should be thick almost to the point of feeling leathery. Its coat is tough, thick, close-fitting and rather wiry. The eyebrows, moustache and beard help create a rather benevolent and knowing expression.

In colour the breed can be white with or without orange or brown markings, or brown roan in which colour there may be larger brown patches. Judges sometimes expect Spinoni to have black pigment, which they do not. In white dogs, the pigment of the skin, nose, eye rims, and pads tends to be a bright fleshy pink, while in the orange and whites and roans it will be slightly deeper. Some Spinone exhibitors will try to justify indifferent movement with some very interesting stories regarding the breed's original purpose, but the Italian judges to whom I have spoken on the subject assure me that the breed should move true up and down, just as the majority of gundog breeds.

THE LARGE MUNSTERLANDER

This is another multi-purpose European gundog which has found favour in Britain. The head is elongated, but fairly broad in skull which is slightly rounded with no definite occiput. The jaw muscles must be strong, the nostrils of the well-formed black nose should be wide and soft. There is a slight rise from the nasal bone to the forehead yet no pronounced stop. The lips are slightly rounded and close fitting. The eyes should be dark-brown and intelligent in expression, the ears broad and high-set, lying close to the head with a rounded tip.

The ears are feathered beyond the tip. The neck is slightly arched, flowing cleanly into the shoulders, and the chest should have width and the brisket good depth. The back is firm, the Munster should be short-coupled, and there is a slight slope from shoulder to croup. The ribs must be well sprung and deep, reaching well up to the loin. There is just a slight tuck-up. Hips should be broad, stifles well-turned, and thighs well-muscled. The feet are tight, fairly round and well-knuckled, with thick hair between the toes. The nails should be black and strong.

The movement of this very unexaggerated breed should be springy yet long-striding and totally free, but judges should not confuse this slight spring in the step with the "style of high order" spring of the Afghan. Tail carriage is horizontal or in a slight upward curve, not over the back, and the set-on should be in line with the back. The coat of the Munsterlander should not be curly or coarse, the head should be solid black with a white blaze or star allowable. The body is white or blue roan with black patches, flecking or ticking.

THE WEIMARANER

One of the most distinctive aspects of the Weimaraner is its colour, and it is one which many non-specialists find difficulty in appreciating. Breed judges tend to be very critical of overly dark specimens. The Standard actually calls for a silver-grey, with shades of mouse or roe-grey being acceptable. Frequently, a darker stripe will be seen along the back, and the whole appearance should be of a metallic sheen. A small white chest spot can be forgiven. The eyes are also distinctive in that they should be a shade of amber or blue-grey, so judges who seek dark eyes in Weimars are in for trouble!

Some judges often relate the Weimaraner to the Vizsla, but they are actually quite different. The "grey ghost" is a heavier and larger breed, and the heads have several acute differences. The Weimaraner skull and muzzle should be the same length, the occiput should be prominent, the nose is grey, and the ears are set high, reaching to within an inch of the nose. The lips and gums are flesh-coloured. The neck should be fairly long and clean, the elbow-wither height the same as the elbow-ground.

In body proportions the distance from the highest point of the withers to the tail-set should equal the height at the withers. The topline is level, but the croup slopes slightly. The chest is strong and deep with well-sprung ribs, and the Weimaraner should be ribbed well back. The abdomen should be firm and the tuck-up moderate. The brisket should reach to the elbow, and the well-muscled hindquarters should be well angulated. Feet are firm and compact, the nails being grey or amber. The tail should be carried assertively. Movement is true and ground covering, always holding a firm topline.

Judges should remember that the long-haired variety, where the coat is 1-2 inches on the body and feathered elsewhere, is just as acceptable as the infinitely more numerous smooth-coated variety.

Chapter Twelve

THE TERRIER GROUP

This Group has a more diverse collection of breeds than may at first be assumed, and it is unfair to simply regard the Group as being split into short-legged and long. The Border, Bull Terriers, the Staffordshire, the Bedlington, the Dandie Dinmont, the Manchester, the Soft Coated Wheaten and the Skye are all quite different from the more "basic" breeds and represent a great challenge to potential Terrier judges.

In my estimation, Terriers without temperament are not Terriers, and to contemplate giving top honours to one of this Group which lacks "spunk" should be unthinkable.

THE AIREDALE TERRIER

"King of The Terriers" is the alias of the Airedale, and when one of the breed steps into the ring it should say just that. The height of nobility and, as the Standard so succinctly puts it, "on the tip-toe of expectation", yet the Airedale is essentially a cobby, rather than leggy breed, and judges should bear this overall picture in mind. The Airedale expression must be keen and alert at all times, fearless but never aggressive. The expression stems from the neat ears, where the top line of the forwardly folded ear is slightly above the skull level, the dark, small and intelligent eyes, the full foreface and the deep jaws, which create an impression of strength.

The skull and muzzle should be of equal length, the forehead free of wrinkle and the stop barely perceptible. Airedales which lack the fill under the eyes will appear weak, but a subtle chiselling gives the head quality and prevents it from appearing plain. Clean cheeks are essential in the Airedale head, the lips are tight and the nose is black. The neck is clean, muscular, of moderate length and thickness, and free of dewlap.

The front must be perfectly straight and well-boned, the chest deep to the elbows (but not broad), the back short, strong, straight and level with no suspicion of length or softness in the topline. The ribs are well sprung and the coupling is short so there should be little space between the ribs and hips. The hindquarters are well angulated, with good length of thigh and well-muscled second thigh. Feet should be small, round and compact with good depth of pad, and should point straight forward. The tail is high set and gaily carried, without being curled over the back; it should also be of good thickness and strength.

Movement is always true, with the forelegs showing the same distance between the elbows as the forefeet. There should be strong rear propulsion too. The coat is harsh, dense and wiry, lying straight and close, with a softer and shorter undercoat. The best textured coats usually exhibit a slight crinkle. The colour is black or grizzle on the saddle, neck top and tail top surface, the remaining area should be bright tan.

THE WELSH TERRIER

To some judges, Welsh Terriers are miniature Airedales – and apart from size there are few subtle differences. The Welsh head tends not to be as long as the Airedale, and in the Welsh Terrier black-and-tan is favoured rather than black grizzle and tan.

THE LAKELAND TERRIER

The uninitiated judge often confuses the Lakeland and the Welsh, and appreciating type in the two breeds tends to be down to experience rather than study of the Breed Standards, for they are in reality quite similar. The Lakeland will tend to have a broader and somewhat shorter head and it is obviously slightly smaller at 14.5 inches maximum compared with the Welsh's 15.5. The Lakeland may not have as small or deep-set an eye as the Welsh and the expression is, to the educated eye, quite different.

The Lakeland's chest is reasonably narrow and his back may not be as ultra-short as the Welsh, but it should still be strong. Colours differ as the Lakie can be black-and-tan, blue-and-tan, red, wheaten, red-grizzle, liver, blue, or black. (Blacks are currently enjoying a revival in popularity in some Continental countries.) Small flecks of white on the feet and chest are permissible but undesirable, and mahogany or deep-tan are not considered typical (presumably in an attempt to avoid the Welsh confusion on the part of some judges!).

THE WIRE FOX TERRIER

This breed is considered by many to be the most glamorous of the Group with its long neck, short back and paintbox markings. It is said to stand like a well-made hunter, short-backed yet standing over a lot of ground. It is a square dog in that the shoulder-buttock distance should equal the wither height. It should have substance but always great quality and must never look cloddy or common. Like the Airedale, the Wire is always on the alert and quite without fear.

The top-skull should be almost flat, sloping and tapering slightly towards the eyes. Skull and foreface should be equal in length, the foreface tapering from the eye to the muzzle, yet still being well-filled under the eyes. The eyes should be full of fire, quite small and round, while the ears should be folded forward, well above the level of the skull. The Wire's neck is clean, muscular, quite long, gracefully curved in profile and free of dewlap. The chest is deep, never broad, and the forelegs well-boned right down to the feet.

The back is short, strong, level and never soft, the loin muscular and slightly arched, and the foreribs are less well-sprung than the rear, facilitating the relatively narrow, clean-looking forehand. The Wire is very short-coupled and well-angulated behind, with round, compact feet. The tail is carried erect but not over the back. Gait is true and driving.

The coat of the Wire should be dense and, obviously, wiry, with an undercoat of shorter and softer hair. The coat on the back and quarters should be harsher than the sides, and the jaw hair should be crisp and be of sufficient length to give added strength to the foreface. The leg hair should also be dense and crisp. In colour, white always predominates with black, black-and-tan, or tan markings. Brindle, red, liver or slate markings are considered undesirable.

THE SMOOTH FOX TERRIER

The Smooth Fox Terrier's Standard is almost identical to the Wire, but obviously the external appearance is affected to an extent by the different coat, particularly in the head. The Smooth's head is described rather differently from the Wire in that there is moderate chiselling of the foreface, which prevents the head from looking too wedge-like. The Smooth's coat is hard, dense and abundant but should lie flat, and be smooth yet hard to the touch.

THE IRISH TERRIER

This breed is much more racy than the other "long" legged Terriers, and an Irish who looks cloddy or dumpy is just plain untypical, as is one who is ultra-short backed. Its character is all-terrier almost to the point of looking for trouble. The head is long, the skull flat, and the Irish is quite narrow between the ears, narrowing further towards the eyes. The stop is very subtle and while the jaws must be strong, the cheeks should never be too developed. The foreface is full but delicately chiselled, the lips almost black and the nose black. The eyes must be small for the real "Mick" expression, and the ear folded well above the top-skull.

For an Irish to be correctly proportioned it should have good length of leg and moderate length of body, unlike the other "similar" terriers who treasure ultra-shortness of back. The chest should be deep and there should not be the impression of width or fullness about the body. Ribs go well back and are noticeably deep. Angulation is moderate and the feet strong, rather round and small. Black toenails are important, along with sound pads. The tail is carried gaily, but not curled over the back. Movement is straight and true.

The coat, while harsh and wiry, should have a broken appearance, yet not be in any way soft or curly. Leg hair is dense and crisp, and a beard enhances the strength of foreface. The colours in this self-coloured breed are red, red wheaten or yellow red. Like so many breeds, a smattering of white on the chest is acceptable, but white on the feet is a bad fault, as is black shading on the body coat.

Stafford Somerfield's Irish Terrier, Ch. Trackways Booger Red, was imported from the United States and won his British Championship at his first three shows. He went on to win many more CCs and was a consistent Group finalist, winning a Terrier Group at Windsor, also qualifying for the Pedigree Chum Champions Stakes Finals. He is proving his worth as a stud dog in his adopted homeland, with Champion progeny at home and abroad. He is handled by Peter Bell.

David Dalton.

THE KERRY BLUE TERRIER

This is another Irish terrier breed with a keen following. The Kerry should appear upstanding and well-muscled, compact and full of terrier style and character. The head is long and lean with slight stop and flat over the skull. The foreface and jaw should be very strong, the jaw deep and punishing. The nose is black and the eyes as dark as possible, small to medium in size, and very keen in expression. The ears are small to medium, carried forward but not too high. Judges should check gums and the mouth-roof which should be darkly pigmented.

The neck is strong and reachy, shoulders as flat as possible with the elbows carried well under. The forehand should appear neither unduly narrow nor wide. The chest is deep, with tremendous spring of rib, and the topline should be level. The hindquarters should appear large and well-developed, with short hocks and good angulation. Feet should be small and round with black nails. Movement should be powerful, free and true.

The coat texture is soft, silky, plentiful and wavy, and it is this, as well as the colour, which foxes a lot of non-specialist judges. The Kerry is born black and the unique blue colouring comes with age. Slight tan is permissible in puppies, but this should grow out. At about twelve months of age, if a Kerry's coat has not yet "turned", but a brownish colouring can be detected around the root of the tail, there is every chance that it will end up an excellent blue. After around eighteen months, the blue colour should be apparent, in any shade and with or without black points. A small white patch on the chest is the only allowable marking. Remember the maximum ideal height of a Kerry is 19 inches.

THE SOFT COATED WHEATEN TERRIER

The relationship between the Soft Coated Wheaten Terrier, another Irish terrier breed, and the Kerry Blue will probably be the subject of debate for generations to come. Certainly they appear very similar in many ways in countries where the Wheaten is presented in a Kerry-style trim, but in reality they are very different. The temperament, to begin with, is quite different. The Kerry

The Soft Coated Wheaten Terrier is shown dramatically trimmed in the USA and several other countries, but the breed is still exhibited quite naturally in Britain, the coat simply being "tidied up". I awarded Sue Munn's Ch. Snowmeadow Blue Baroo Best in Show All Breeds at a Dorking Open show, and soon after he won his title.

should display "disciplined gameness", whereas the Wheaten should come across as a happy, but characterful, dog. They are similar in size and shape, and the Wheaten should have a natural coat which falls in loose curls or waves.

Colour is very important, for it is this which gives the breed its name. The colour in the adult should be the shade of "ripening wheat". White and red are equally objectionable, but darker shading on the ears should be considered typical. Wheatens tend to be darker as youngsters, but should lighten to their true mature colour by two years of age – a point for judges to bear in mind.

The head of the Wheaten is very distinct from that of the Kerry. It should be fairly long, moderately wide in skull (unlike the leaner Kerry) yet never coarse. It has a well-defined stop (unlike the Kerry), and the muzzle should be shorter than the skull. The muzzle should be square and straight and parallel with the skull. The nose is black and quite large. The head should have a look of power about it, while the bright, dark eyes should be medium in size and have dark eye-rims. The ears are set forward, lying closely along the cheek, the outer edge standing away from the head, again quite unlike the Kerry. The ears should be thin and well-coated. The lips should be black, the neck strong and slightly arched without dewlap. The shoulders should be muscular yet fine, and the forelegs always straight with good bone and muscle. The pasterns are strong but springy and the chest moderately wide. The body is deep-chested, ribs well-sprung, and there should be a squareness of outline, the Wheaten being short-coupled and equal (or even slightly less) in wither-tail length to wither-ground. The thighs are strong, muscular, well-angulated, and the feet strong and compact. There should be black toenails and good depth of pad.

The gait is free, graceful and lively, with long, low strides (in other words, no high-stepping), yet the Wheaten should move gracefully with head and tail carried high. The coat texture should not be woolly nor wiry. It should be loosely waved or curly, and the curls should be soft and silky, light and loose. The coat is abundant, especially on the head and legs. The UK Standard does allow tidying up of the coat to neaten the outline, but the British breeders remain adamant that over-trimming and stylising should be penalised, so judges beware!

THE AUSTRALIAN TERRIER

This is a low-set dog, rather long for its height, so judges should not be looking for a short-backed dog as they would be with a Norwich Terrier, for example. The Aussie should look as rugged as its homeland suggests, with a definite ruff around the neck and a harsh untrimmed coat. It should look "hard bitten", alert, active and totally sound. The head is long with a flat skull of moderate width, and full between the eyes. There is a slight but definite stop, the muzzle is strong and powerful and should be the same length as the skull. The skull has a silky top-knot and the nose is black. Eyes should be small, keen in expression and dark-brown. They should not be prominent, or too close-set.

The neck is long, strong and arched, the forelegs should be well-boned and perfectly straight (not always easy to find!). There is no slope to the pastern and the forelegs should be coated to the knee. The body is long in relation to the dog's height, but the ribs are well sprung and the flanks deep, so there is no obvious tuck-up. The topline should be straight and the tail high set and carried erect. The thighs should be muscular, and the hocks well let down. The feet are well-padded and close, with strong dark toenails. The gait of the Aussie is described as free, springy and forceful. The body coat has a harsh, straight and dense top coat, with a soft-textured undercoat. The muzzle, lower legs and feet should be free of long hair. Blue-and-tans should be richly coloured, with the topknot a lighter shade than the head colour. Puppies will lighten with age and may be quite black to start with. The reds should be free of smuttiness.

THE CAIRN TERRIER

This is another short-legged terrier where ultra-shortness is not required, as the body should be of medium length. It should stand well forward on its paws and have a rugged, weather-resistant coat. The head is not over-large but the skull should be broad, have a definite stop and a powerful muzzle. The jaws are strong, but not long or heavy. The nose is black and the whole head well-coated. Shaggy eyebrows should complement the wide-set, medium size, dark-hazel eyes which appear slightly sunk. The ears are small, pointed, erect but not too closely set and should not be too heavily furnished.

The neck should not be short, there is medium length of leg but the bone should not be too heavy. The forelegs should be tight at the elbow and harsh-coated. The back is level, ribs deep and well-sprung, with a strong and supple loin. The thighs should be very strong and muscular, and bend of stifle should not be exaggerated. Being a digging breed, the forefeet of the Cairn will be larger than its hind, and they may turn out slightly, but the pads should always be thick and serviceable. Poor feet should be penalised.

The short tail is well coated but not feathered as such, and it is not as high-set as some of the terriers. It should be carried "up and out", never over the back. Like most of the terriers, Cairn movement is uncomplicated, being free and true and showing both reach and drive. The Cairn coat is very important and it has alarmed British judges to find the breed being very severely trimmed in some countries. It must be double-coated and weather-resistant, the outer coat being profuse and harsh, with a soft, close undercoat. Open coats are considered a bad fault, and judges should remember that a slight wave in the coat is acceptable. In colour, the Cairn may be cream, wheaten, red, grey or almost black, with or without brindling. Dark points on the muzzle and ears are typical, but black, white, or black-and-tan Cairns are taboo.

THE NORFOLK TERRIER, THE NORWICH TERRIER

For many years the Norfolk and the Norwich were registered as one breed, but for some years they have been separated and regarded as two breeds. The Norfolk has drop-ears which are slightly rounded at the tip, the Norwich has erect ears which have pointed tips. Experts in the breed will tell you that there are subtle differences between the two breeds, particularly in disposition, but for the non-specialist judge this is of little help as the Breed Standards for the two breeds are virtually identical.

They are small, compact, strongly-made terriers with lovable dispositions yet alert and fearless. The skull is broad, just slightly rounded with good width between the ears, which should not be set too closely. The muzzle is strong and wedge-shaped and shorter than the skull which shows definite stop. The eyes are oval, deep-set and dark-brown or black. The expression is always keen and alert. The Norfolk asks for medium length of neck; the Norwich stipulates good length. In reality, there would appear little difference.

The forelegs are short, powerful and straight with round, thick-padded feet. The body is compact, short-backed, with ribs well sprung, and level topline. Hindquarters should be well muscled with good turn of stifle and the tail is set level with the topline and carried erect. The Norfolk and Norwich are one of the few breeds which have anticipated the anti-docking legislation and their Breed Standards make provision for undocked tails which should be as straight as possible, thick at the root, tapering towards the tip and not excessively gay in carriage. On the move the Norwich and Norfolk should have a true, low, driving gait with the hind legs following through the track of the fore. The stifles and hocks should flex well and the topline remain level. The coat is hard, wiry and straight, lying close to the body, and the neck and shoulder hair is longer and rougher. Hair on the head and ears is short except for whiskers and eyebrows. All shades of wheaten, red, black and tan or grizzle are allowed.

The Norwich Terrier, Ch. Sebzevar Claret And Blue, was taken to Spain when his owner/breeders, Frank and Cherry Anne Atkinson, emigrated. However, he did not take to the heat and so came back to the UK where he lived with Marjorie Bunting. Sadly he died when he was just four years old from leishmaniasis, but despite his early death, he had quite an influence on top-winning Norwich Terriers. He sired five Champions including the highly successful sire, Ch. Ragus Leo The Lark. The multiple Group winners, Ch. Ragus The Devil's Own, Ch. Ragus Lucifer's Luck, Ch. Elve The Alchemist and Int. Ch. Elve The Sorcerer, are all line-bred to him.

At a show in Solihull I awarded Claret And Blue Best Puppy All Breeds, and also Reserve Best in Show, when "Sid" was barely six months old, in March 1983. He won Best Puppy in Show at the Norwich Club Open show a fortnight later, taking the same award plus Best in Show at the Club's second Open show of the year. In coming years his progeny was to dominate the Norwich Club's shows. He is pictured as a puppy. Diane Pearce.

THE SCOTTISH TERRIER

This is a thick-set dog which was bred to go to ground. The impression a Scottie gives is of being low, short-backed, big-ribbed and long-headed. While the head should always appear rather long, there should still be decent width of skull, and yet the length of skull is such that it will always appear long and narrow. The skull is nearly flat, clean-cheeked and the foreface strong and deep. Skull and muzzle should be equal in length. The stop is slight, and, in profile, the set of the underjaw is such that the large nose appears to slope downwards and backwards. The eyes are almond-shaped, dark-brown and fairly wide set. They are set deep under bushy eyebrows and have

The Scottish Terrier bitch, Ch. Stuane Highland Empress, was bred and campaigned by Stuart Plane and was one of four Champions from Ch. Stuane Princess Royale and Ch. Kennelgarth Edwin. She won her first CC and BOB plus the Terrier Group at Crufts 1982, but withdrew from the Best in Show competition due to her owner's close association with the judge, the late Reg Gadsden. Empress then won the CC and BOB and Reserve in the Terrier Group at Crufts 1983, and retired from further competition after winning the CC at Crufts 1984 at the age of three, having won a total of twenty-six CCs, eight Terrier Groups and a Best in Show All Breeds, as well as two Pedigree Chum Champions Stakes.

Anne Roslin-Williams.

a sagacious expression. Ears are neat and fine in texture, with large ears being undesirable. They are set high but not too close together. The muscular neck should be fairly long. The deep chest is fairly broad and tends to be hung between the forelegs rather than on top of them. Forelegs which are out at the elbow or well under the body of a Scottie are not typical. Judges should ascertain the lowness of the Scottie body and the correctness of the forehand construction by "going in" through the coat between the forelegs and checking how much "daylight" there actually is between dog and ground. Sometimes profuse coat can be deceiving!

The ribs are well sprung and carried well back and the back is short and muscular, with deep muscular loin which couples the ribs powerfully to the hindquarters. A level topline and bang-on tail-set, with a very thick tail, completes the Scottie outline, bearing in mind that the hindquarters should be unusually powerful, with wide buttocks and well-bent stifles. A thin tail will destroy the outline and balance of an otherwise good specimen. The hocks are short and the feet of good size, close knit and, as with so many terriers, larger in front than behind. The Scottie coat is close lying and consists of a short, dense and soft undercoat with harsh, wiry top coat. Black, brindle or wheaten in any shade are acceptable Scottie colours.

THE SEALYHAM TERRIER

This is another low terrier whose body is rather let down between the forelegs, yet it should be oblong, whereas the Scottie is more square. The Sealyham skull is slightly domed and has width between the ears, but it should be clean-cheeked and square-jawed if a look of quality is to be maintained. The nose should always be black, and the ears are medium-sized and rather rounded at the tip, carried close to the cheek. The neck is moderately long, thick and muscular, and the forelegs short, strong and as straight as possible, bearing in mind that the chest is well let down between them. Elbows should be close to the chest wall and in line with the point of the shoulder.

The topline is level, ribs well sprung, and the chest should be both broad and deep. Strong hindquarters are called for, well bent in stifle, and the hindquarters should extend well beyond the tail-root, creating a definite "bottom" on the Sealyham. The breed should have round cat-feet, thick-padded, and with the forefeet pointed directly forward. The Sealyham coat is wiry on top, with a weather-resistant undercoat beneath. In colour, the Sealyham is predominantly white with lemon, brown, blue or badger pied markings on the head and ears. Noticeable black and heavy ticking is undesirable. The Sealyham movement is vigorous and driving.

THE WEST HIGHLAND WHITE TERRIER

The Westie is considerably more "up on leg" than the Scottie and Sealie, but it is still a deep-bodied dog with typical terrier gameness. The skull is slightly domed, and when you feel across the forehead a smooth contour is noticeable. The skull tapers slightly from ears to eyes and is slightly longer than the foreface. There is a distinct stop with definite forehead and a slight indentation between the eyes. The foreface is well-filled under the eyes, and the rather blunt nose is black. There is a tendency for many modern Westies to be over-long and weak in muzzle. Eyes should be set wide apart and slightly sunk. They are medium size, as dark as possible, and should never appear full. The expression from beneath bushy eyebrows is a piercing one.

Ears are small, erect and carried firmly and end in a sharp point. They are moderately wide apart and free of fringe. The Westie's teeth should be large for its size, and between the canine teeth there should be definite breadth. The neck is long and muscular, thickening into the shoulders. The forelegs are muscular, short and straight, and the elbows well in. The body is compact with a level back and broad loins, the chest deep, and the ribs well-arched in the upper half which creates a rather flat-sided appearance (not to be confused with slab sides which indicate flatness due to lack of any spring).

The back ribs are unusually deep and the Westie is short-coupled, so there is very little tuck-up. The hindquarters are wide across the top, muscular and the thighs not too wide apart. The hocks are well set under the body in such a way that they are quite close to each other when moving or standing. The forefeet are larger than the hind, strong and thickly padded. Judges should check that the underside of the pads and also the nails are black, which is preferred. The tail should be as straight as possible, free of feathering and carried jauntily. The Westie moves freely and with scope, but its hind action is closer than one would expect of some other terrier breeds. The coat consists of an outer coat which is harsh, long and straight, and an undercoat which is furry, soft and close. Open coats should not be considered. The Westie is white, of course.

THE DANDIE DINMONT TERRIER

Of all the Terrier breeds, the Dandie Dinmont is arguably one of the most difficult to judge, possibly because it is so far removed from the "average" in construction, with its low and weasely body. The most obvious "deviation" which hits you about a Dandie is its topline, which is low at the shoulders, then dips downwards and rises in an arch over the loins from where it drops to the root of the tail. The backbone should be well-muscled to make this topline workable, and the ribs are well sprung and rounded, with a well-developed chest which is well let down between the forelegs. The forelegs are short with great musculation and bone, they are set wide apart and the forearms should follow the line of the chest, with feet pointing straight forward or turning slightly out. Bow-legs are not typical.

The hindquarters are – again, unusually – rather longer than the fore, they too are set wide apart but not spread out weakly. The thighs are well developed, the stifles still well-angulated, and the feet are round and well padded with, typically, forefeet larger than hind. Ideally, nails should be dark. The head of the Dandie is very strongly-made and appears large, its muscles showing unusual development, especially those of the jaw. The skull is broad and narrows towards the eyes, which should be set in such a way that the distance from the inner corner to the back of skull should be the same as from ear to ear. The forehead is well-domed, and the muzzle is strong but shorter than the skull. On the top side of the muzzle is a bare triangle pointing backwards to the eyes, otherwise the head should be covered with soft, silky hair which is pronounced in the top knot. The eyes of the Dandie are very distinctive, being large, bright, full and round, set wide apart and low, and of a rich dark-hazel colour, but they should still not bolt. The ears, set well back and low, are pendulous, wide apart and close to the cheeks, but they stand off very slightly at the base. They taper from a broad base, almost to a point, and are very thin with a thin feather of light hair starting a couple of inches from the tip, and of nearly the same colour as the topknot. This may not appear in young dogs until they are about two years of age.

The Dandie should have remarkably large canine teeth for its size, and judges should remember that the inside of the mouth should be dark or black. The neck is very muscular, well-developed and strong, and at the other end the tail is quite short, thick at the root, becoming even thicker for about four inches and then tapering off. It should curve in a distinctive scimitar-style, and when excited the tip should be carried perpendicular to the root. It should not be too highly-set, and on the underside there is neat feathering of hair, which is much softer than the upper side. The coat of the Dandie is very much its own with a soft linty undercoat and crisp (but not wiry) top coat. The coat lies unusually, which is caused by the harder hair coming through the undercoat. Forelegs are feathered.

There are two colours in the Dandie. "Pepper" ranges from a dark bluish-black to silvery-grey, with middle shades preferred. The body colour should come well down the shoulder and hip, and then merge into the tan or fawn of the legs and feet, and the top-knot is silvery white. "Mustard" varies from red to fawn with a creamy white top-knot, and legs and feet slightly darker than the top-knot. The top side of the tail tends to be darker than the body, but the underside is considerably lighter. Despite the Dandie's rather unusual conformation, it should still move quite straightforwardly, having a fluid and easy stride with good rear drive and forehand reach. In temperament, the Dandie is a little more laid-back than many of its competitors in the Terrier Group ring.

THE SKYE TERRIER

The Skye should be long, low and level – twice as long as it is tall, and profusely coated. Judges should remember that Skye ears may be pricked or dropped – some judges have been known to throw out drop-eared specimens, revealing their ignorance of the Breed Standard in the process. The Skye is wary; it should not be vicious, but it is naturally distrustful, and the breed is not always the easiest to judge because of this natural suspicion. The head is long and powerful, with moderate width at the back of the skull, which tapers towards a slight stop and strong muzzle. The nose is black. Eyes should be brown, the darker the better, fairly close-set and full of expression.

Contrary to popular belief, the Skye ear is not that large, but the pricked ear appears so, due to the graceful fall of feathering. In a drop-eared Skye the ears should hang straight, lying flat and close at the front edge. The neck should be long and crested, the chest deep, and legs short and muscular. The ribcage is oval rather than round, deep, and the Skye is ribbed well back. However, the loin should still be short and strong, and the coat-fall will create the impression of a certain flatness. Hindquarters must be well-angulated and muscular. The forefeet should point directly forward, and be larger than the hind. There should be thick serviceable pads and strong nails. The tail should not curl over the back, and is gracefully feathered.

Movement should be straight and true, free and active with strong rear drive. The feet should be as far apart as the elbows, so the front movement is very straight and should also have considerable reach. The Skye is double-coated, with a soft woolly undercoat and a long, hard and dead-straight top coat, which is the breed's crowning glory. The head hair veils the forehead and eyes. In colour, the Skye can be black, either dark or light-grey, fawn or cream, all with black points on the ears. A small white chest-spot is tolerable.

THE BEDLINGTON TERRIER

This is a specialist terrier breed, with a topline which suggests Whippet ancestry, the unusual set of the forelegs, its mincing gait and unique coat. It should be lithe and elegant, yet never weak. It is one of the most mild-mannered terriers in the show-ring, but should still show gameness when aroused. The skull is narrow, but deep and well-rounded, the jaw long and tapering with no stop at all. It is well-filled below the eyes and the lips should be taut with large nostrils. The head is furnished with a profuse silky top-knot which is very light in colour.

The Bedlington has small, deep-set eyes, which should appear almost triangular in shape, and very bright in expression. Blues should have dark eyes, but in the other colours they may be lighter. Ears are low-set, medium size, and "filbert-shaped". They hang flat to the cheek, are thin and velvety in texture, with a "tassle" of silky hair at the tip. The neck is deep-based and long with no dewlap, and the chest deep and quite broad. The forelegs should be appended in such a way that, while they are straight, they are wider apart at the chest than at the feet, so a Bedlington will stand naturally close in front. Judges give themselves away when they try hard to prise apart a Bedlington's forefeet so that the legs appear dead parallel.

The pasterns should be long and rather sloping. The brisket should reach to the elbow, and the back arches over the loin, creating a definite tuck-up. The Bedlington is longer in body than square. The hind legs are of sufficient sweep and length as to create the impression of being longer than the forelegs. The feet are not tight and cat-like, but rather hare-footed with well-closed pads. The tail is thick-rooted and low-set and should never be carried over the back, though its carriage should be in a graceful curve. The flexibility of the Bedlington should suggest ability to gallop at speed, but in the show ring its movement will appear light, springy and mincing, yet always retaining its typical curving topline.

The coat is thick and linty, and should stand well out from the skin, with apparent guard hairs on the back and body of a correctly-coated dog. Bedlingtons can be blue, liver or sandy, with or without tan. Darker pigment is sought after, and judges should remember that while blues should have black noses, brown noses are correct in liver and sandy-coloured dogs.

The Border Terrier, Ch. Brannigan of Brumberhill, was not only the top-winning Border of all time with thirty-one CCs to his credit, but he won seven Terrier Groups, six Reserve Groups and was Best of Breed at Crufts in 1987/88/89. He was a finalist in the Pedigree Chum Champions Stakes in 1987/88/89/90 and won Best in Show at Driffield and the prestigious National Terrier Show, as well as three times taking Reserve Best in Show at All Breeds Championship events. He has sired eight British Champions to date and was owned and campaigned by Stewart McPherson and Ted Hutchinson.   *Dave Robinson.*

THE BORDER TERRIER

This breed is possibly the most workmanlike of the Group, with its no-nonsense expression and entirely functional conformation. One of its trademarks is its otter-like head, with fairly broad skull and short strong muzzle. Black noses are preferred but not essential. The eyes should always be dark and keen in expression, the ears small, moderately thick and dropped forward close to the cheek. The neck is moderately long, forelegs straight, and the bone should never be too heavy.

Rather than being "boxy", the Border should be fairly long-bodied, deep and relatively narrow, so judges who look for short backs and great spring of rib are doomed. The ribs should extend well back, the loins should be strong, and the Border should be capable of being spanned by both hands behind the shoulder. (Though, I must confess, I find this requirement rather odd as it does not take into account the varying size of judges' hands!) The Border has racy hindquarters so they should never appear overbuilt. The feet are small and thick-padded, the tail is fairly short and thick at the base. It should be carried up, but never over the back.

The coat is harsh and dense, with a close undercoat and the skin or pelt must always be thick, and judges should ascertain this when going over a Border. Colours are red, wheaten, grizzle and tan or blue-and-tan.

THE BULL TERRIER

This is the gladiator of the canine world, and has for years remained the province of its specialist judges. Its trademark is its unique egg-shaped head, which should be completely down-faced, of good length and strong, and deep right down to the end of the muzzle. Under the eyes the head should be so well filled in as to give this smooth-contoured egg-like appearance, free of humps, bumps and hollows. The skull should be virtually flat from ear to ear. The head profile curves smoothly downwards to the nose, which should be black and, in turn, curves downwards with the contour of the head. Maybe because of the unusual construction of the head, despite requiring a perfect scissor bite, some Bull Terriers' mouths are not their fortune, and it is up to the individual judge as to how he will deal with a less than perfect bite in an otherwise excellent dog. Certainly, many breed specialists tend to be forgiving of shortcomings in the bite.

The eyes are also very distinctive, being narrow, triangular, set obliquely and well-sunken. They should be as dark as possible and are piercing in their expression. There should be greater length from the eyes to the nose-tip than from the eyes to the top-skull, and the head should exude power. Interestingly, the Bull Terrier Standard is one of the few which stresses the need for dogs to look masculine and bitches feminine. The ears are small, close-set and capable of standing erect. While being strong-shouldered, the Bull Terrier should not be loaded or coarse, yet the forehand should convey an impression of breadth and strength. The pasterns are upright and the feet round and compact with well-arched toes. The bone of the forelegs should radiate strength, roundness and quality, and the foreleg length should equal the depth of chest in mature dogs.

The ribs are very well sprung, and the back should be short, strong, with a slight arch over the broad and muscular loins. The underline should have a distinct, yet very gentle, upward curve so that there is shape, but not a decided tuck-up. Hindquarters are well angulated with good development of second thigh, and good strong bone right down to the foot. The tail should be short and thick-rooted, not wispy, and it should be carried horizontally. The Bull Terrier should move jauntily but show reach and drive with great power. The skin should fit the entire dog tautly, and the coat is short and harsh with a glossy appearance. Colours are white – with or without head markings – and "coloured" dogs may be predominantly brindle, red, fawn or tricolour, though the Standard suggests brindle is preferable. Ticking in the white is not to be encouraged. The Bull Terrier is unusual in that its Standard does not give weight or height limits, it merely suggests that there should be the impression of maximum substance for size, consistent with quality and sex.

THE MINIATURE BULL TERRIER

The Miniature should be judged by exactly the same Standard as the Bull Terrier, but its height limit is 14 inches.

THE MANCHESTER TERRIER

This an elegant close-coated breed, whose colour is only jet-black with rich mahogany markings. Its skull is long and wedge-shaped, clean-cheeked with good fill-up under the eyes. The muzzle tapers consistent with the wedge-shape, and it should be tight-lipped. The small almond-shaped eyes should be dark and sparkle with expression, and they should never be prominent. Ears are small, V-shaped, and tip forward well above the top line of the head in such a way that their tips lie close to the head above the eyes. The neck is quite long, arched at the crest, and thicker towards the base. The forehand should appear fairly narrow but deep, the forelegs being straight and well under the body.

The body is short, the ribs well-sprung, and there is a definite slight arch over the loin, accentuating the tuck-up. Hindquarters should be muscular and well-angulated, and the feet, while small, are mid-way between the cat and hare foot, still showing well-arched toes. The thick-rooted tail should complement the graceful outline with its set-on, and should not be carried higher than the level of the back. The coat is very glossy and tight, and the mahogany markings should be located as follows: on the muzzle to the nose, a spot on each cheek and above each eye, on the underjaw and throat in a distinct V-shape, from the knee down (but the toes should have black pencilling and the distinctive "thumbprint" on the pastern), inside the hind legs, under the tail (sufficiently narrow to be covered by the tail), and on each side of the chest. It is important that the two colours should never merge, but always be clearly defined.

THE STAFFORDSHIRE BULL TERRIER

The most numerically popular of the Group, and the secret of judging the breed well is to get the ideal balance between the "bull" and "terrier". Some specimens favour one or the other and end up appearing rather leggy and racy, or alternatively too low-set and cloddy. Being a fighting dog, the Stafford should be well-boned and constructed in such a way that it is extremely solid and stable and it should be fit, hard and with no loose bits which could be torn off in combat. The head is relatively short and deep, with great breadth of skull and unusually pronounced and developed cheek muscles. There is a distinct stop, short and strong foreface, which should be tight-lipped, and the nose should be black. The ears should be rose or half-pricked, and the neater and less

Illustrating an ideal blend of "bull" and "terrier" is Bryn Cadogan's aptly-named pied Staffordshire Bull Terrier dog, Ch. Bullseye of Dogan. He was the top-winning Stafford of 1991, winning ten CCs in all, and went on to Reserve in the Terrier Group at Crufts 1992. His wins include Best in Show at the parent club's Championship show in both 1990 and 1991.
        Alan Raymond.

obtrusive the better. The neck is quite short but very muscular and clean, widening well into the shoulders. The forelegs are set wide apart to give stability. They are straight and well-boned, with strong pasterns and slightly outward-turning feet. The elbows should be tight with no play. The body is close-coupled with wide front, well-sprung ribs, deep brisket, and the hindquarters should be well-muscled and let down. The feet are well-padded and nails should be black in solid-coloured dogs. The "pump handle" tail (not always easy to find these days) is low-set and carried low. The gait is free, powerful and agile, with the minimum of effort being expended. There should be great rear drive. Black-and-tan or liver are very undesirable colours, but otherwise all colours with or without white are acceptable, when the white predominates the term "pied" being used.

SUMMARY

Despite their varying shapes and sizes, most of the Terriers call for movement which is straight and true, showing drive and animation, the Bedlington having its unusual mincing gait and the West Highland moving a little narrower through the rear than some judges would normally expect. As I have said earlier, the original purpose of these breeds should be borne in mind when assessing them in the show ring, and courage and gameness should be high on the list of priorities.

Chapter Thirteen

THE UTILITY GROUP

The present Utility Group contains a wide variety of breeds which, it was evidently decided, did not slot neatly into any of the other more specifically functional groups. The entire grouping system is currently under review in the UK, and it will be interesting to see what changes, if any, are made among the Utility breeds. Many feel that the interests of the Akita would best be served in the Working Group, that the Toy Poodle should be classified as a Toy, and that the Japanese Spitz and Keeshond would lend themselves to a newly-formed Spitz Group. Time will tell. For the most part, our Utility breeds presently encompass those which can loosely be described as companion dogs, yet not so diminutive as to be regarded as Toys.

THE BOSTON TERRIER
This is an American creation of Bulldog descent, and its Standard poses something of a problem in that the variation in size is so wide. While the breed in Britain is now fairly stable, it must be remembered that the Boston can be up to 25lbs in weight. The current Standard still makes provision for three weights – Lightweights (under 15lbs), Middleweights (15-20lbs) and Heavyweights (20-25lbs). Most of the specimens seen in the show ring tend to be light or lower middleweights, and this seems the most popular size.

The Boston head is clean and square, flat on top, wrinkle-free and clean-cheeked. There is a distinct brow and deep stop, with a very short, square muzzle. This is exceptionally wide and deep, with no suggestion of narrowing, and totally proportionate to the skull. The muzzle tends to be one-third of the skull length (but is sometimes, I suspect, rather less), and the upper lines of the foreface and skull should be parallel. The nose is black and wide, with a distinct line between the nostrils. Jaws are broad and square with deep, but not "lippy" flews. The eyes are set wide apart, large, round, dark, and alert yet kindly in expression. The outer corners of the eyes should be in line with the cheeks when studying the dog head-on. The ears are carried erect, thin, and are wide set. In order to maintain the correct expression and strength of underjaw, the bite should be level or slightly undershot. The classic Boston head is a thing of great quality and beauty.

The arched neck is fairly long and flows cleanly into the shoulders. The forelegs are set a little wide apart in line with the shoulders, they are straight-boned and well-muscled with short, strong pasterns and firm elbows. The body should have width and depth, the back is short, and the croup curves slightly to the tail which is low-set, short and can be straight or screw. There is slight tuck-up, and the body should appear short without being dumpy. There is good turn of stifle in the hindquarters and musculation should be evident. Feet should be compact and round with well-arched toes. The Boston's gait is smart, straight and true, and the coat is short, fine and gleaming.

Brindle is the preferred colour, with the brindling showing through the base colour in distinct relief, but black is acceptable, and both colours should have white markings. Perfection in markings is achieved with a white muzzle, even white blaze right over the skull, full collar, breast, part or all of the forelegs, and the hind feet.

THE BULLDOG

Most people will admit to finding the Bulldog one of the most perplexing breeds to judge – in many respects it is so different from the "average". The movement of the breed is most important, and when a Bulldog is correctly constructed it will appear to move quickly on tip-toes, leading with one shoulder and almost skimming the ground with the hind feet. Imagine a Bulldog as a rugby-forward and you won't go far wrong.

Obviously, the head is a characteristic of the breed. It should be large in circumference, and there should be great depth between the corner of the jaw and the top of the skull. The cheeks are well developed and wide of the eyes. The forehead is flat with loose wrinkled skin, but this should not overhang the face Bloodhound-style. There is a wide indentation between the eyes, and a furrow runs from the stop to the middle of the skull. The foreface is short and broad with great sweep of underjaw, and while the Bulldog Standard does not actually say, in so many words, that the mouth is undershot, it always is – sometimes extremely so. The canine teeth should be wide apart with incisors in a straight line, and judges should remember that the Standard is explicit in requiring the teeth to be out of sight when the mouth is closed – so don't let exhibitors try to tell you otherwise!

There should be great depth from eye to jaw, with large, broad and black nostrils. The Bulldog's nose should be laid back towards the eyes, and the stop to nose-tip should be no longer than the nose-tip to lower lip. The chops should be thick, broad and deep, hanging well over the jaws at the sides, yet not in front so as to obscure the upturned underjaw. The eyes are set low in the skull and wide apart. They are round and dark and should show no white when looking ahead. The ears are high-set, small, and rose-shaped, always carried backwards. The neck should not be long, but it should be very thick, deep, and strong and well-arched at the back. Unlike many breeds the Bulldog should have plenty of thick, loose and wrinkled skin around the throat, which forms dewlap on either side. The shoulders appear to be almost tagged-on as an afterthought, for they are wide of the cavernous ribcage which is well let down between the forelegs. The forelegs are stout-boned and very muscular, set wide apart, straight, and the immediate impression is of a rather bowed front. Despite this illusion, the forelegs must, in actuality, be straight. The elbows are low and sit well away from the ribs. The topline of the Bulldog dips behind the shoulders and rises to a definite roach back, dropping more sharply to the tail. The massive chest and neater loin create a pear-shaped body with a good tuck-up.

The hindquarters of the breed are very distinctive, having length and musculation to raise the loins. There is no great angulation, and as the stifles tend to stand out from the body, the hocks will appear quite close and the rear feet turn outwards. The feet are rounded, and the rear more compact than the fore. The tail is also unique, sticking out at first, then turning downwards. It varies in length, but should be short rather than long. In colour, the Bulldog can be whole-coloured, where black masks or muzzles are optional, or pied. Black or black-and-tan are highly undesirable.

THE CHOW CHOW

This is another difficult breed for non-specialists with its short, stilted gait, minimally angulated hindquarters, and blue tongue and gums. The breed is essentially dignified and aloof and carries itself with unhurried style, its tail proudly over its back. The skull is flat and broad with no pronounced stop. It is well filled under the eyes, which are small, dark, almond-shaped, and should be free of the entropion which has haunted the breed for so long. Happily, breeders now seem to be heeding the revised Standard, and clean, healthy, yet still relatively small eyes can often be found.

The muzzle is not very long and should have good breadth, never appearing pointed. The nose should be black, but creams can have a light-coloured nose, and in the blues and fawns it may be self-coloured. The ears are small, thick and slightly rounded at the tip, they are set wide apart and tilt noticeably forward and towards the centre of the top-skull. This creates the typical "scowl" which should never be confused with a wrinkled forehead, though some Chow exhibitors have a tendency to exaggerate the scowl by pushing the skin of the head forward.

The tongue should be blue-black, as should the mouth-roof and flews, preferably with black gums. Judges have to check this, and not all Chows are keen to co-operate. Thankfully, most handlers automatically show these points to the judge. The neck is not short, but strong and full and slightly arched. The forelegs are perfectly straight, well-boned and with small, round cat-feet. The chest is deep and broad with well-sprung ribs, powerful loins, and the back should be short and level with no softness in the topline. The tail is high-set and carried right over the back. The hindquarters are rather straight, but still muscular, and the hocks never flex forward. A Chow who has great turn of stifle and drives behind will not have the typical action. This is not a ground-covering breed.

There are two coats, though, sadly, smooths are seldom seen winning top honours as their rich, plushy coat is most attractive and not really "smooth" at all! The rough coat should have a soft woolly undercoat and then a profuse, straight and coarse outer coat which stands off. Coat should be thicker on the mane and pants, the mane on the male helping to create the "leonine" appearance.

THE DALMATIAN

Bred as a carriage dog, the Dalmatian should be biddable and supremely fit, capable of considerable endurance, and I feel judges should attach great importance to movement in such a breed. It is, of course, spotted with either liver or black, and the spots should be round and well-defined, evenly distributed, and larger on the body than elsewhere. They are coin-size and should never merge into large irregular patches.

The Dalmatian head is fairly long, flat in skull and quite broad between the ears, which are high-set, wide at the base, moderate in size and taper to a rounded point. They should be fine to the touch, carried close to the head, and should, ideally, be spotted. There is moderate stop, and the head should be completely free of wrinkle. The muzzle is long and powerful, but should never be mean or pointed. There should be no hanging flews, the lips being clean, and the nose should be black in black-spotted dogs and brown in livers. The eyes are fairly wide-set, medium size, round and sparkling with intelligence. They should be dark in black-spotted dogs and amber in liver. The eye rims should be correspondingly pigmented.

The neck is quite long and elegantly arched, free of throat and thickness. The elbows are set close to the body, and the forelegs are quite straight with strong, round bone right down to the feet, though there is a certain flexibility in the pasterns. The feet are round and compact, with well-arched toes, and the nails can be black or white, or brown or white, depending on the spotting. The body should not be too wide, yet it is deep with well-sprung ribs, facilitating plenty of heart and lung room, which is essential in an endurance dog. There is a slight arch to the loin, though the back should be level and strong. The Dalmatian's hindquarters should be well rounded with noticeable strength of second thigh, and good turn of stifle. The tail reaches more or less to the hock, is strong-rooted and tapers. It should never be set too low or too high, and is carried with a graceful upward curve, but never curled. Ideally, it should be spotted. On the move, the Dalmatian should exhibit great freedom, fluidity and a long stride, and it should look as if it could go on all day. The coat is hard, short and dense with a definite gloss. Beware of patches, tricolours and lemon spots, and bronzing on spots is not desirable in mature dogs.

THE FRENCH BULLDOG

This breed is said to have "clown-like" qualities, though these are difficult for a judge to ascertain in the environs of the show ring! The Frenchie is a sturdy and compact breed, whose "bat ears" give its head a unique expression. The head is square, large and broad, but not so much so that it is out of balance with the whole dog. The skull is almost flat between the ears, the forehead is rather domed, and there is a little loose skin which should form noticeable wrinkles. The muzzle is deep and broad, and the cheeks well-developed without giving the head a "football" appearance.

The nose and lips should be black, and the stop is very well defined. The underjaw should be

I first judged Jill Keates' French Bulldog, Ch. Nokomis Omeme, at the West of England Ladies Kennel Society's Members' Limited show when she was eight months old. I made her Best Puppy and Best in Show. She went on to become the top-winning French Bulldog of all time, winning the last of her thirty CCs at Crufts 1992 from the Veteran class. She also won two Utility Groups during her illustrious career. A classic example of line-breeding, she was from a half-brother to half-sister mating which produced four Champions. Diane Pearce.

broad and deep, well turned-up with a slightly undershot mouth. The lips are thick and should hide the teeth, and while there is ample cushioning of the muzzle, it should not be so exaggerated as to hang below the jaw level. Eyes should be dark, medium size and round, set wide apart and low in the skull, and there should be no white showing when the dog looks ahead. The distinctive "bat ears" are wide at the base, medium size and definitely rounded at the top, creating a tulip-shape. They are high-set, carried upright and parallel, and should not be too close together.

The neck is powerful with just a little dewlap, it is thick and nicely arched and should not appear too short and stuffy. The cobby body is short and well-rounded with plenty of width of brisket, and a definite roach back. There is something of a pear-shaped appearance created by the width at the shoulders narrowing to the loins, and a decided tuck-up. The hind legs are longer than the fore which raises the loins, and while the hocks are well let down, there is no great hind angulation. The feet should be small and compact with sound pasterns, and the hind feet tend to be a little longer than the fore. They should be well-knuckled, and preferably, the thick, short nails should be dark. The tail is short and low-set, thick-rooted and can be straight or kinked.

The movement of the Frenchie should be free and flowing, and it tends to have rather a "busy" demeanour. The fine coat is lustrous and can be brindle, fawn or pied. In brindles there can be white, provided the brindle predominates. Fawns must have black eye lashes and rims, and a few brindle hairs are acceptable. In pied dogs the white predominates over the brindle patches, and include white specimens in which the eye lashes and rims must be black.

THE JAPANESE AKITA

The Akita has rapidly risen to the fore in the UK as a popular show dog, the breed being founded primarily on American imports. There is currently a move afoot in FCI countries to stick rigidly to the advocated Japanese Standard, which calls for a lighter-built dog in which there are only three solid colours allowed, and no "pintos" – which are, by far, the most popular colour both here and in the USA. Judges officiating in the UK can only go by our accepted Standard.

The Akita is a large and powerful dog with heavy bone and lots of substance. It has a large, broad head with large, flat skull and broad forehead, and quite small eyes, which are almond-shaped, dark in colour, set apart, dark, and tight-rimmed. The ears are a breed characteristic, being small, thick, triangular, but somewhat hooded, and high-set. When the ears are alert, their forward-pointing will, in profile, be seen as a continuation of the markedly crested neck.

The cheeks are well developed, and the nose bridge is straight. The muzzle is strong, broad, and shorter than the skull. The large nose and tight lips should be black, but in white dogs flesh-colour is allowed. The thick, muscular neck should be relatively short, and the forehand should be tight-elbowed with straight, well-boned legs, and pasterns inclined slightly forward. Feet should be thick and well-knuckled with hard nails. The balance of the Akita body is fractionally longer than tall (10 to 9), with allowance being made for a little extra length in bitches, so judges should not be looking for an ultra-short dog with a long neck. The Akita is wide and deep-chested, with its depth of chest equalling the chest-ground height. There should be a well developed forechest with just moderate tuck-up. Hindquarters are strong and very muscular, with just moderate turn of stifle. The tail of the Akita is large and full, high-set and carried over the back in a curl, which should always dip to or below the backline. It should be strong-rooted, and when relaxed the tail should reach to the hock. The tail hair is coarse and straight. In action the Akita exhibits strength and vigour, and a moderate length of stride. It will single-track when gaiting.

The coat texture is important, with a soft and dense undercoat topped with a coarse, straight and rather stand-off outer coat. On the withers and rump the hair will be longer than on the body, but there should be no suggestion of either a mane or feathering. In the UK we accept any brilliant colour, and in the particolour (pinto) dogs, the markings should be well defined. A mask or blaze is optional with the UK Standard. A word of advice to judges – it is not advisable to crouch down and view the Akita's expression at eye-level. They may feel the need to establish their dominance.

THE JAPANESE SPITZ

Some judges seem to view the Japanese Spitz as a miniature Samoyed because of its colour, yet it is quite different in build and head. The breed should stand up to 14 inches at the shoulder, it has a profuse coat which is pure white and stands off. It is marginally longer in body than tall. The head should be free of coarseness, moderately broad and slightly rounded in skull, which is broadest at the occiput. There is a definite stop and the forehead should not protrude, so beware of rather "bulbous" skulls. The muzzle should be pointed but not too thick or too long. The lips are tight and should be black, as should the relatively small nose. The eye-rims should also be black, and the eyes should be dark, medium size and oval, set slightly obliquely and not too wide. Ears should be small, triangular, set high and fairly close, and tilting forward.

The Japanese Spitz neck is strong, arched, neither obviously long or short, and the forelegs should be straight with firm elbows and slightly sloping pasterns. They should not be too heavily-boned, and the feet are small and cat-like, with black pads and preferably dark nails. The chest is broad and deep, ribs well-sprung. There is a definite tuck-up to the broad loins, and the croup is slightly arched with a straight back. The tail is high-set and curled over the back, and the coat is double with a soft, short and dense undercoat and a long and straight top-coat. The coat pattern should form a definite mane on the shoulders which drops down to the brisket, and the tail should be very profuse. In action, the Japanese Spitz is very light on its feet, nimble and true.

THE KEESHOND
Another Spitz breed, with the typical Spitz characteristics of small, pricked ears, a wedgey head, and tail curling over the back. The Keeshond is a short-backed and compact dog who can be up to 18 inches at the shoulder. The head is wedge-shaped, but in profile the stop is noticeable. The muzzle should be dark and equal in length to the rather flat skull. The muzzle should not be too "blocky", but at the same time it should never appear snipey. The lips should be black. The eyes

Jean Sharp-Bale's Keeshond, Ch. Neradmik Jupiter, is the top winning Keeshond of all time with thirty-eight CCs, twelve Utility Groups, four All Breeds Best in Show awards and three Best in Show wins at Breed Club Championship shows. He was also an overall winner one year of the Pedigree Chum Champion Stakes Finals. Jupiter was my winner when I judged my first Utility Group.
                                                                          Dave Freeman.

are dark, medium size and almond-shaped. They are set obliquely, and the eyes should be framed by the breed's unique "spectacles", which consist of a line of black hair from the outer eye to the lower ear, along with a contrasting shade of coat around the eye surrounded by explanatory markings. The ears should be dark, small and erect, set neither too wide nor too close.

The neck is actually quite long and well-arched, but it is covered with a thick ruff of coat which makes it look shorter than it is. The forelegs are straight and well-boned, and the front of good width, with well-padded, round cat-feet. The feet should be cream in colour but with black nails. The body is square with well-sprung ribs, and good depth of brisket. The muscled hindquarters do not have too much angulation, and the tail is quite long, high-set and curled well over the back. A double curl is highly-prized, and the tail is lighter on its upper side when curled, with a black tip.

The Keeshond coat is harsh and stands off, the top coat being straight and the lighter-coloured undercoat soft and thick. There should be no feathering below the hock. In colour, the Keeshond is a blend of grey and black, with pale grey or cream undercoat. Various shades of grey are equally acceptable, and the body hairs are black-tipped. Shoulder markings are distinct, and while pencilling is acceptable, there should be no black below the wrist or hock.

THE LHASA APSO
The Lhasa Apso and Tibetan Terrier were originally classified as one breed, and both are

At a Members' Limited show in Sheffield, I gave a first Best in Show to a young Lhasa Apso bitch who was giving her owner, Jean Blyth, rather a hard time. Saxonsprings Fresno went on to create history, not only in her breed but in variety competition, later passing into the ownership of her handler Geoff Corish. She was BOB at Crufts four times between 1981 and 1989, winning the Group there in 1988 and Reserve in 1981 and 1989. She was Dog of the Year All Breeds in 1982, won the Contest of Champions, and the finals of both the Pedigree Chum Champions and Veteran Stakes. Through her children, notably Norwegian Ch. Saxonsprings Fol de Rol and Danish Ch. Saxonsprings Famous Flyer, she has influenced the breed worldwide. She won forty-seven CCs in all, the last of which was awarded by me. She remains, in my opinion, the most exceptional dog I have ever judged.   Thomas Fall.

undeniably related to the Tibetan Spaniel and the Shih Tzu. Today the four breeds are quite distinct, and judges would seldom confuse any two, though it is worth remembering that the Lhasa is smaller than the Shih Tzu, being a maximum of 10 inches at the shoulder, with Shih Tzus half-an-inch taller.

The Lhasa moves jauntily and is an alert dog, but can be a little aloof with strangers. Its skull is moderately narrow and seems to fall away behind the eyes. While it is not quite flat, it is certainly not dome or apple-headed. There is moderate stop, and the muzzle should be about one-third the length of the entire head, and not too blunt. The eyes are forward-looking, medium size, dark and oval, with no white showing and never bolting or sunken. The ears hang close and are heavily feathered, the coat blending in with that of the head and neck.

As with all the Oriental breeds, a certain strength of underjaw is vital to get the arrogance of expression, and with this goes the typical Lhasa mouth which is fractionally undershot, or a reverse scissor – whichever you prefer! The incisors should be in a broad and straight line, and be warned ... the breed is not known for outstanding mouths. The neck is strong and noticeably arched, with forelegs straight and feet round, firm-padded and cat-like. The Lhasa is not a square dog, as its wither-buttock length is greater than its wither height. The topline should be level, loin strong, and the breed should always appear compact and well-knit. The Lhasa should have well-developed hindquarters which are well-muscled, and there should be good angulation – but this should not be so excessive as to create weakness. The tail is set high and carried well over the back, and there can be a kink at the end.

The Lhasa is profusely coated all over its body. There is only moderate undercoat and the top coat should be long, heavy, straight and rather hard. Far too many Lhasas have a silky top coat, which is quite untypical. The action of the Lhasa is free and jaunty, and not as forcefully driving as the Shih Tzu, but the movement of the two breeds these days seems to be getting very similar. In colour, the Lhasa can be any shade of red or grey, dark grizzle, black, white or particolour.

THE POODLE

There are three sizes of Poodles recognised in the UK – Standard (over 15 inches), Miniature (11-15 inches) and Toy (under 11 inches), and in Europe a fourth size has been accepted, so that sizes there are now Standard, Miniature, Toy and Dwarf. Whatever size is being judged, the Breed Standard remains the same, and the smaller specimens should ideally be merely scaled-down versions of the larger. It is also worth remembering that in the UK, when judging Standards, the only requirement as regards size is that the dog should be over 15 inches. The British Standard does not say "the bigger the better!" Indeed, on the Continent, the Standards have a maximum height, which seems quite logical when the other sizes have to.

To me, the very essence of a Poodle is its elegance, balance and very proud carriage. It is light on its feet, and should move freely, effortlessly and with lots of rear drive. No matter how exquisite a Poodle may look when standing, or how brilliantly it is barbered, if it moves around the ring with a clunking, laboured action, it is not a typical Poodle. A recent bone of contention has proved to be the method of presentation, as the British Breed Standard still calls for adherence to the traditional lion clip, although the Continental and Scandinavian "pants trim" are being seen more and more in our rings – much to the disgust of some long-serving Poodle breeders.

The Poodle's head, at its best, is truly wondrous. It should be long and fine with a slight occipital peak. The skull is never broad, and there is just moderate stop, though this sometimes appears more severe due to exaggerated spraying and forcing forward of the topknot. The cheeks are clean and smooth, and the foreface well chiselled yet never falling away under the eyes. The lips should

The Standard Poodle dog, Int. Ch. Rackateer Exquisit Sinner, owned by Charlotte Sandele and breeder Margareth Vear, enjoyed a spectacular career in Scandinavia where he was Sweden's Dog of the Year All Breeds in 1991. During his Scandinavian campaign he had won Best of Breed under such notable British Poodle specialists as Ken Bullock, Clare Coxall and Peter Young. In 1992 he entered the British show ring, being campaigned under the ownership of Roger Stone and Graham Thompson, and quickly won his title. His major British win was that of the Utility Group and Best in Show at the Scottish Kennel Club show in August 1992 where the author was judging. Both in Sweden and Britain, Sinner has proved to be an outstanding sire with many excellent progeny.
Andre Giercksky.

be tight and the chin strong but not protruding. The eyes are dark, almond-shaped and should be full of character, almost to the point of wickedness. The low-set leathers are long and wide, and should frame the face. The whole head should have a beautifully moulded appearance, full of quality and refinement.

The Poodle neck should be fairly long and strong, there is no dewlap and it should carry the head in a very dignified and self-possessed manner. The forelegs are straight, the feet tight, quite small and oval, with arched toes and thick, hard pads which are well cushioned. The chest is deep and fairly wide, the ribs well-sprung and rounded, and the back is short and strong, yet with a slight hollow. Loins should be broad and muscular, leading into well-muscled and angulated hindquarters. The thick-rooted tail is set on high and should be carried up, but at an angle away from the body. In some countries the fashion seems to be for a tail carriage which is almost over the back. This is quite wrong and spoils the naturally elegant outline of the breed.

The coat texture is very important, being profuse, dense and very harsh in texture. When you put your hand into a Poodle's body coat, it should spring straight back into position. Soft, floppy coats are not typical. In colour, the Poodle may be any solid colour. Ideally, blacks, silvers, blues, whites and creams should have black nose, lips, eye rims and nails. Browns can have amber eyes, dark liver nose, lips, eye rims and nails. Apricots have dark eyes with black points, or deep amber eyes and liver points. There should be allowance made for colours in young dogs, which are a little varied in intensity in the creams, apricots, browns, silvers and blues, but beyond 18 months the colour should be even.

THE SCHIPPERKE

This breed was once described to me as looking like "a little highwayman on horseback" – a good description, in view of its keen expression and abundant cape. While black may be the most popular colour, any whole colour is acceptable. The Schip should look distinctly cobby and have a lively, foxy expression. The skull is fairly broad and flat with little stop. The ears are of medium length, not too broad-based and should taper to a point. They should be carried erect and be very firm. The eyes are dark-brown, oval rather than round. The muzzle is of moderate length and although rather fine, never weak or underdone, with plenty of work under the eyes.

The neck is strong, broadly set on the shoulders, and slightly arched. It is rather short, and this shortness is accentuated with the mane and frill of thick, stand-off hair. The forelegs should be completely straight and of enough bone to balance the body. Feet are small and cat-like, and the Schip should stand well on its toes. The forelegs should be set well under the chest, which is broad and deep-brisketed. The back is short, strong and straight, and there is an acute tuck-up.

The hindquarters are rather light in comparison with the fore, but should still be well-muscled with a nicely rounded rump and well let-down hocks.

The gait of the Schipperke indicates quite a short, but very brisk, stride and should be true from all angles. The coat is abundant, dense and harsh, smooth on the head, ears and legs, and close-lying on the back and sides. Around the neck is the typical mane and frill, and to the rear should be plentiful "culottes".

THE SCHNAUZER

There are three sizes of Schnauzer. All

Pictured here with his owners' young son, is Jeff and Sandra Sampson's Schipperke, Ch. Hallbower Hans. This dog was the top CC winner in his breed for 1989, 90 and 91 and the top Schipperke stud dog for 1992. I awarded him his first Utility Group at Darlington in 1991, and I also gave him the CC and BOB at Windsor that year.

Diane Pearce.

share basically the same Standard, apart from size. The Schnauzer and the Miniature Schnauzer currently appear in the Utility Group, the Schnauzer being up to 19 inches at the shoulder, and the Miniature, ideally, 14 inches for males. The Giant Schnauzer is classified in the Working Group and should be 23.5-27.5 inches in height. Schnauzers are square-bodied dogs, very robust and sinewy, and judges would be well advised to remember that the Breed Standards stress that conformation should always triumph over colour, and what it describes as "purely beauty points".

The Schnauzer head is strong and fairly long. It narrows from the ears to the eyes and then further to the nose. The skull is quite broad with muscular but not bulging cheeks, and the forehead should be flat and without wrinkle. There is a medium stop, accentuated by the bushy eyebrows, and the muzzle should be powerful. I find that some Miniature Schnauzers tend to fall away under the eyes and are rather weak in the muzzle, which is quite alien to the breed. In profile, the foreface and forehead should appear virtually parallel, and the muzzle terminates quite bluntly, finishing off with moustache and beard.

The nose should be black and the nostrils wide. The lips are tight and the eyes dark, oval, forward-looking and medium size, creating a sagacious but keen expression when coupled with the eyebrows and beard. The ears are high-set, neat and drop forward. The Schnauzer has a

The Miniature Schnauzer bitch, Ch. Risepark Remember Me To Armorique, owned by Shaune Frost and David Bates, won her first CC as a youngster under me in May 1991. She won her title later that year and was the top CC winner for her breed in 1992, becoming a finalist in the Pedigree Chum Champions Stakes that year, and also winning Best in Show at the Schnauzer Club of Great Britain's three-variety Championship show.

John Hartley.

moderately long neck (but not exaggeratedly so), which has a slight arch, and there is no dewlap. The forehand should be quite broad-chested, with straight forelegs which are well-boned. Short cat-feet are required with firm, black pads and dark nails.

The musculation should be clean and smooth rather than bulging, and while there is width about the front, the elbows should be close to the body. The breastbone is apparent, and the back should be straight and strong, yet slope very slightly towards the hindquarters. There is good spring of rib, and the thighs, while flat, are well muscled, with good rear angulation. The Schnauzer tail is set on and carried high. Study the profile in action – the Schnauzer should retain its firm topline at all times, and demonstrate excellent reach and drive.

The coat is smart with a dense undercoat and a short, wiry top coat. The leg furnishings should be of thick, harsh hair (not silky – many Miniatures, in particular, fail in this respect). In Miniatures it should be remembered that specimens who appear "Toyish" are to be avoided. The colours in Miniatures are pepper-and-salt, black, and black-and-silver. In the latter, the silver should appear on the eyebrows, muzzle, chest and brisket, below the elbows and stifles, on the vent, and under the tail. Schnauzers and Giant Schnauzers may be pepper-and-salt or solid black. Pepper-and-salts should have a dark facial mask, which blends with the coat colour, and the pepper-and-salt should be an equal mix of what are technically black and white hairs, banded alternately, with no brown.

THE SHIH TZU

The growth of hair on the Shih Tzu's head creates a chrysanthemum effect quite naturally, but modern-day presentation has resulted in a much more stylized top-knot. The breed has a naturally arrogant carriage, and when the Shih Tzu moves its gait should be smooth and flowing, reaching well forward, driving strongly from the rear and showing the full pad as it goes. The head is broad and round, wide between the eyes, which are large, round and set well apart with a kindly expression.

The muzzle is of proportionate width, square, short (but no shorter than about an inch, as are many of the breed these days) and flat, but not wrinkled. The nose should be black, but dark-liver is acceptable in liver-marked dogs. As Pekingese blood was introduced into the Shih Tzu not that long ago, judges should be on the look-out for Pekingese traits in the breed (e.g. wrinkles about the foreface, ultra-short muzzles, bowed forelegs etc.) as the contemporary specimen should be as pure as possible in type.

The nose should be level or slightly tilted upwards, and the top of the noseline should almost be level with the lower eye rims. Nostrils should be wide open, and pinched nostrils or down-noses are highly undesirable. On the muzzle, the pigment should be as solid as possible. The ears are large and long, set fairly low and carried drooping close to the head. They are heavily furnished and appear to blend in with the hair on the neck. As I have mentioned before, in these Oriental breeds strength of underjaw is vital to the arrogant expression, and the Shih Tzu mouth should be level or slightly undershot, with level lips.

The neck is well arched and long enough to facilitate proud carriage. The legs are short, muscular, well-boned and as straight as possible (not easy to find, as it should be remembered that the broad chest is rather let down between the legs). The feet are rounded, firm and well-padded, and they appear rather large because of the hair. The Shih Tzu's body is longer from withers to tail-set than the wither-height, but is well coupled and sturdy with deep, broad chest and a level backline. The hind legs are short and muscular with strong bone, and the thighs are well-rounded and muscular showing moderate turn of stifle.

When I judged the Puppy Stakes on the second day of the legendary snowbound LKA, I awarded both Dog and Bitch classes to Shih Tzu littermates owned and bred by Judy Franks. The bitch (pictured) became Ch. Hashanah Take Me To The Top and won sixteen CCs with twelve BOBs and three Utility Groups. Her litter brother is now Ch. Hashanah Hot Pursuit, who has twelve CCs with eight BOBs and one Group. Interestingly, this precocious pair were bred from two Champions, both bred by Margaret Stangeland of the highly successful Weatsom affix. She won her first-ever CC under me with her lovely bitch, Ch. Weatsom Only You.

Mick Franks.

The high-set tail is well furnished and carried gaily over the back, and it should be remembered that the height of the tail where it curves forward and downward to the back should be level with the skull. In some countries, the craze is for very long necks, ultra-short backs, and tails which are carried right down on the back almost like a Pug! This totally destroys the natural balance of the correct Shih Tzu outline. The coat is long and dense with no curl, and a good undercoat. A slight wave is acceptable. All colours are permitted, and in particoloured dogs a white blaze on the forehead and also a white tail-tip are considered very desirable.

THE TIBETAN SPANIEL

Gone are the days when Tibetan Spaniels were mistaken for bad Pekingese, as the breed has made great strides in Britain where it becomes increasingly popular. The Tibetan should be a small dog with a relatively small head, and it should be slightly longer in body than its height at the withers. It is an assertive little dog, which is quick-moving, but it can be aloof with strangers, so judges should exercise a little tolerance when dealing with puppies, especially.

The head should not dominate the profile of the Tibetan, as it should be relatively small. It should be masculine in males, but never coarse. The skull is slightly domed and of moderate width

Ch. Kensing Rusk is the first combined British and American Tibetan Spaniel Champion and was the top winner in his breed in the USA for 1986. He won his first CC when I was judging at Bath 1982 when he was just ten months old. Before being exported, Rusk helped himself to his owner/breeder Jane Lilley's bitch, Ch. Kensing Dahlia. This clandestine union resulted in Ch. Kensing Glory Be who was Top Tibetan Spaniel brood bitch for three years, having produced at least one Champion in each of her three litters. One of her offspring, American Ch. Kensing Pongo, became the first-ever Tibetan Spaniel to win Best in Show All Breeds at an AKC general Championship show. Both Pongo and Rusk are owned by Dick and Carole Jeffery of Maryland. McFarlane.

and length. The ears are of medium size, fairly high-set, and they should have a definite lift from the skull before dropping forward. It is this ear-lift which is essential to a classical Tibetan expression, and it is one aspect of the breed which seems to be getting lost internationally. The low-set, heavy ear, which folds completely forward with no lift, will create a bland expression lacking alertness.

The muzzle is of medium length, with no side wrinkles, blunt and well-cushioned, but not short and cushioned to the extent of the Pekingese. I feel the Tibetan muzzle should just be sufficiently padded to prevent it from appearing boney. There should be good depth and width of underjaw, with a slightly undershot mouth which should be wide between the canines. The eyes are black-rimmed, dark-brown in colour and oval. They are set fairly well apart and forward looking. The old Breed Standard included the invaluable "ape-like expression", which will come to life when you see a really excellent Tibetan head. The ears should be well feathered in adults.

The neck is quite short but strong, and a gentle crest enhances the outline. It carries a shawl of longer hair, which is usually more marked in dogs than bitches. The forehand of the Tibetan causes some judges problems. The Tibetan is only moderately-boned and any hint of heaviness or great bulk is to be avoided. Although the forelegs should have a slight bow, they should be firm at the elbow. So, in other words, the top of the foreleg begins directly above the foot, then curves down, gently outwards and inwards to the foot. The feet are small and hare-shaped, neat, and feathered between and beyond the toes. Cat-feet are taboo in the breed, and judges who praise tight feet are in big trouble!

The body has good rib-spring, a level back, and the length should be just slightly more than the shoulder height. Far too many Tibetans are getting low to ground, long in back, and with these traits invariably come a more Pekingese-like forehand. The hindquarters are moderately angulated and strong, with a high-set tail, which is well feathered and carried in a gentle curl over the back when moving. Many Tibetans will down-tail when static, and judges should never penalise this.

The top coat is silky and flat-lying, and there is a fine and dense undercoat. Ears and the back of the forelegs should be well feathered, and the buttocks and tail furnished with even longer hair. The breed should never carry a stand-off coat which destroys its natural outline. All colours and markings are allowed – a boon for judges! Remember that the maximum weight is 15lbs.

THE TIBETAN TERRIER

While the Tibetan Terrier was originally lumped together with what is now the Lhasa Apso, it has for several years been classified as a quite separate breed with a maximum shoulder height of 16 inches. Like all Oriental breeds, it can be a little reserved. The head is of medium length, never broad or coarse, and it narrows slightly from ear to eye. It should not be domed, but neither should it be totally flat between the ears. It should not appear cheeky, and there is a definite but not exaggerated stop. The muzzle is strong with a well-developed lower jaw and the skull-muzzle ratio should be about equal. The nose should be black, the ears not too large and carried slightly away from the head. Eyes are large and round, fairly wide-set, and dark-brown with black rims. The Standard now allows for a scissor bite, but it still accepts the traditional slightly undershot (or reverse scissor). The incisors are set in a slight curve.

Forelegs should be straight and with slightly sloping pasterns. The body should be square, well-ribbed, with a short, slightly arched loin and level back. The hindquarters are well angulated with low hocks and the tail high-set and carried well over the back in a curl. A kinked end is no fault. The feet are large and round, and the TT stands well down on its feet – something which some judges tend not to appreciate. The gait is smooth and free with good reach and drive. The coat has a fine woolly undercoat, and a top coat which is fine but fairly dry and never silky or woolly. It can be straight or slightly waved, but never curly. In colour the TT can be any colour except chocolate or liver, particolours being equally acceptable as solids.

Chapter Fourteen

THE WORKING GROUP

There are several sub-groups to be found within the Working Group. Breeds such as the Bearded Collie, Belgian Shepherd Dog (with its four varieties), Border Collie, Briard, Rough Collie, Smooth Collie, Hungarian Puli, Old English Sheepdog, Shetland Sheepdog, Cardigan and Pembroke Welsh Corgis are essentially herding, or pastoral, breeds. Others, like the Bouvier des Flandres, German Shepherd Dog, Maremma Sheepdog, Pyrenean Mountain Dog and Swedish Vallhund may have originally been bred as herding dogs but have developed into dogs which fulfil guarding and other roles too. Breeds such as Boxers, Dobermanns, Bullmastiffs, Giant Schnauzers, Mastiffs and Rottweilers are basically guarding breeds, while the Group also contains breeds which had a specific original purpose, like the St Bernard, Newfoundland and Siberian Husky. Others such as the Bernese Mountain Dog, Great Dane, Norwegian Buhund and Samoyed are arguably multi-purpose dogs.

   Britain's Working Group is now unmanageably large with almost fifty breeds, many of them not as yet awarded Challenge Certificate status, and, as I write, the Kennel Club is currently investigating the possibility of a total re-grouping. The USA, Canada and Australasia have for some years split their Working Group into two, removing the relevant pastoral breeds into a separate Herding Group, a possibility that could well come into being here. All of the breeds which appear in the Group were developed by Man to do a specific job of work, and their original function should be understood before embarking on a judging career. The first Standards were drawn up around function, and soundness and stamina remain important.

THE BEARDED COLLIE

The Beardie is a fit and active dog, slightly longer than its height which should still show some daylight under its body and consequently never appear "dumpy". The skull is broad, flat and square with skull, muzzle and ear-to-ear being the same length. This creates a head which has ample brain room and good strength of foreface. The stop is moderate, nose large and square and usually black but in blues and browns it will often follow the coat colour which is quite acceptable. The lips should be solidly coloured and, like the eye rims, should follow the coat colour. The eyes are wide set, large, soft and kindly. The eyebrows tend to arch up and forward but should not hide the eyes. Ears are moderate size and hang down, but when alert they will lift at the base which gives the skull greater apparent width. A level bite in the breed may be tolerated, but is undesirable, the normal scissor being preferred.

   The neck is of moderate length, muscular and slightly arched. The forelegs are straight, well-boned, but with flexible pasterns. Feet should be well padded, oval in shape and with close and arched toes. The length of the Beardie comes from the ribcage and not the loin, the chest is deep and ribs well-sprung, so there is the requisite heart and lung room for a functional working sheepdog. The topline is level and tail set low, with no kink or twist, and in length it should reach to the hock. It is carried low and there is an upward swirl at the end. The tail flattens out at speed, but should not be carried over the back.

The hindquarters are well muscled with strongly developed second thighs, good turn of stifle and low hocks. On the move, the Beardie should cover ground effortlessly, having suppleness and a long-reaching stride. Its coat should have a soft, furry undercoat, while the top coat is flat, harsh and shaggy with a slight wave being permissible. The hair should not be so profuse as to mask the basic outline of the dog, and trimming is definitely out! The typical Beardie expression is enhanced with longer hair on the sides of the muzzle while the hair length increases from the cheeks to the lower lips and chin towards the chest.

Judges may be forgiven for thinking that the only colour allowed in Beardies is grey-and-white, but acceptable colours are slate, red-fawn, black, blue, all shades of grey, brown or sandy, and these can be self-coloured or with white markings! In "flashy" dogs, the white is typically situated on the foreface, as a blaze, on the tail-tip, on the chest, legs and feet, and in a collar. White should not extend beyond the shoulder or appear above the hocks. Slight tan is allowed on the eyebrows, inside the ears, on the cheeks, under the tail-root, and on the legs where the white joins the base colour.

THE BELGIAN SHEPHERD DOG

The Belgian Shepherd Dog has been the subject of a raging controversy in Britain due to the Kennel Club's decision to classify the four distinct varieties as one breed, competing in one ring for one set of Challenge Certificates. I do not propose to go into the pros and cons of this action, or to speculate as to the consequences. For the purpose of this book, what we should remember is that the four varieties share the same Breed Standard – the only difference is coat and colour.

The Belgian is a guarding sheepdog which is wary, but never timid or sharp. Its movement is brisk, free and true, and when gaiting it gives the impression of an almost skimming motion. The head is delicately chiselled and long without being unbalanced. The skull and muzzle are approximately the same length, with the skull being of moderate width. In profile, there is moderate stop and the flat forehead should be parallel to the topline of the muzzle. The muzzle tapers gently to the nose, which is black and with wide nostrils. Under the eyes is fine chiselling which creates a look of quality, and while the cheeks are flat, they should be noticeably muscled. The forehead should not appear prominent over the eyes.

The Belgian's lips are thin but firm, and strongly pigmented. A pincer bite is tolerated but scissor preferred. Eyes are medium size, tending towards an almond-shape and preferably dark-brown. Eye rims should be black and the expression is direct and inquisitive. The ears are triangular, high-set, stiffly erect and of fair length, with the outer ear rounded at the base. The neck is quite long, supple, well-muscled and free of dewlap. The nape is arched. The Belgian should give the impression of being a rather wiry dog, but with strong bone and powerful muscle. The withers are distinct, the forelegs long, straight and with short, strong pasterns and a clearly defined wrist. The body combines strength and elegance. Males should be fairly square-bodied, with females tending to have a little more length. The chest is deep, ribs just moderately well sprung, and there is no marked tuck-up. The rump slopes slightly from the level back.

Hind angulation should not be excessive, but there should be strong muscling and the hocks should be well let-down. The forefeet are round, the hind rather more oval, but all should be close-

Sue and Mike Young's Belgian Shepherd (Tervueren), Ch. Vallivue Bon Chance is proof that not all great dogs take off dramatically as puppies. Having attended thirteen Championship shows and won fourteen Second prizes his owners nick-named him "Second Chance"! However, he went on to distinguish himself with seven Groups (including Crufts 1992) and six Reserve Groups. He currently holds the breed record with thirty-four CCs (twenty-eight with BOB), he has been Best of Breed at Crufts in 1991/92/93 and twice qualified for the Finals of the Pedigree Chum Champions Stakes. He has been Best in Show at both the National Working Breeds and Working Breeds Association of Wales' Championship shows.

David Dalton.

toed with thick, springy soles and strong nails. The tail is strong-rooted and hangs to the hock, at which level its tip will turn slightly backwards. In action, it will raise in a curve and the tip may be carried just slightly above the back line

THE GROENENDAEL: This variety is solid black, with permitted white in a small star or stripe on the chest, between the pads and on the tips of the hind toes, or subtle frosting on the muzzle. The outer coat texture is long, straight, moderately harsh and plentiful, with the undercoat being very dense. There is a definite ruff around the neck, which is more pronounced in males who are generally heavier coated and more lavishly furnished than bitches. The opening of the ear is protected by hair, the forelegs carry a rear fringe, and the hindquarters and tail are well coated.

THE LAEKENOIS: This is reddish-fawn with black shading, mainly in the muzzle and tail areas. Its coat texture is harsh, dry and wiry, but not curly. The hair lies in locks all over the body, and the muzzle hair is sufficiently short to prevent a heavy or blocky appearance. Fluffy and fine hair amongst the locks is undesirable.

THE MALINOIS: This variety can be any shade of red, fawn or grey with a black overlay, which means that the individual hairs have a lighter base colour with black tips. The blackening becomes more definite with maturity, especially in males, and noticeably around the shoulders, back and ribs. There is a black mask no further up than the eyes, and the ears are mainly black. The tail should have a darker tip. White is allowed to the same extent as the Groenendael. Once a dog has reached the age of 18 months, a wishy-washy or too black colour is not considered desirable. The actual texture of the coat is thick, close and firm on top with a woolly undercoat. The hair is thicker on the tail, and neck where it lies like a collar, running from the base of the ear to the throat.

THE TERVUEREN: Exactly the same colour as the Malinois, and the same texture as the Groenendael.

THE BERNESE MOUNTAIN DOG

This is a draught dog of great versatility. It is a very strong and sturdy breed, whose stunning coat pattern of jet-black, rich red and pearly white make it a real eye-catcher. It should be friendly and fearless, but never aggressive. The head is strong with a flat skull, slight furrow, and well defined stop. The muzzle is straight and strong, with lips developed sufficiently to comfortably cover the

When Pam Aze entered her pet Bernese Mountain Dog puppy for a Redditch Limited show in 1981, she entered him in every single class for which he was eligible! I was so impressed with the young Forgeman Footpad that I gave him eight First Prizes, Best Puppy and Best in Show All Breeds. Footpad went on to win thirty CCs, and was for some time the Breed Record holder. He won his last CC from the Veteran class at the Bernese Mountain Dog Club Championship show when he was ten years old. Apart from being a highly successful show dog, "Paddy" was a much loved companion and an active P.A.T. dog, visiting hospitals and schools, a job he enjoyed enormously.

jaw, but not so much so that they appear to hang loosely. The eyes are dark-brown, almond-shaped, and the eyelids should fit well, not loose or showing haw. Ears are medium size, high-set and triangular, lying flat when relaxed but raised at the base and brought rather forward when aroused.

The neck is strong and muscular and of moderate length, the forelegs straight and well-boned, with slight flexibility of the pasterns, and short, round, compact feet. Contrary to some judges' belief, the Bernese should be compact rather than long, about 9 parts tall to 10 long. The chest is broad, with well-sprung ribs, and brisket deep enough to reach to the elbow or beyond. The back should be strong and straight with a cleanly rounded rump. The hindquarters are broad, strong and well-muscled, with well-bent stifles and hocks well let down. The tail should reach to just below the hock, it is raised when alert, but never curled or carried too gaily over the back.

The Bernese movement should exhibit good reach in front and drive behind, with a balanced stride. The breed has a huge problem with front action, the majority coming on extremely wide and loose. The coat is long, soft and silky with a natural gloss, and while there can be a slight wave, it should never curl. The main body coat is shining jet-black. The rich red markings should appear on the cheeks, over the eyes, on all four legs, and on the chest. A balanced white blaze and white chest marking are considered essential, and, ideally, there should be white on the paws (extending no higher than the pastern) and tail-tip. There are sometimes a few white hairs on the nape of the neck and in the anal region. These are undesirable but tolerable.

THE BORDER COLLIE

This is a relatively recent addition to the British show ring and the breed has, inevitably, developed into more of a "show dog" than some of the original workers which appeared in the ring. This is largely due to the influence of several imports from Australia and New Zealand where the breed has for many years been developed as a high-quality exhibition animal. (I was a little taken aback however, when attending, some years ago, a seminar given in Sydney on "The Australian National Breeds", to find that the Border Collie was included. I became unbelievably Celtic on that subject!)

While the present-day Border Collie may be getting aesthetically more and more impressive, breeders remain keen to maintain the functional aspects of the breed, particularly as far as movement is concerned. The Border moves stealthily with little lift of the feet. Its gait is smooth and effortless, and somewhat low in that it is not a head-high, tail-high, proud carriage, but rather a scopy, reachy and purposeful action. Moderation is essential in the Border. It should never appear bulky and coarse, but on the other hand it should never appear underdone or weedy.

The skull is fairly broad with no pronounced occiput. The cheeks are full or rounded, and the muzzle, although tapering, is quite short and strong. The skull and foreface should be equal in length. There is a definite stop, well-developed nostrils, and the nose should be black except in the case of brown dogs where it can be brown. The eyes should be set wide, oval in shape, and medium size. They should be brown, but merles can have one or two blue eyes. The expression should at all times be mild and indicate intelligence. The Border ears may be either erect or semi-erect, where the tip drops forward neatly. They are set well apart and medium size.

The neck is long, strong, arched and muscular, with forelegs straight but with slightly sloping pasterns. Elbows should be well under the body, and while the bone should be strong, it should not appear unduly heavy. The chest is deep rather than broad, the ribs well-sprung, and the loins muscular and deep so there is no tuck-up. The Border should be slightly longer in body than its shoulder height. Thighs should be long and deep, with good turn of stifle and obvious musculation. The hocks should be short, and the feet should be oval with deep, strong pads, and well-arched toes, close together and with strong, short nails.

The tail is quite long, reaching at least to the hock, is low-set, and has an upward swirl to the end. It can be raised when the dog is excited, but should not be carried over the back. The Border can be fairly long-coated, in which case there is a dense top coat with a soft dense undercoat, and abundant coat which forms a mane, breeches and profuse tail. It can also be smooth-coated, which specimens lack the "furnishings" previously described. The colour can be virtually any, but white should never predominate. In many show specimens the traditional collie markings of white collar, shirt front, legs, feet and tail-tip are apparent.

THE BOUVIER DES FLANDRES

This is a herding and guarding breed, fairly new to the UK, where it is nothing like as popular as it is in Europe where Bouviers are to be found on every street corner. The Bouvier is short-bodied and should impress instantly with his overall power and apparently massive head, which is made to look even more so by the profuse beard and moustache. The skull should be well developed but clean-cheeked, flat and slightly longer than wide, the muzzle being shorter as 2 is to 3. The stop is in reality quite shallow, but it appears more accentuated because of the upstanding bushy eyebrows.

For several years the USA's Kennel Review magazine organised a Tournament of Champions at which the nation's top rated dogs were invited to compete. One of the recipients of the "Show Dog of the Year" title was Gloria and Nathan Reese's Bouvier des Flandres, Ch. Galbraith's Iron Eyes, handled by Corky Vroom. They are pictured with three of my co-judges for the event, Denny Kodner, R. William Taylor and Sari Brewster Tietjen.

The muzzle is broad, powerful, and slopes slightly towards the nose, which must never appear pointed. The nose should always be black with wide nostrils and rather rounded. There is a definite moustache on the upper lip, while the lower carries a full harsh beard, and these help create the typical forbidding expression of the breed. The eyes should be alert, rather oval, and fairly wide set on the horizontal. They should be as dark as possible. Ears are high-set, triangular, and fall forward towards the cheeks. The Bouvier's neck should be shorter than the length of its head with a definite arch and strong nape. It should be free of dewlap.

Forelegs are straight, parallel, well-muscled and heavy in bone, with slightly sloping pasterns. Feet should be short, round and compact, with strong, black nails and hard, thick pads. The body should be square with the chest deep to the elbows and ribs well-sprung, but the underline should be such that there is hardly any tuck-up. The rump curves slightly from the horizontal topline, and the tail is carried gaily when in action. Hindquarters show just moderate angulation and should be obviously well-muscled. The Bouvier's gait is driving and free; it sometimes has a tendency to amble, and this is permissible if not desirable.

The Bouvier can be from fawn to black (the "fawns" sometimes bordering on cream), and are more usually brindle of varying shades. Interestingly, the breed changes colour markedly as it darkens with age. A white chest-spot is permissible, but predominating white or chocolate are highly undesirable, and wishy-washy colours are not to be encouraged. The coat should be plentiful and the density should be such that, when a judge separates the body coat by hand, the skin is difficult to see. The hair should be coarse, dry and matt rather than glossy. The Bouvier should look unkempt, but never woolly or curly. Lack of undercoat is quite untypical and the undercoat must be really dense. Size should vary from 23 inches in bitches to 27 inches for dogs, these being the recommended minimum and maximum.

THE BOXER

The first two words of the Boxer Breed Standard are "great nobility", and I feel that judges should have this uppermost in their minds when judging the breed. The sight of a stallion male Boxer, arching his neck, kicking his heels and strutting around as if to say "I am the king", is a thrilling sight. I must confess to loathing the current fashion of stacking Boxers with a chunk of liver in one hand and a tail in the other! The most ordinary Boxer can, with clever handling, be screwed into position to throw out a quite eye-catching outline, but let it stand naturally on a loose lead and the picture tells a different story. The Boxer should be biddable but self-assured and fearless and, as the good ones have no problem standing their ground unaided, I find them much easier to judge when they stand naturally, than when they are turned into cardboard cut-outs!

It has often been said that this is a "head breed" and it is true that, no matter how brilliantly constructed a Boxer may be, if it has a head like a plank, it cannot be an outstanding Boxer. The skull should be lean, the cheeks clean, and the muzzle should be broad, deep and powerful. There is forehead wrinkle when the dog is aroused, but otherwise the skull should appear dry. There should be noticeable creases at the side of the muzzle, and the dark mask should be clearly defined, rather than running into the base colour. The profile of the Boxer head shows great rise of skull, a distinct stop, and at the end of the muzzle (which should be one-third the length from nose to occiput) the broad, black nose should be tilted upwards. Lack of this tilting will create a down-face and bland expression.

The muzzle should be very well padded, and its fullness is enhanced by support from the well-developed lower canines. The mouth should be undershot, with the incisors of the lower jaw sitting in a straight line. This is not easy to find, and wry mouths and rounded underjaws are

At her last show as a puppy, I awarded Walker and Yvonne Miller's Boxer bitch, Ch. Crackers at Walkon her first CC. I still considers her to be one of the most correct Boxer bitches I have ever judged.

commonplace. Vital to the Boxer expression is tremendous depth and width of underjaw with a noticeable upward sweep, so that the upper lip rests perfectly on the lower. Lack of chin gives a "frog face", which makes the Boxer look positively gormless. The eyes should be dark-brown, forward facing, never too small or bolting, with well-pigmented rims and haws. Ears should be medium size, set wide apart on the skull and lying close to the cheek when relaxed. Alert, the Boxer's ears will fall forward with a definite crease.

The Boxer's neck should be aristocratically arched, quite long, and free of dewlap with the nape quite marked. The strongly-boned forelegs should be straight and parallel, with very slightly sloping pasterns, and well-arched cat-feet. The forehand construction should be such that the elbows are well under the body when seen in profile. From the front they should be sufficiently wide to allow great depth of chest, but not so much so as to appear "Bulldoggy". The body is square with well-arched ribs which extend well back. The Boxer is short-coupled, has a pronounced but gentle tuck-up, and the topline is straight and slopes slightly to the high-set tail.

The hindquarters should be very strong with obvious musculation standing out from underneath the skin, and should be really "hammy". There should be good angulation with well-developed second thighs and short hocks. The Boxer's movement should have great reach, rear drive, and be totally free and powerful. Interestingly, the Boxer Standard makes no mention of the accuracy of "up and down" movement which can, perhaps, account for the shortcomings seen in this direction, but as it stresses the profile action in detail, why do so few Boxer judges appear to really study this aspect of the dog in action?

The coat is short, tight-fitting and glossy and can be fawn or brindle, with or without flashy white markings, which should never be more than one-third of the base colour. Something which has crept in, almost undetected, over the years is the poor quality of brindling. The Standard specifically requires the black stripes to contrast against the base colour, and they should run parallel to the ribs all over the body. Today, you will find many brindle Boxers where the stripes merge indistinguishably with the base colour to create the appearance of a dog which is almost black. It can be argued that this is not the most important feature of a Boxer, but it is a clearly detailed aspect of the Standard which is obviously, in some instances, being ignored.

THE BRIARD

This is a rugged, herding dog, with a long, dry coat, marginally longer than tall, with double dewclaws and a hooked tail-tip. It is fearless and intelligent, and its gait indicates suppleness, also showing great ground-covering qualities and strong rear drive. The skull is slightly rounded, and the skull and muzzle should be proportioned as two equal rectangles. While the skull has sufficient width for brain room, it is fractionally narrower, cheek-to-cheek, than the distance from occiput to stop. The stop is distinct and the muzzle very strong. Snipiness is a major fault. The nose is noticeably large, square, and always black.

Ears should be high-set and well fringed, and they do not lie too close to the cheeks. In fact, when the Briard is alert it will lift its ears forward and out, which will create a wider-skulled appearance. Eyes should be horizontally placed and rather large without being bolting. They should be benign and intelligent in expression, dark-brown and always with black rims. The neck is long, strong, muscular and well arched giving proud carriage.

Forelegs should be well-boned and straight, the chest should be quite broad and there is moderate spring of rib. The back is firm and level with a minimal slope to the croup. Thus, the tail is rather low-set. Hindquarters are well angulated, but the hocks should not be set too low. Double dewclaws should be present on the hind legs. The tail should reach to the hock or beyond, and it should have a distinct crochet-hook at the end, though this small breed characteristic seems to be fast disappearing.

The body coat should be long, slightly wavy and dry rather than shiny. There is a dense and finer undercoat, and the head hair should consist of moustache, beard, and eyebrows which fall over, but should not completely obscure, the eyes. In colour, the Briard can be slate-grey, black or fawn, and blacks can have a few individual white hairs distributed through the coat. Fawn varies in shade, though the darker hues are preferred. However, in my experience many light-coloured youngsters mature to a much richer and darker fawn. Fawns can have dark shading on the ears, muzzle, back and tail, but these should merge gradually into the fawn. Often you will find black hair which is so solid that there is a definite demarcation line between the fawn and black. This fault constitutes a bi-colour, which is not acceptable.

THE BULLMASTIFF

This breed is a reliable guard which, despite its overall bulk, should never appear cumbersome but rather serviceable. The square skull is large, and its squareness should be apparent from any angle. It has a degree of wrinkle when alert, but otherwise should appear clean-skulled. The circumference of the skull can equal the height at the shoulder, but few judges take a tailor's tape measure into the ring to establish that fact! The cheeks should be full, and there is a pronounced stop. The short muzzle should be one-third the length from nose to occiput. Interestingly, these are the same proportions as given for the Boxer, yet when you compare the profiles of the two breeds, generally speaking, the Bullmastiff will appear rather shorter in foreface than the average Boxer. Which has remained more faithful to their Standard, I will leave you to ponder.

The Bullmastiff should be broad under the eyes, and this width should persist almost to the end of the nose. The muzzle is square with the underjaw broad, and the bite may be level or slightly undershot. The incisors should be strong and well spaced. The nose is broad with well flared nostrils and, unlike the Boxer, should be flat rather than having any turn-up. The lips are well developed but should not hang below the jaw. Eyes should be hazel to dark-brown, set apart, with a furrow between. Ears are V-shaped, set high and wide. The point of the ear should be at eye-level when the dog is alert, and rose ears are very undesirable.

The neck is very muscular, but should still show an arch. The chest is wide and deep, well let down between the straight and well-boned forelegs. Pasterns are straight and strong, and feet well-arched and cat-like. Dark toe nails are a plus, and the pads should be hard. The back should be short and straight, and the tail set high, strong-rooted and tapering, reaching to the hocks and carried straight or curved, but not scimitar-fashion. The Bullmastiff's hindquarters should be muscular with wide loins and well-developed second thighs. On the move the Bullmastiff gaits purposefully, true in front and back, and with good rear drive.

The coat is short and hard, but weather-resistant and lies close. In colour, the Bullmastiff can be any shade of brindle, fawn or red, and the colour should always be bright and not dilute. A small white spot on the chest can be forgiven, and a black muzzle is essential, toning off towards the eyes rather than distinctly contrasting as in the Boxer. Dark markings around the eyes help create the typical expression.

ROUGH AND SMOOTH COLLIES

The two Collies do not, as is often supposed, share the same Breed Standard with differences only in coat. The Smooth's ears are larger and wider-based, and its pasterns are more flexible. Students of the two breeds will soon realise that a detail such as the ears can create quite a different expression. Otherwise, the breeds are basically identical. Non-specialists have a problem reconciling the indifferent movement often found in this breed along with unusually gay tail carriage. It has to be said that breeder-judges seem to be almost obsessive about heads and expressions, and when these take priority over basic construction and movement it is hardly surprising that the breed fares poorly at Group level.

The head is reminiscent of a blunt wedge; it is very clean and smooth in outline with no lumps or bumps, and the skull is flat. The sides gradually taper from the ears to the black nose, and the muzzle should be well-moulded, with no suggestion of being pinched or fluted. The profile should show two parallel lines in the toplines of skull and muzzle, and the stop should be minimal yet noticeable, and the centre of the stop should also be the central point of the entire head. The muzzle ends bluntly, but is well-rounded and smooth. The underjaw should have strength, but the depth of the skull should never be excessive as this will detract from the overall quality of the head. The eyes should be medium size (not too small, as some seem to be getting), set rather obliquely and almond-shaped. They are dark-brown, but in blue merles one or both may be blue or blue-flecked (some judges get nervous when they encounter such a blue-flecked eye, but it is quite acceptable in the appropriate colour).

The ears should always be carried semi-erect, with the top third tipping forward. The neck is fairly long and well arched, forelegs straight and muscular, and the body is a little longer than high. The chest is deep, ribs well-sprung, and there should be fair breadth behind the shoulders. The loin has a slight rise, and the tail should be carried low with a slight upward swirl at the tip. Gay carriage is acceptable when a Collie is excited, but the tail must never curl over the back. Hindquarters should be muscular about the thighs, but apparently sinewy below and with powerful but well let down hocks.

My choice for Best of Breed the first time I awarded CCs in Rough Collies was John and Lynn Stinchcombe's Ch. Silvermoor's Hollyberry at Amalie. She won ten CCs in all, the other nine coming from breeder-judges.

I gave the young Ch. Colonel Mustard of Mistoff his first CC from the Novice class when I first awarded CCs to Smooth Collies. This red and white dog soon won his title and was later acquired by Trevor and Birgit Hayward of the famous Foxearth Smooths, whose bloodlines greatly influenced his pedigree.

David Dalton.

The true Collie movement is not easy to understand. The breed should never be out at the elbow, should never plait or cross in front, yet the forefeet are quite close together when the dog moves. The hind legs should be parallel when going away, but never too close. In profile, there should be noticeable rear drive and a long stride, and the whole picture should be of a functional dog moving effortlessly and fairly light on its feet. The coat should enhance the outline of the body in the Rough. The outer coat is straight and harsh, the undercoat extremely dense, soft and furry. The hair of the frill, mane, hind legs above the hock and tail is profuse whilst the forelegs are well feathered. The Smooth coat also has a dense undercoat, but its top coat is short, harsh, and lies quite flat.

The colours in both varieties are sable (any shade of gold to rich mahogany or shaded), tricolour (black without rustiness, with tan markings on the legs and head) and blue merle (clear silver-blue – never slate-grey – with splashes of black, preferably with tan markings. The black patches should not be too large, and rusty tinges in either top or undercoat are undesirable). All of these three colours should be combined with the traditional Collie white markings, which consist of a full or part collar, shirt front, legs, feet and tail-tip. A white blaze is also acceptable on the face.

THE DOBERMANN

This is a breed in which, I feel, British breeders have done a good job of combining the strength and substance of the European dogs with the style and elegance of the Americans, and it is a breed in which a number of high-quality animals can usually readily be found when judging. While the breed is an extremely stylish one, its functional aspects should never be forgotten, and temperament should be of paramount importance. The Dobermann's demeanour should be proud and alert, and it should be supremely fit and clean-cut.

The head should resemble a fairly long but blunt wedge. It is well filled under the eyes, free of wrinkle, and there is just a slight stop. In profile, the topline of the skull and the muzzle should be quite parallel – not always easy to find when judging, as some Dobermanns tend to have decidedly rounded (rather than flat) skulls which seem to fall away to the occiput. The whole head should be clean with no loose skin or undue lip, the cheeks should be flat and smooth, and the muzzle should have good depth. The nose should be black in black dogs, dark-brown in browns, dark-grey in blues, and light-brown in fawns. (The fawn colour in the breed is traditionally referred to as "Isabella".)

Ears should be small, neat, and set high. Some judges are unaware that the Dobermann's ears can, in fact, be erect but more usually they are dropped neatly forward. The eyes are important to the true Dobermann expression, as they should be almond-shaped, fairly deep-set and dark. Round eyes will give a totally untypical expression for the breed. In colours other than black, the eyes can be slightly lighter, but they should never be lighter than the markings. All colours should have clearly defined rust markings – over each eye, on the muzzle, throat and forechest, on all legs and feet, and below the tail. Any white markings are considered undesirable.

The neck is quite long and relatively lean, elegantly arched and affording proud carriage of the head. There should be no dewlap and the nape should be well muscled. The forelegs are straight, parallel, muscular and sinewy with good round bone, and the cat-feet are well arched and compact. The elbows should be well under the dog and there must be well-developed forechest, in which respect many Dobermanns lack. In body shape, the Dobermann should be square, measuring the same from withers to ground as from forechest to buttocks. The back is short and firm, and slopes slightly from the withers to the croup. It is acceptable for a bitch to be a little longer in loin than a male. The ribs should be well sprung and deep to the elbow, and there is noticeable tuck-up.

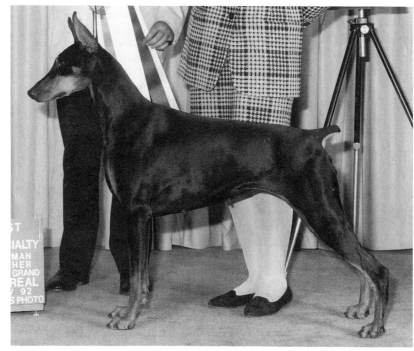

My choice for Best in Show at a Dobermann Specialty in Canada in 1992 was the much-titled bitch, American, Canadian & Bermuda Champion Simca's Dream Academy, owned by Lana Sniderman and Bob Krol. She was rated Number Two All Breeds in Canada that year.

Paw Prints Inc.

Hindquarters should be quite wide apart, the croup well filled out, and the whole rear assembly very muscular with good length and bend of stifle. The tail should appear to be a continuation of the spine without any definite drop. The Dobermann movement is elastic and true, with good forehand reach and great drive behind, the hind action appearing to be rotary. The coat is short, hard, thick and lies close. Occasionally you will find Dobermanns (as you do Boxers and some other short-coated working breeds) which have a cow-lick or ridge of hair on the back of the neck or spine. This is undesirable.

THE GERMAN SHEPHERD DOG

Of all the breeds where type has evolved in different directions, resulting in two "camps", the German Shepherd is the most obvious example. In Britain today, there are the "Alsatian" afficianados, and the faithful "German Shepherd Dog" followers who take their lead from the Fatherland. Each advocates a type of dog which is quite different from the other, and both maintain that theirs is correct. Sadly, the majority of "German" fanciers tend to dismiss All- Rounder judges as being of the "English Alsatian" persuasion, and consequently few non-specialists ever get the opportunity to judge the many excellent German-type dogs which have come into this country in recent years. In some ways this is the fault of the judges, who were so enraptured with the image of the Rin-Tin-Tin type of animal, they ridiculed the majority of imported dogs they saw as "banana-backed", without taking the time to try and understand the rationale of the progressive breeders.

The German Shepherd is essentially a working machine, with a far-reaching, effortless and enduring gait. It should always be judged from a functional standpoint rather than mere aesthetics, and it is one of the few breeds which insists on overt masculinity and femininity. Again,

Many top-quality German Shepherd Dogs have recently been imported into the UK. Wendy and Graham Stephens' Ch. Laios van Noort Sch. H3 FH was bred in Germany and in 1990 attained a V5 placing at the German Sieger Show and a VA4 at the Austrian Sieger Show. Since his release from quarantine in January 1992, he has become the Top male German Shepherd Dog in the United Kingdom. Although a highly qualified Schutzhund H3 dog, Laios' friendly disposition has enabled him to be accepted as an ideal PAT-dog.

temperament is absolutely vital, and the Shepherd has to be steady and self-assured under any conditions. The head should never be coarse, but similarly, it should never be too fine or over-long. The forehead is slightly domed, the cheeks rounding gently but never bulging. The stop is not too pronounced, and the skull should be equal in length to the muzzle, the whole head gently tapering towards the nose.

The muzzle should be powerful and wedge-shaped, and in width the skull should be slightly greater than its length in the male, slightly less in the female – an unusual requirement and one judges should remember. Eyes are almond-shaped, moderate in size, and preferably dark-brown. Lighter eyes can be accepted if the expression is maintained. The ears are high set and virtually parallel, firm and wide-based, and tapering to a point. The neck is fairly long, well-developed, muscular and free of dewlap. It tends to be lowered at speed. The forelegs are parallel, straight from the pasterns to the elbows, but the pasterns should be firm yet supple and slightly angulated.

Feet should be rounded with well-arched toes, serviceable pads, and short, strong nails, well-pigmented. Many in the breed seem to have poor feet. The length of foreleg should always be greater than the depth of chest (not always so with some "Alsatians"). The Shepherd is slightly longer from the breast bone to the rear of the pelvis than the wither height. The chest should be deep and about 45-48 per cent of the height, but never greater than the length of foreleg. The brisket is well developed, with well-formed, long ribs, never flat, but not overly sprung, so that the elbows can move freely when gaiting. The loin is quite short, the belly firm and just slightly drawn up, and the back between the withers and croup should be straight, strong, and not too long.

The withers should be of good height and well defined, flowing into the topline, which slopes slightly from the front to the back. The loin should be broad and well-muscled, the croup long, and gently curving down to the tail, the whole spinal column indicating a smooth, flowing outline. The hindquarters are strong, broad, well-muscled and well-angulated, with strong hocks. Over-angulation should not be encouraged. The well coated tail should reach to the hock or beyond, hanging in a gentle curve when the dog is relaxed. On the move, the curve will increase and the whole tail raise, but it should not come above the backline. The gait of the Shepherd should be fluid and steady, exhibiting great reach and scope, the topline remaining virtually static. Only on the move will the true beauty of the Shepherd be seen.

There is a thick undercoat and a harsher, but close-lying top coat, and it will vary in length. Blues, albinos, livers, whites and creams are highly undesirable, but given an acceptable coat colour, this is considered very much of secondary importance when judging the breed.

THE GREAT DANE

The Great Dane's key-word is "dash and daring", and those who have been fortunate to see an outstanding example of this noble breed will know exactly what that phrase means. The Dane has the air of a thoroughbred horse, and must combine those apparent opposites of strength and elegance. The expression should always be alert and, despite its substance, the Dane's Standard insists on grace of form.

The head should appear to have great length and strength of jaw. The foreface is broad, and the skull quite narrow, which results in the head appearing to be of equal breadth throughout. In balance, the muzzle should be as long as, if not longer than the skull, which is flat with a slight indentation running up its centre to the occiput, which should never be prominent. There is a definite brow over the eyes, but in reality the stop is not that acute. The head should be well filled below the eyes and the muzzle should be consistent in its depth all through. The cheeks are clean and in no way Mastiff-looking. The head profile is quite angular and brick-like, with a noticeable ridge on the bridge of the very wide nose, giving a slight "budgerigar bump".

The eyes are fairly deeply set and should be of medium size, ideally dark, but one or both wall eyes are permissible in harlequins. Ears should be triangular, not large, high-set and folded forward. Large, pendulous ears are not typical and give an alien "hang-dog" expression, rather than the alert outlook which is so essential. The neck is long, nicely crested, and free of dewlap. The nape is well defined. The forelegs are straight, parallel with big bone which should be flat – not round, as some judges have been known to say ... and write! The body is deep with the brisket coming down to the elbow, and the ribs well-sprung, but a keel reminiscent of a Dachshund is quite untypical – some Danes seem rather overdone in this respect.

There is definite (but not Whippety) tuck-up, and the loins are strong and slightly arched. The hindquarters are strong, well-angulated with low-set hocks, and good development of second thigh. The cat-feet should have well-arched toes with strong and curved nails. In all colours the nails should be dark, other than harlequin where they may be light. The tail is thick-rooted, reaching to the hocks and should be carried in a straight line out from the back, slightly curving towards its tapered end, but not carried curled or over the back. The Dane movement is free, ground-covering, lithe, and with a certain effortless spring in the step. The head should always be carried proudly.

Ann Foxwell's young Great Dane bitch, Ch. Auldmoor American Honey, won the coveted title of "Dane of the Year" in 1993. She is by an American imported sire, Honey Lane's Incahoots with Auldmoor (who died tragically young) out of Auldmoor Asa, the daughter of a Swedish import and a male who combined American lines with those of the Auldmoor foundation bitch, Ch. Oldmanor Manthem of Auldmoor.

The coat is short and dense, and coarse coats are quite untypical. The colours allowed are fawn, brindle, blue, black and harlequin. Blues can have blue eyes and nose. Harlequins should have a pure white base coat with black or blue patches which should be completely irregular, with a "torn" appearance. They can have pink or butterfly noses. In the other colours, white is only acceptable on the chest and feet, but this is to be discouraged.

THE HUNGARIAN PULI

This is a nimble and wiry worker, whose heavy corded coat disguises the fact that it is, in fact, a rather fine-boned breed. The head is actually quite small and fine, with a slightly domed skull, and a bluntly rounded muzzle one-third of the head-length. There is a definite stop and the arches of the eye-socket are well defined. The nose should be large and black, with eye rims and lips black in all cases. The eyes (yes, Pulis do have them, and judges should check!) should be medium in size, dark-brown and lively in expression. The ears are set slightly below the level of the skull, V-shaped and about half the length of the head, but the coat pattern is such that ears are never really detectable. The Puli should have a uniformly dark roof to its mouth or alternatively can have dense pigment patches on a dark base. The lips are tight and black.

The neck should be set at an angle of 45 degrees to the horizontal, the forelegs straight and muscular, with elbows tight to the chest. The withers are slightly higher than the backline, the back is of medium length, and the well-sprung ribs are deep, with the ribcage broadening noticeably

Gibbs

Hungarian Pulis take a long time for their corded coats to fully mature, as illustrated by Heidi Thomas' six-year old Ch. & Irish Ch. Mournebrake Flying Teapot, whose movement has so impressed many judges. She has won eleven CCs and eleven Reserve CCs, was Best in Show at the Working Breeds of Scotland Championship show in 1992 and Reserve in the Working Group at Southern Counties the same year. In Ireland her career has been equally successful and in 1992 she was Top Puli in both the UK and Ireland.   Gerwyn Gibbs.

behind the elbows. The rump slopes slightly and the loin is short and broad. There is a slight tuck-up, and the hindquarters are strong, well-muscled, with good bend of stifle and low-set hocks. The feet are short, round and tight, but the hind feet are slightly longer than the fore. Nails should always be strong, black or dark-grey in colour. The pads should be springy and dark-grey in colour.

   The Puli's tail is of medium length, curled closely over the rump, and its cords blend in with those of the rump, appearing to be indistinguishable. The Puli does not move with great reach, rather it is quick but short-stepping, and the impression should always be of a nimble, lively dog. The typical coat hangs in rather oily cords, and this is brought about by careful training of the coat in the young dog. Cords lengthen considerably with maturity, which is why many Pulis are still winning top honours in their breed when similarly aged dogs in other breeds are thinking only of Veteran classes.

   In colour, the Puli can be black, rusty-black, white, grey of various shades, or apricot. It is quite acceptable for the black to appear weathered, rusty or with occasional white hairs. Grey and apricot should show some black or white hairs, with or without a black mask, ear-tips and tail-tip. While the overall appearance of the Puli should always be that of a self-coloured dog, a white chest spot is acceptable and a few white hairs on the feet are in order. Judges should remember that the Puli body-skin should always be well-pigmented and of a slate-grey colour.

THE MAREMMA SHEEPDOG

To the uninitiated, this breed is reminiscent of a finer Pyrenean, but the two breeds are quite different, particularly in head. The head should appear conical, and rather large for the body size. The skull is quite wide, narrowing towards the muzzle. The occiput is not very noticeable and the stop moderate with slight chiselling under the eyes. The muzzle is slightly shorter than the skull, and tapers without being snipey. The jaws are powerful with a strong foreface, and the lips clean and close, and black like the nose. The eyes are required to be bold, but not too large, and yet from a judge's standpoint, boldness does not seem that compatible with the requirement to also appear almond-shaped. They should be preferably dark and the rims must be black.

Ears are quite small, V-shaped, high-set, and hang flat to the cheeks when the dog is relaxed, moving forward when alert, and the ear tips are narrowly pointed rather than rounded. The neck is strong, of fair length and free of dewlap. The forelegs are well-boned without undue heaviness and lumber, straight and parallel, with the elbows close to the chest. The pasterns should slope slightly forward. The Maremma should be quite high-withered, with a broad and straight back, and a slightly arched loin which falls to a broad, strong rump. The ribs are well sprung, the chest deep to the elbow, and the sternum is long, curving up to the abdomen, giving the impression of a waist without obvious tuck-up. In length the Maremma is slightly longer than its shoulder height.

The hindquarters are moderate in angulation, wide and powerful, with hocks well let down. The tail is low-set, reaches to below the hock and is gently curved at the tip. In repose, it hangs loosely but when alert it can be carried level with the back. It should be thickly-coated but not fringed. The Maremma in action should appear supple and active, its gait being free, and able to turn quickly. The white coat, with or without a little ivory or pale-fawn shading, should be plentiful and rather harsh to the touch on the neck and body, with a thick collar. A slight wave is allowed but never a tight curl. There is a thick, close undercoat which is more pronounced in winter.

THE MASTIFF

Not that long ago this breed was in danger of disappearing in Britain, so depleted were numbers in wartime. However, thanks to some American imports it was saved and continues to make steady progress. In the past the breed seemed to have problems with regard to general soundness, many breed specialists placing great emphasis on the magnificence of head qualities. The head should appear fundamentally square with great breadth. The proportion of breadth to length of head should be as 2 is to 3. The body is also massive, and great substance and height are advocated in the Standard, without reference to any actual measurements. This would seem to indicate to judges that the breed should be judged on a "the bigger the better" basis, provided type, balance and quality are maintained. In reality, the breed appears very stable in size with no dramatic variation.

The skull is broad between the ears, and though the forehead should be flat, there appear distinct wrinkles when the dog is aroused. These are further accentuated by the slightly raised brows. The muscles of cheeks and temples are well developed, and the arch of the top-skull is rather like a flattened curve, with an indentation running from the centre of the stop up the forehead. The muzzle is short and broad under the eyes, and should be virtually the same width to the end of the nose. It is blunt and cuts off squarely, with great depth from the broad, wide-nostrilled nose to the underjaw, which should be broad. In profile, the nose should be flat, not upturned like the Boxer. The lips should have enough drop to maintain the squareness of the whole head.

The length of the muzzle in relation to the whole head is 1:3 (interestingly, exactly the same proportions as called for in the Boxer and Bullmastiff). The massiveness of the muzzle is indicated by the fact that proportionately it should be three fifths of the skull circumference. The eyes are

There was a time when the head of a Mastiff was considered all-important by some breed judges, almost to the exclusion of all else! Happily, Mastiffs can now be found in the show ring which have size, bone, substance and soundness. This is in no small way due to the importation from America of the outstanding male, Ch. & Am. Ch. Arciniega's Lion of Bredwardine, by Richard Thomas and Peter Tugwell. In 1986 Richard Thomas judged the Mastiff Club of America's National Specialty, where he drew a record entry of 157 dogs including 45 Champions, however he selected the young Lion – then untitled – as his Best of Breed and expressed a great interest in bringing him to Britain. Within a matter of months Lion had finished his American Championship and his owners agreed to let him join the Bredwardine kennel. At his first three shows fresh out of quarantine, Lion won his British title, taking Best of Breed each time, and ended up with twenty-one CCs. He went on to sire many British Champions; his ability to stamp his type doubtless resulting from his being the result of a half-brother to half-sister mating on a daughter of the legendary Am. Ch. Deer Run Wycliff. In this photograph, Lion illustrates the breed's great bone and substance, coupled with sound conformation and intense overall quality. Diane Pearce.

small, dark-hazel (the darker the better), wide-set, showing no haw, and the stop is fairly obvious without being too severe. The ears should be small, thin, and set wide apart on the highest points of the skull in such a way that they continue with the outline of the top-skull. They lie flat and close to the cheeks. The Mastiff's mouth should have canine teeth wide apart, the incisors sitting level or marginally undershot, but the teeth should never be visible when the mouth is closed.

The neck is fairly long, slightly arched and very well muscled, and while the Standard makes no mention of dewlap, most Mastiffs have a generous helping! The forelegs are heavy and muscular, with plenty of width between them, yet still straight and parallel with upright pasterns. The chest is wide, well let down between the forelegs, the ribs well rounded, deep, and carried well back with great depth of flank and consequently no visible tuck-up. The back and loins are wide, with males being slightly arched over the loin, whereas bitches tend to be wider and flatter. The hindquarters are broad, wide, well-muscled with strongly developed second thighs. Feet should be large but round, with well-arched toes and black nails.

The tail is high-set, reaches to the hocks or below, is wide-rooted and tapers, hanging loosely when relaxed, but curving and pointing upward (though never over the back) when excited. The Mastiff should move powerfully and extend freely. Its coat is close and short, but over the shoulders, neck and back it tends to be coarser. The colours are apricot-fawn, silver-fawn, fawn or dark brindle, in all cases the mask, ears and nose being black.

THE NEWFOUNDLAND

This is a water-dog of massive bone, yet it should still maintain an active and majestic appearance. Its temperament is one of its great strengths, being extremely docile and gentle, and consequently no concessions should be made as to aggression or nervousness. The head is broad and massive, almost bear-like, with a well developed occiput, a barely noticeable stop, and a short, rather square, but clean-cut muzzle. In some countries the Newfoundland heads seem to be getting too deep in stop and rather "jowly", which creates almost a St Bernard type head. This is quite wrong and totally alien to the classic Newfoundland. The eyes are small, dark and rather deep-set with no visible haw, wide-set and give the breed its totally benevolent, tranquil expression. The ears are set well back, square to the skull and carried close to the head. A level bite is tolerated, but ideally it should be scissor. The neck is strong and not unduly long, the forelegs straight and parallel, well-muscled with elbows fitting close to the deep, well-ribbed body. The topline is level with a very broad back, and strong, well-muscled loins. The feet are large, webbed and well made, and the hindquarters should be well built and strong with moderate angulation.

In view of the Newfoundland's bulk, soundness without slackness is important. The gait is free, and the Newfoundland has a slight roll. The breed also tends to toe-in slightly in front. The tail should reach to just beyond the hock, should be fairly thick and well coated, but not actually fringed to such an extent that it appears flagged. When relaxed the tail will hang down with a slight curve at the end. When moving, it will be raised to the level of the back but some Newfoundlands, males particularly, have an unacceptably gay tail carriage.

The coat is important in that it should be water-resistant, thus it must be double with a dense undercoat and flat, coarse, rather oily top coat. Judges should be able to brush their hands against the grain of the coat and watch it naturally fall back into place. Open and severely sculpted coats are not typical. The forelegs are well feathered and the hind legs less so. There are three colours – black, brown and Landseer. Blacks should be dull and may be tinged with bronze. White splashes on the chest, toes and tail-tip are acceptable. Browns can be chocolate or bronze, with white acceptable as in the blacks. Landseers should have a clear white base-colour with a black head on which is a narrow white blaze, an evenly marked black saddle, and a black rump extending as far as the tail. It is extremely difficult to breed a beautifully-marked Landseer free of ticking, but when one is discovered it is breathtaking.

THE NORWEGIAN BUHUND

This is an unexaggerated Spitz breed of fairly light build, but capable of great endurance. Its head is lean and light yet rather broad between the ears, wedge-shaped and narrowing to the nose. The skull is almost flat with a definite but not too deep stop, and a moderate length muzzle which tapers evenly both from above and in profile. The topline of the muzzle is straight and the lips tight. The nose is always black, and the eyes are dark-brown, bright and lively with a fearless expression and not protruding. The ears are set high, carried erect, and longer than their width at the base. They are sharply pointed and very mobile.

The neck is moderately long and lean with noticeable arch and no dewlap. The forelegs are lean, straight and strong with tight elbows, and the feet should be small, oval and with tightly closed toes. The body should be short, deep-chested, with a straight topline and short couplings. There is slight tuck-up and the hindquarters are not too angulated. The tail is high-set, short and thick, tightly curled, and well coated. The Buhund should move lightly, covering the ground well.

It has a soft and woolly undercoat with close, harsh outer coat, and in colour the breed can be wheaten, black, red (but not too dark a shade) or wolf-sable. White markings on the chest and legs, a blaze on the head and narrow ring on the neck, or a black mask, ears and tail-tip are also permissible. There should always be sufficient daylight under the Buhund for it never to appear low-built or "squat"

THE OLD ENGLISH SHEEPDOG

The "Bobtail" is a square-looking dog which, contrary to what some judges believe, has no upper height limit. It should be a somewhat cobby looking dog, devoid of any suggestion of legginess. The skull is sizeable and rather square, it is well arched over the eyes and has a well-defined stop. The muzzle is strong and square and should be approximately the same length as the skull. The nose is noticeably large and black, with wide nostrils. The eyes should be set wide and, ideally, there should be black eye-rims. The eyes can be dark-brown, blue or they can be wall eyes. (The

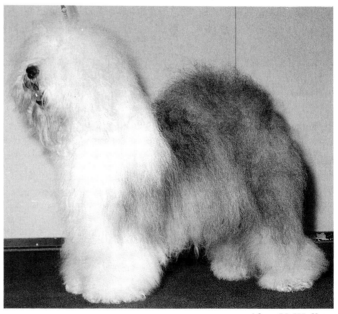

Not all top-winning bitches prove outstanding brood bitches, yet Ch. Lamedazottel Flamboyant, John and Christina Smith's Old English Sheepdog male, is a son of the former record-holding Ch. Zottel's Miss Marple of Lameda, whose record he has recently beaten. Pictured here as a young dog, Flamboyant has won fifty-two CCs to date, along with an amazing ten Best in Show awards at All Breeds Championship shows. He has won sixteen Breed Club Bests in Show and sixteen Working Groups and is now making his mark as a sire.

Alan V. Walker.

wall eye is a flecked blue eye, commonly found in breeds carrying the blue merle colour gene.) Ears are small and carried close to the skull, the coat merging in with the head coat. A level bite is tolerated, but the scissor is the ideal.

The gracefully arched neck should be fairly long and muscular, the forelegs well-boned and straight, and the feet small, round and tight with thick, hard pads and well-arched toes. The body should be short and compact, with well-sprung ribs and good depth of brisket. The Bobtail should be lower at the withers as the back rises to the broad and gently arched loin, giving the body almost a pear-shape. The hindquarters are well muscled, rounded, with the second thigh being long and well developed. There should be good turn of stifle, low hocks, and when the Bobtail walks, it appears to have a bear-like roll at the rear. At a trot, there should be effortless extension and strong, driving rear action. At slow speeds, the breed may pace, and in action its natural head carriage is quite low.

There is a dense waterproof undercoat, and the top coat is harsh, shaggy and free of curl. The head and skull are well covered with hair as are the neck, forequarters and body, with the hindquarters more profusely coated. Texture should be regarded as more important than length. In colour, the breed can be any shade of grey, grizzle or blue, with head, neck, forequarters and under the belly white. White patches ("splashes") on the solid body colour are to be discouraged, and any shade of brown is undesirable. Coat will improve in colour and texture with age, puppies tending to be darker and softer than the mature dog.

THE PYRENEAN MOUNTAIN DOG

This is a substantial and powerful breed with a definite elegance. Its head is strong but never coarse, and should not be massive, as in the case of the Newfoundland. In profile and head-on, the skull should be definitely curved to give a rounded appearance, and at its widest point it should be as broad as it is long from occiput-stop. The cheeks are almost flat, but the skull is still of good depth. The stop is not obvious, having a slight furrow at the point where the muzzle gently slopes up into the forehead. The muzzle is of moderate length and tapers more acutely towards the tip of the nose, which is black. There should be ample fill-in under the eyes, and the bird's-eye view of a good Pyrenean head should be that of a blunt wedge, rather than the cone of the Maremma.

The eyes should be almond-shaped, dark-brown, with tightly fitting lids, and they are set rather obliquely, with black eye rims. Exposed haw and drooping eyelids should be avoided. The ears are small, triangular, with rounded tips, and they are set on level with the eyes. They lie flat against the head and can be raised somewhat when alert. The roof of the mouth and lips should be black, or at least heavily pigmented with black. The ideal Pyrenean bite is a scissor, but a level bite can be tolerated. Two central lower incisors are sometimes a little deeper set than the others.

This is not a "necky" breed, the neck being quite short, thick and muscular with a little dewlap being tolerated. The forelegs are straight, heavily-boned and strongly muscled. It is important, if the Pyrenean body is sufficiently broad and deep, that the elbows are not set too tightly under the chest, but neither should they stand off Bulldog-fashion. The Pyrenean should have a look of width, and its pasterns should be flexible without weakness. Feet are short and compact, with slightly arched toes and strong nails. The chest is broad and in depth reaches to slightly beyond the elbows, with slightly rounded sides and ribs extending well back. There should be fair length of back which is broad, muscular and level. Males tend to have more of a tuck-up than bitches.

The hindquarters display prominent haunches, and a slightly sloping croup where the topline curves smoothly into the tail. The thighs should be strongly muscled, and there should be moderate angulation of the stifle. Strong double dewclaws are considered a very important breed

The Pyrenean Mountain Dog, Ch. Benacia Alexander of Lukeanna, owned by Ann and Paul Butcher, won his first CC when I judged Border Union. He subsequently won CCs in England, Wales and Scotland and was retired before he was three and a half years of age.

characteristic as is the "wheeled tail", which would be considered an ugly fault in many similar breeds. The tail is thick-rooted and tapering, ideally with a slight curl. It should reach to beyond the hocks and is thickly coated with long hair. When relaxed, the tail will hang low, the tip turning slightly out to one side. When aroused, however, the tail should rise until it curls high above the back in a full circle. In action, the Pyrenean moves with a leisurely, but still steady and powerful, gait. At slow speeds it will pace.

There is a fine undercoat and a longer, coarser top coat which is straight or slightly waved but never curly. The coat will usually be longer around the neck and shoulders, and the forelegs should be fringed. On the hindquarters, the hair will be very dense and much more woolly which creates the effect of breeches. Bitches are usually less heavily-coated than males, certainly around the neck. In colour, the breed should be mainly white with patches of badger, wolf-grey or pale-yellow, or alternatively pure white. Patches should be on the head, ears or base of tail, and may be allowed to a small extent on the body. Black patches which go right down to the roots are highly undesirable.

THE ROTTWEILER

This breed has suffered a grossly unfair press in the wake of its population explosion, and sadly the quality of the breed seen in the show ring is not always as high as it could be. Having said that, the hard-core of British breeders have maintained a very high standard, and it is now the opinion of many overseas experts that Britain is producing some of the best Rottweilers in the world. The Rottweiler should be bold, powerful and yet calm. Its temperament must be flawless, and judges should penalise shortcomings in this direction accordingly. In colour, it should always be black with clearly defined tan markings, which appear as a spot over each eye, on the cheeks, as a strip around each side of the muzzle (but not on the bridge of the nose), on the throat, two distinct triangles on either side of the breast-bone, on the forelegs from the wrist to the toes, on the inside of the hind legs from the hock to the toes, and under the tail. Black pencilling on the toes is

Ch. Fantasa Clockwork Orange won her first CC at thirteen months of age when I first awarded Challenge Certificates in Rottweilers. She went on to win seven CCs and nine Reserves, becoming the top-winning Rottweiler bitch of 1992 and subsequently produced an excellent litter to Ch. Fernwood Enforcer.

John Hartley.

desirable and there should be no white. The head is of moderate length, broad between the ears, with rather small ears set high and wide apart, hanging flat and close to the cheek. In profile, the forehead will appear gently arched, and while the occiput is well developed, it should not be noticeable. The cheeks are well developed and muscular, but not bulging. The head should be completely dry, with no loose skin, but when the dog's attention is caught, a moderate amount of wrinkle will appear on the forehead. The muzzle is fairly deep with the top completely straight, and flews firm and black, and it should be shorter than the skull (as 2 is to 3). The nose is well developed, with large nostrils, and always black. Eyes should be dark-brown, almond-shaped, and with close-fitting lids.

The Rottweiler should have a fairly long, muscular neck with a slight arch and no dewlap. Forelegs are straight, muscular and with strong bone and substance, while the elbows are well let down. Pasterns slope slightly, and the feet should be strong, round and compact, with well-arched toes, very hard pads and short, dark, strong nails. The chest should be capacious, broad, deep, and with well-sprung ribs. The brisket depth should be ideally 50 per cent of the shoulder height. The back is straight and strong, and the Rottweiler is proportioned in such a way that it is slightly longer than square, as 10 is to 9. The loins are strong and deep, there is no great tuck-up, and the croup slopes very slightly.

The hindquarters should be well muscled, strong, with fairly well bent stifles. The tail should not be too low set. Movement in the Rottweiler is most important and should indicate a dog capable of great endurance. Its gait is free, supple and powerful, with plenty of forehand reach and rear drive. There is an imperceptible undercoat which can be grey, fawn or black, while the top coat is of medium length, coarse and flat. Long or very wavy coats are not desirable, though in many dogs a slight wave is detectable. The hair will usually be longer on the back of the legs. It is worth remembering that while the Rottweiler is a substantial breed, bitches may be as small as 23 inches at the shoulder, so judges should think hard before dismissing bitches which they may consider initially to be under-sized.

THE ST BERNARD

This is a dog of great substance with a massive head. The muzzle is short, perfectly straight and broad, well filled in front of the eyes and square. The cheeks are flat rather than bulging, and there should be great depth from the eye to the lower jaw. The skull is broad, rather rounded on top with a prominent brow. The stop is quite marked and deep, and the lips deep without being unduly pendulous. The nose should be black, and nostrils well developed. The eyes should be of medium size, not too deep set, and the lids should be fairly tight without any excessive haw. This has been a problem in the breed for some time, with many very obvious haws and unacceptably loose eyes. The eyes should be dark, and the Standard now stresses that the loose wrinkle on the brow should not be so excessive that it would detract from a healthy eye.

Ears are of moderate size, lying close to the cheeks and not heavily feathered. The neck is long, thick and well-muscled, with a noticeable arch and well-developed dewlap. The forelegs are straight, heavily-boned and of good length. The chest is wide and deep, but never so deep that it descends below the elbows. The back is broad, topline straight and the ribs well-sprung. The loin should be well-muscled and wide, and the hindquarters heavily-boned, with muscular thighs and well angulated hocks. The feet are large but still compact, with well-arched toes.

The Saint's tail is rather high-set, long, and carried low in repose. It should never curl over the back, even when the dog is moving. The movement should indicate easy extension, but it is a smooth and sedate gait. There are two coat types, Rough and Smooth. In Roughs, the coat is dense and flat, more profuse around the neck, thighs and tail. In Smooths, it is close with just slight feathering on thighs and tail. The colour is white with patches which can be orange, mahogany-brindle, red-brindle. There should be a white muzzle, blaze, collar, chest, forelegs, feet and tail-tip, and there should be black shading on the face and ears. There is no specified size in the breed, and the taller a dog is the better, but symmetry should always be maintained.

THE SAMOYED

This is another member of the Spitz group, and judges should acquaint themselves with correct size in this breed (18-20 inches for bitches and 20-22 inches for dogs), as size has tended to creep up somewhat. Its best-known characteristic is probably its "smiling expression", which is achieved through correct head balance and eye placement. The shimmering appearance of the Samoyed is due to its coat (which can be white, with or without biscuit shading, or cream) having a top coat which consists of silver-tipped hairs.

The head is a strong wedge with broad, flat skull and muzzle of only medium length. The foreface should taper, but not too sharply as a snipey appearance is quite alien. The ears are thick, not too long, rounded at the tips, set wide apart, and they are fully erect in mature dogs. The eyes are most important. They should be set aslant, almond-shaped, and medium to dark-brown. They should be set wide apart, and the eye rims should be black, as should the lips. Ideally, the nose should be black, but brown or flesh-coloured noses are acceptable, and the strength of pigment will sometimes vary seasonally.

There should be a good arch to the neck which should be strong and not too short. Forelegs are straight, parallel, muscular and of good length. The back is of moderate length, broad and well-muscled with a very strong loin. The chest should be deep but not too broad, and the ribs should have good spring and great depth for heart and lung room. The muscular hindquarters should have good turn of stifle, low hocks, and the feet are long, rather flat and slightly spread, with soles that are well cushioned with hair. It is a mistake for judges to look for Samoyeds who are well up on cat-feet. If you don't understand why, research the function of the breed.

The tail is long, high-set and carried over the back and to one side when the dog is alert. The movement should be free with great drive and indicate power with a certain elegance and style. There is a thick, close and soft undercoat, and the top coat, which is harsher, grows through it and creates a rather stand-off weatherproof layer.

THE SHETLAND SHEEPDOG

The Sheltie is not a Miniature Collie, though their Standards are very similar. The Sheltie should never be cloddy or heavy in appearance. The head should be refined and rather like the ubiquitous blunt wedge. The skull is flat and moderately wide between the ears, which are small, quite wide-based and placed quite close together (which would seem to be a contradiction in terms in a breed which is "moderately wide between the ears" – in reality, the ears should appear to be set not too far apart or too low). The ears tip forward as with the Rough Collie.

The cheeks should be flat, blending smoothly into a well-rounded muzzle, which is equal in length to the skull. The stop is slight, and the skull and muzzle should be parallel in their toplines. The eyes are almond-shaped, obliquely set and of medium size, dark-brown in colour except in blue merles where one or both can be blue or wall. The Sheltie has a good length of neck which is well arched, and the head should always be carried proudly.

The elbow-wither height should equal the elbow-ground, and the forelegs should be straight and parallel, clean, muscular and with strong bone which should never be too heavy. The pasterns are flexible. The Sheltie should be marginally longer than it is tall at the withers, and the chest should be deep to the elbow, with well-sprung ribs, the lower half of the ribs being noticeably less rounded, to allow freedom of forelegs and shoulders. The back is level, but there is a gentle curve over the loins with the croup gradually sloping to the low-set tail which should reach to at least the hock.

The tail should be free of kinks and never carried over the back level; ideally it should just be slightly raised when the dog is moving. There is good bend of stifle in the broad and well-muscled hindquarters, and the hocks should be clean and well let down. Feet are oval with well-padded soles, the toes arched and close together. In motion, the Sheltie comes across as lithe and graceful, with good rear drive and plenty of ground-covering ability. It should move proudly but still be workmanlike in its gait. The breed should be true up and down with no plaiting or crossing of the legs.

The coat is double with a soft, close undercoat and a harsh but straight top coat. There should be a profuse mane and frill, and the forelegs should be well feathered. Above the hocks the hindlegs should also be very profusely coated. In colours, the more usual tend to be sable, tricolour or blue merle, but black-and-white and black-and-tan are also recognised. White markings follow the standard coat pattern of the Rough Collie.

THE SIBERIAN HUSKY

This breed has few challengers in combining functional conformation with exotic colours and luxurious coats. The breed in the UK remains in the hands of ardent breed fanciers, whose aim is to combine original purpose with exhibiting. In the past, some Siberians have appeared in Group rings which seemed rather underweight, but the breed should always be fit and indicating sufficient strength to withstand sustained physical demands. The Siberian is not a draught animal, but neither is it a sprinter.

The head is fox-like, of medium size, and finely chiselled. The skull is slightly rounded on top and tapers gradually toward the eyes. The muzzle is equal in length to the skull, quite wide but never coarse, and tapers gradually to a rounded nose. The stop is definite without being too severe, and the topline of the muzzle is straight. The eyes are almond-shaped, set obliquely, and any shade of blue or brown. Odd eyes and particolour eyes are quite acceptable, and the wide variety of eyes seen in the breed is one of their great charms. The expression should be keen and interested, and there should always be the proverbial "twinkle" in the eye of the Siberian.

The ears are quite close-set, triangular and not too long, but longer than their base-width. They are strongly erect, and when the dog is alert they should appear almost parallel. They are arched at the back, thick, slightly round-tipped and well-furred. The lips should be well pigmented and tight. The neck is moderately long, gracefully arched, and carried high and proud when standing, though in action the head will lower and push forward. The forelegs are parallel and straight with elbows well in, the pasterns slope slightly, and the feet are oval, not too long, compact, well-furred, and slightly webbed. The pads should be tough and well cushioned.

In balance, the Siberian should be slightly longer from elbow to ground than from withers to elbow. It should be well-boned but not heavily so, and there should be moderate forehand width. The back is straight and strong, of moderate length and never "boxy". The chest should be deep but not overly wide, and while there is good rib spring from the spinal column, the lower sides should appear somewhat flattened to allow freedom of forelegs. The loin is slightly arched and well-muscled, the croup slightly sloping, and the tail continues with a slightly low set-on. It should be like a fox's brush, well-furred and carried in a graceful sickle curve. It should never curl too tightly or be flat on the back, and in repose may hang naturally.

The hindquarters are well muscled, powerful, with good bend of stifle and short hocks. In action, the Siberian is smooth, effortless, and with good forehand extension and rear drive. At speed, it will single-track and the topline should remain level at all times. The coat has a soft, dense undercoat with a protective outer coat of hair which is rather flat-lying. The whole impression is of rather a plushy coat which at all times complements the natural outline of the dog. All colours are allowed – and Siberians come in many wondrous coat patterns not usually found in other breeds.

Judges should remember that the nose should be black in grey, tan or black dogs; liver in copper dogs; flesh-coloured in white dogs; and that in winter a pink-streaked or "winter" nose is allowed. There seems to be the mistaken belief amongst some multi-breed judges that if they are to achieve credibility with the Siberian breeders, they should put up the thinnest ("fittest") dogs when they judge. This is not true, and dogs can be fit without appearing to be half-starved!

THE SWEDISH VALLHUND

This breed has been likened to the Welsh Corgi, but they are very different in many ways. To begin with, the Vallhund's proportions should be such that its height at the withers to length of body is as 2 is to 3. The head is quite long, clean-cut, and bluntly wedge-shaped with an almost flat skull and definite stop. From above, the head is distinctly wedge-shaped, whereas in profile the muzzle looks rather square and is shorter than the skull. The lips should be tight, the nose black, and a well defined mask is highly sought after, with lighter hair around the eyes, on the muzzle and under the throat, so that there is a distinct contrast with the mask.

The eyes are medium size, oval and very dark-brown. The ears are moderate in size, pointed and firm. The neck is long, reachy and well-muscled. While most breeds tend to aim for equal length in shoulder and upper arm, the Vallhund has a slightly shorter upper arm, but this should not be so short as to prevent the forelegs reaching well forward with little lift. The forelegs of the Vallhund appear slightly bent to accommodate the deep chest, and they should be well-boned with quite short but oval feet pointing forward. The pads should be strong and the feet well knuckled-up.

The back is level and muscular, the chest long and loin short. The ribs should be well sprung, and the forehand should reveal a rather oval chest. There is a slight tuck-up, and the broad croup slopes slightly. On the forechest "harness markings" should be easily visible. The hindquarters are well angulated with strong, muscular thighs. The movement is free, and the Vallhund should be tight-elbowed in action with noticeable rear drive. The undercoat should be soft and woolly, while the top coat is moderate in length, harsh and close.

The Vallhund can be various mixes of grey and brown with darker top coat on the back, neck and sides. The muzzle, throat, chest, belly, buttocks, feet and hocks should be lighter in shade but still of the same base colour, and while white markings can be acceptable, these should never be more than one-third of the total surface area.

THE WELSH CORGI

There are two varieties of Welsh Corgi – the Cardigan and the Pembroke. Up until now, judges have had it easy, as Cardigans are shown with tails; Pembrokes are docked. Should we have to face life with undocked Pembrokes, appreciating type in the two varieties may be considerably more important! Both varieties should have "foxy" heads with skulls which are quite wide and flat, though the Cardigan has a suggestion of fullness and roundness over the eyes. Both have moderate stops and muzzles which are three-fifths the overall head length, and in both, the muzzle tapers gently to a black nose.

The eyes should be medium in size, definitely round in the Pembroke, but the Cardigan Standard is more vague about shape, merely requiring the corners to be well defined. Certainly, the Cardigan's eyes tend to be set wider apart than the Pembroke's. In expression, ear-set and size help distinguish the two varieties. If you were to draw an imaginary line from the centre of the nose through the centre of the eyes, the Cardigan's ear-tips will lie rather wide of that line, whereas the Pembroke's will more or less be central to the line. The Cardigan's ears are rather large and rounded at the tip, the Pembroke's are pricked, not large, and only slightly rounded.

Both varieties should have a fairly long and well developed neck, but the forehand appears quite different in the two. The Cardigan tends to have a definite, if slight, bow of the well-boned forelegs, this rather moulded around the chest. The feet are quite large, round, well-padded and tend to turn slightly outwards. The Pembroke, on the other hand, has forelegs which are as straight as possible, but they should still complement the contours of the chest. They should also have good bone, but the feet are oval, with strong, well-arched toes, the two centre toes extending slightly beyond the outer two. The pads should be strong and the nails short.

The Cardigan's chest should be quite broad with a prominent breast-bone, its body should be long and strong, with deep brisket, good spring of rib, and a clearly defined waist. The Pembroke may not be as prominent in breastbone, should be of only medium length, but should still have well-sprung ribs and a broad and deep chest, which is well let down between the forelegs. It is not short-coupled and should taper slightly in body. Both varieties should have a level topline and well-angulated, strongly-muscled hindquarters. The Cardigan's tail is like a fox's brush and this should not be carried over the back. The Pembroke should have a short tail, preferably natural. (Pembrokes are sometimes born with "natural bobs", and several breeders are currently working hard to produce these consistently, in view of the docking situation.)

Both Pembroke and Cardigan should have short legs, but it should be remembered that they are working dogs which should be able to move freely, actively, with good forehand reach and drive behind. In colour, the Pembroke is only ever red, sable, fawn or black-and-tan, with or without white markings on the legs, brisket and neck. Some white is also allowed on the head and foreface.

Idris Jones and Allan Taylor's Pembroke Welsh Corgi, Ch. Belroyd Nutcracker, is a classic example of an outstanding show dog who also made his mark as a sire. He won thirty-two CCs and several Working Groups, including the Group at the Crufts Centenary show. He sired thirteen British Champions and more overseas, many of which went on to produce Champions themselves. When I first awarded CCs in the breed, Nutcracker won Best of Breed. The Reserve Dog CC was won by the Minor Puppy, Llyswen Break Every Rule, who went on to win many CCs and was himself a Crufts Best of Breed winner. The Bitch CC that day was a first for Ch. Blands Starlight Express who won from the Post Graduate class, while the Reserve Bitch CC winner was Ch. Headholme Custom Maid. All three were sired by Nutcracker.   *Sally Anne Thompson.*

Cardigans can be any colour, with or without white markings, but white should never predominate. While Pembrokes will always have brown eyes appropriate to their coat colour, Cardigans should have dark eyes blending with the coat, but they can have one or both blue or wall eyes if they are blue merles. The coat texture should be quite harsh and straight with a dense undercoat. Cardigans can sometimes have more of a wavy coat than would be forgiven in Pembrokes, and also their coat can be shorter than the Pembroke.

SUMMARY

In judging the Working breeds, as I have said before, it is important that judges should be acquainted with a breed's original function and purpose. When we understand why certain aspects of the Breed Standard are as required, we find it a lot easier to establish a basic list of priorities when judging that breed. Certainly in the Working breeds, movement, general stamina and temperament are extremely important, and while our top show dogs should have obvious quality, we should never forget the basics. Judges have a responsibility to the breeds, and once we start "forgiving" we will soon find ourselves "forgetting".

Chapter Fifteen

THE TOY GROUP

The Toy breeds were bred specifically to be good-looking companions. In this Group will be found miniaturised versions of other breeds from the Working, Gundog, Hound and Terrier Groups, as well as breeds whose roots seem historically to stem purely from companion animals. In view of this Group's "function", soundness and temperament should be major priorities as well as aesthetic beauty. What use is a bad-tempered pet? Or one who cannot enjoy a rough-and-tumble because of its constructional shortcomings?

THE AFFENPINSCHER
This is a new recruit to the CC-honoured breeds in the UK, and it is important that its rough-coated, sturdy appearance is maintained. It has a monkey-like expression in a fairly small head, domed at the forehead, with a broad brow and marked stop. The muzzle is blunt and short but not

The Affenpinscher has only recently achieved Challenge Certificate status in the UK. I awarded the first Championship show Toy Group for the breed to Rita Turner's Avantgarde Osiria von Gerbraes, who won at a Scottish Kennel Club show when she was just a puppy. Note the desirable unkempt appearance of the head.

Stuart Cordon.

exaggeratedly so – it should not have a "flat face". (The eyes and nose should form an equilateral triangle.) The chin should be strong and upturned, and the mouth slightly undershot. The lively eyes are round and full of expression without being bolting, and the ears are high-set with upright or neatly dropped ears.

The neck is short and clean, the body square with well-sprung ribs and straight forelegs. There is neither excessive tuck-up nor rear angulation, and the dark-nailed feet should be small and round. The tail is set and carried high in a gentle curve. The Affenpinscher has a strutting movement in which it lifts its feet high without hackneying. Its coat is rough and harsh, untrimmed, and is preferably black, but some grey shading is permitted.

THE BICHON FRISÉ
This breed has proved a golden opportunity for the hairdressers of the show world, yet the Standard still only allows for tidying up of the feet and muzzle! Having said that, if judges were to discard all the dogs which had been scissored, they would be left with few Bichons to judge. The proportion of muzzle to skull is as 3 is to 5, and a major fault in the breed is over-long muzzles. In my experience, this failing often crops up in dogs which also have almond eyes and harsh coats, suggesting that there may be more Poodle lurking in the background of some Bichons than we have been led to believe!

When you consider that, like the Affenpinscher, the Bichon's eyes and nose create an equilateral

The Bichon Frisé, Ch. Tiopepi Mad Louie at Pamplona, owned by Michael Coad and handled by Geoff Corish, is seen winning under the late Mrs Ena Bassett. Louie's first major award came when he was a Junior winning the Green Star and BOB when I judged at a St. Patrick's Day Show in Dublin, before he, and his owner left Ireland for England. That day he beat the previous month's Crufts BOB winner. He went on to take twenty-one CCs, still a breed record for males, and won eleven Toy Groups in the U.K. as well as Best in Show All Breeds. He has sired Champions in Britain, Europe, America and South Africa.

John Hartley.

triangle (imagine the heads of those two breeds side by side), it brings the question of the correct head balance into context. The skull is rather rounded, cheeks flat and not very muscular, the stop is moderate, and a hollow between the eyebrows should be detectable. The muzzle is thick and never snipey, the nose large, round, black, soft and shining. The eyes must be dark, round and with black eye rims, surrounded by rings of well pigmented skin which form the "haloes". The eyes look forward and are alive with expression. The ears hang close and should reach halfway along the muzzle. They are set just higher than the eye-level and rather to the fore of the skull. The lips are fine, tight and black.

The Bichon's neck is quite long, carried high and proud, and tapering towards the skull. The forelegs are straight and parallel (not always easy to find) with moderate bone, the feet tight, round and well-knuckled, with black pads and nails. The forechest should be well developed, the brisket deep and ribs nicely sprung. There is good tuck-up, and the Bichon should be the same length from withers to tail-set as it is from the withers to the ground. The hindquarters are well angulated and with broad thighs, the tail carried in an upward-and-forward sweep, with only the tail hair touching the back.

The Bichon should show reach and drive and should display the rear pads clearly when moving away. The coat is fine and silky, hanging in corkscrew curls. The breed is white but shading of cream or apricot can be allowed up to around 18 months. It is advisable for judges to ascertain that there is dark pigment on the skin. The maximum height of the Bichon is 11 inches.

THE CAVALIER KING CHARLES SPANIEL

This is a hardy, sporting dog, but he is also a Toy Spaniel, and so judges should keep an eye on weight – 15lbs being the ideal weight, with 3lbs leeway on either side. The skull should be almost

When I judged Cavalier Dogs at Leeds in 1985, I gave a first CC to the winner of Junior, Ch. Homerbrent Pentilly. The Reserve CC that day also went to the Homerbrent kennel of Molly Coaker, whose kennel has been so prepotent in the breed. Earlier in the year I had judged bitches at Bath and given a first CC to Ch. Homerbrent Emerald, who also came up from Junior. These two accounted for the CCs at Crufts in 1986 when the breed judge was Caroline Gatheral. Pentilly went on to become a Toy Group winner and won thirteen CCs in all.

flat between the ears, the stop is shallow, and the muzzle is of moderate length, tapered, but full-lipped without being pendulous. The face is well filled in below the eyes, and snipey muzzles are untypical. The nose is black, and pigment in the breed can be quite weak, especially in some Blenheims. The eyes must be large, round, dark and expressive, and set wide. The ears are high-set, long and luxuriously feathered. The mouth should have a scissor bite, but it is surprising how many imperfect mouths in young Cavaliers end up quite correct.

The neck is nicely arched, forelegs straight and medium-boned, and feet compact, cushioned and well-feathered (scissor-happy exhibitors please note!). The body is square with good spring of rib and level topline, the hindquarters well-angulated. The Cavalier tail should be carried gaily, but never much above the backline. Movement is free, elegant and driving. The coat should be long, silky and never curly, with plenty of feathering and no trimming! The Blenheim has well-broken chestnut markings on a brilliant white background and, ideally, should have a white blaze in which is situated a chestnut spot – the "lozenge" – a major breed characteristic. Black-and-tans should be jet black with tan markings over the eyes, on the cheeks, inside the ears, on the chest and legs and under the tail. Rubies should be solid rich red. White is undesirable on the whole-colours. Tricolours are black-and-white, with tan over the eyes, on the cheeks, inside the ears, inside the legs and under the tail.

THE CHIHUAHUA
There are two varieties of Chihuahua, Long Coat and Smooth, and the Standard tells us that if two dogs are equally good in type, the smaller should be preferred. In reality, a judge is seldom faced with two dogs which are actually equal in merit, so type really must be totally assessed before implementing the "smaller the better" yardstick. The Chihuahua should have a saucy expression and be alert, with swift moving and forceful action. Despite their diminutive size (2-4lbs being preferred), they should be soundly made dogs, with true and powerful action. They should also be spirited little dogs without ever being snappy or introvert.

The head is important and the skull should resemble a ping-pong ball with a pronounced stop and a quite short muzzle, which is pointed rather than snub-nosed. The eyes should be large, full and round but not bolting, set wide, and while they should be dark, they can be lighter in lighter coloured coats. The ears enhance the characteristic expression, and must be large and flared, and set on quite low at an angle of 45 degrees (these typical, large ears are a fast-disappearing breed feature). The neck is of medium length and slightly arched, and the straight and parallel forelegs should be set well under the body. The back is level, the ribs well-sprung and brisket deep, and the Chihuahua is slightly longer than its height at the withers, so don't go searching for ultra short-backed Chihuahuas.

The hindquarters are muscular and well angulated, and the feet should be small and dainty, but the toes are divided in such a way that the foot is not a cat-foot, yet the foot should not be spread or a hare-foot. The tail is of medium length, high-set and carried sickle-style. It is very much a characteristic of the breed and should appear thick and flat, broadening in the centre and then tapering. Fine "rat" tails are quite untypical. In the Smooth the tail should appear noticeably furry. On the move, the Chihuahua should have great reach and drive and not high-step or hackney. The topline should remain level and up and down movement should be true.

The Smooth has an undercoat and permissible ruff, with a soft, smooth, close and glossy top coat. Longs have a soft textured top coat, which is flat or slightly wavy with well feathered ears, feet and legs, and full coat on the hindquarters and tail. Any colour is allowed in the breed.

THE CHINESE CRESTED DOG

This is a recent addition to British show rings, and even more recent in the USA. The breed was first shown with only the hairless variety being permitted, but now their coated siblings can be shown, and there have been several of these (known as "Powder Puffs") which have won top honours. Although the Breed Standard allows for two distinct types – the deer type (racy and fine-boned) and cobby type (heavier in bone and body), the breed seems to have levelled out and the majority of Cresteds shown are not obviously of one type or the other, but rather of a middle-of-the-road size and type. This would appear far more logical than trying to maintain a breed with two very different basic types whilst still trying to judge them against the same Standard!

The Crested is not a short-backed breed, it should be medium to long with a fairly broad and deep chest and no prominence of the breast-bone. The brisket should come down to the elbows, and there is slight tuck-up. The forelegs should be long and slender, set well under the body, and the feet are long, narrow with unusually long bones which create the impression of the forefeet almost having an extra joint. The hindquarters are well let down and moderately angulated, with nicely rounded rump. The tail should be carried up or out when moving, but should not be curled

Ch. Donsal Dirty Dancing for Valdejenlo was the first Chinese Crested "Powderpuff" to win a Challenge Certificate at Crufts. I gave her a first CC when she was a Junior and she soon completed her title. She was the first CC winner to be owned by David Lodge and Valerie Jennings, who had previously been involved with Afghan Hounds for some twenty years. Dave Freeman.

Toy breeds tend to mature earlier than their larger cousins, as this photograph of the Chinese Crested Dog, Ch. Totsdown Trixie of Freelane, illustrates as it was taken shortly after she had won her first CC and BOB, at barely six months old, when I was judging. She won her other qualifying Certificates under Toy specialists Pamela Cross Stern and Bob Flavell, and went on to be a Champion producer.

or twisted. The skull is rounded and quite long, the cheeks clean and flat and tapering towards the muzzle. There is a moderate stop, and the head should be dry. The skull and muzzle should be the same length, the muzzle tapering without being too sharply pointed, and the lips tight and thin. The nose is quite narrow and may be any colour. The eyes should be very dark, of moderate size, not set close, and tend to be quite round without fullness. The ears are low-set, large and erect in the Hairless, but in Powder Puffs the ears can be completely dropped.

Judges should note that it is not essential to have fringed ears in the Hairless. The essential coating is the crest, which should, ideally, begin at the stop and continue over the skull and down the neck. There are socks of hair on the four feet, and the tail should have a long, flowing plume. The Hairless' skin should feel warm, smooth and almost "clammy". In the Powder Puff, the hair should cover the body in a fine veil of soft, long undercoat. The coat should never be too dense, harsh or stand-off.

Mouths have always presented a problem with this breed, as missing teeth (and sometimes nails too) is related to the hairless factor. The current Standard, however, requires a normal scissor bite. The Crested can be any colour or pattern, and some very exotic terms are proffered by breeders in an attempt to describe same! On the move, the Crested should have plenty of reach and drive, and its gait should be elegant. In its Hairless form, with the appropriate furnishings, the breed can be reminiscent of a little prancing pony. As regards size, 12lbs is the recommended maximum weight with height varying from 9-13 inches.

THE ENGLISH TOY TERRIER (BLACK AND TAN)

This breed should have terrier character, even though it may never be required to acquit itself in the rat pit as suggested by the Standard! The black should be as ebony, and the tan is that of a new chestnut. The two colours should be distinct and never run into each other. The forelegs are tanned up to the knees on the front of the leg, and on the back the tan continues to just below the elbows. There is thin, black pencilling up each toe and a definite thumb mark on the centre of each pastern, and also under the chin. The hind legs are tanned in front and inside, but heavy tan breeching on the outer hindquarters is undesirable. The muzzle is well tanned, but black should run from the black nose along the top of the muzzle and curve below the eyes to the base of the throat. There is a tan spot over each eye and small tan cheek-spots. The underjaw and throat is tanned, but the line of the lips should be black. There should be tan inside the ears, on either side of the chest and under the tail. White spots and patches are taboo.

The ETT's head is long, narrow and flat-skulled, basically wedge-shaped with no great development of the cheeks. It is well filled under the eyes and the stop is slight. The wedge appearance should be apparent both in profile and from above. The eyes are very dark, small, almond-shaped and obliquely set, and should always sparkle with character. The ETT ears are a characteristic of the breed and should be the shape of a candle-flame. They are set well back on the skull and quite close together. When brought forward over the forehead, the ears should not be long enough to reach the eye. The ears should be fully erect in adult dogs, always fully forward-facing with rather thin leathers.

The neck is long, elegant and delicately arched with no dewlap. Forelegs should be fine-boned, straight and parallel, with compact and dainty feet which should be split up between the well-arched toes and have black nails. The two central toes of the forelegs are slightly longer, but the hind feet should be cat-like. The body is compact and the chest deep but rather narrow, yet there should still be detectable rib-spring. The topline curves gently up over the loin and down again to the low-set tail, with a well-rounded rump, and the underline shows good tuck-up.

The English Toy Terrier, Ch. Brynlythe Tannia, owned and bred by Ted and Shirley Ellis-Jones from two Champions, won four CCs as a puppy and enjoyed a consistently successful career which saw her winning twenty-six CCs (with twenty-one BOBs) and the Toy Group at Bath Championship show in 1989 – a rare feat for the breed.
Diane Pearce.

The hindquarters are moderately angulated and well let down, and should be sufficiently set back to avoid a hunched-up appearance. The tail is thick-rooted, no longer than the distance to the hock, and tapers. The forehand gait is something of an extended trot, with hackney action being undesirable, while the hind action should be driving, the whole being fluid and free. The coat is dense, close and glossy.

THE GRIFFON BRUXELLOIS

This breed has two coat types, the Griffon Bruxellois proper being rough-coated, the smooth coat also being known as the Petit Brabancon. It has terrier character, but that is not to say that judges should be looking for too terrier-like construction. The Griffon should look square and cobby, it is solid and heavy for its size, and its head has a monkey-like expression. The head is actually quite large in relation to the body, the skull is gently rounded but not domed, and wide between the ears. The nose is always black, short and open-nostrilled, set high and sloping back towards the skull in such a way that the face appears almost flat, with very pronounced stop.

The muzzle is wide with neat lips and good turn-up and depth of underjaw. Consequently, the ideal Griffon mouth will be slightly undershot. The eyes should be round, dark, fairly large and black-rimmed, and should be very alert in expression. The ears are set high, semi-erect, and should be small and neat. The Griffon has fair length of neck which should be elegantly arched. The chest is fairly deep and wide, with good spring of rib, and the forelegs are straight, parallel and of moderate length and bone. The Griffon should never appear leggy, but by the same token, it should never look "dumpy". The feet are small, thick cat-feet with black nails. The back is short and level, well-ribbed, with a short and strong loin, the tail is set high and carried gaily, and the hindquarters

Ann Fenn's Griffon Bruxellois, Ch. Starbeck Rainbow Quest, was just nine and a half months old when I gave him the CC and BOB at Windsor. He became the latest in a long line of home-bred Champions produced by this most remarkable Griffon breeder whose bloodlines have had a major impact on the breed in both the UK and USA.
Hans Bleeker.

are well-muscled with good bend of stifle and neat, short hocks.

The movement of the Griffon should be free and driving with no trace of hackney action. In colour, the breed can be red, black, or black-and-tan. In the reds, dark shading on the mask and ears is desirable. In Roughs, the coat should be harsh and wiry, ideally with undercoat, traditionally marked with a well furnished beard. In Smooths, the coat is short and tight. The Griffon is one of the most characterful of all breeds, and it is interesting to discover how many leading judges and breeders of other breeds keep a Griffon as a companion. Once under your skin, you will never be free of them!

THE ITALIAN GREYHOUND

Olive Parsons' Italian Greyhound, Ch. Parpico Rosetta, was a Junior when she won her first CC when I was judging at Bath. Appropriately, it was an Italian judge, Paolo Dondina, who gave her her third and qualifying CC and also BOB.
Martin Leigh.

This is the Sight Hound of the Toy Group, and it is an elegant and quick-moving dog whose forehand gait is high-stepping and free, with strong drive from behind. Its head is long, flat and narrow with slight stop and a dark-coloured nose. The rose ears are set well back and soft and fine in texture. They should never be erect. The Italian's eyes are like precious stones – large, bright and sparkling with expression. The forelegs are straight and parallel with bone which is both fine and strong, leading down to hare-feet. The body is deep and narrow-chested with good depth of ribs. The back is slightly arched over the loin, gently curving down to the low-set tail and long, well-muscled and well-angulated hindquarters. The tail is carried low, and the skin should be fine and supple with a fine, short and glossy coat.

In colour the Italian can be red, fawn, cream, black or blue, with or without white markings, or white as a base colour with or without markings in any of these colours. Black-and-tan, blue-and-tan and brindle are not allowed.

THE JAPANESE CHIN

This is one of the aristocratic Orientals of the Group, and the daintier the Chin, the better. One of the major characteristics is the unique "astonished" look, which comes from white showing in the inner corners of the large, dark, wide-set eyes. This expression should always be present. Another breed point, which some judges overlook, is the stylish movement in which the feet are lifted high, this resulting from a rather steeper forehand construction than the norm.

The Chin head is large for the size of the dog, the skull is broad and gently rounded, both in profile and between the ears, but never so much so as to be domed like the Chihuahua. The muzzle is short and wide and very well cushioned, with the upper lips noticeably rounded and padded on each side of the wide nostrils. The ears are small, wide-set, carried slightly forward, V-shaped and

Tom and Margaret Paxton's Japanese Chin bitch, Ch. Swietenia Evettee, won her first CC when I was judging at Midland Counties in 1991, winning her second under breed authority, Pamela Cross Stern. She returned to Midland Counties the following year as a Champion and repeated the win with BOB uner Ferelith Somerfield. Michael Trafford.

well fringed. The mouth should be level or slightly undershot, and if the jaws are to be level, there will be good strength of underjaw. The neck is quite long and carried proudly, the forelegs straight and parallel, fine-boned and nicely feathered, with slender hare-feet which are also feathered at their tips.

The body is square and cobby, wide-chested, compact and quite square in profile. A lot of Chins are far too narrow. They must have a certain width about them to be cobby and thus, typical. The hindquarters have good turn of stifle, and the tail is high-set, well feathered and carried closely over the back. The coat is plentiful, soft, straight and silky. There should be no curl or wave, and it tends to stand off, particularly around the neck. The Chin can be black-and-white (in which case the nose must be black) or red-and-white in any shade (when the nose can match the coat colour). The white should be clear, not flecked, and it is worth remembering that the British Standard does not allow tricolour dogs. This is far from being an easy breed to judge, as some "all-rounders" discover to their cost.

THE KING CHARLES SPANIEL

The King Charles and the Cavalier are now quite separate breeds, the major difference being their size and heads. The King Charles is, ideally, between 8-14lbs, the Cavalier 12-18lbs. There was a time, not that long ago, when the King Charles was considered the ultimate "head breed", to such an extent that the original Breed Standard devoted very little space to anything other than this aspect of the dog.

The breed should be compact and cobby, refined, and yet with width. Its body should be wide and deep, its back short and level – far too many King Charles are longer in back than the ideal, and considerably narrower. The forelegs are quite short and straight, and the hindquarters well-angulated and muscular. The feet are compact, well-padded and knuckled, round and cat-like with good feathering.

The King Charles head seems to cause some judges problems and some obviously have difficulty discerning between the King Charles and the Cavalier! The King Charles head must be noticeably domed between the ears, it is a large head in relation to body size, and it is unusually full over the eyes. The stop is very deep, the muzzle square and wide with great depth too. It should be well turned-up, to such an extent that the lips meet perfectly, showing good width of underjaw, and the mouth should be slightly undershot. The muzzle is well cushioned, and there should be good finish under the eyes so that the whole head retains a look of smooth quality. The eyes are very large and dark, wide-set and benevolent in expression. The head is completed by low-set, very long and profusely feathered ears, which should hang flat, framing the face.

The tail should be well feathered and never carried over the backline. The coat should be long, silky and straight, and while a slight wave can be forgiven, there should never be an obvious curl. The legs, ears and tail should always be heavily feathered. The colours are exactly the same as in the Cavalier.

THE LÖWCHEN (LITTLE LION DOG)

This is a 10-13 inch tall breed, whose name comes from the traditional style of clipping the coat in a lion pattern. The head is rather short and proportionately wide in skull, the eyes dark, round, quite large and intelligent. The muzzle should not be over-long and the ears are quite long, well-fringed, and they lie in such a way that they blend in with the coat of the head and mane. The neck is quite long, elegantly arched, the forelegs fine, straight and parallel, and the feet small and round. The back should be short and level, the ribs well-sprung, and there should be moderate tuck-up and a strong loin. The hindquarters should be well muscled with rounded rump and good turn of stifle, though it has to be said that one of the breed's major failings is its lack of rear angulation.

The tail is clipped with a plume of hair and carried gaily over the back. On the move, the Löwchen should be parallel in front and behind with no hackneying. The coat should be long, wavy, fine and silky, and it can be any colour or pattern. The nose will be black or brown, depending on the coat colour. The Löwchen is a very basic breed in many ways, with no exaggeration, but sometimes size can be a problem. Also, exhibitors with rather long-backed dogs sometimes fool judges by leaving a greater length of body-coat. The relatively short, clipped area to the rear can create an illusion of a short back to the untrained eye, so use your hands as well as your eyes!

THE MALTESE

This is essentially a short and cobby breed, and, therefore, should not be as long-backed as some judges seem to think. It is bright and showy, has a proud carriage, and a smart white coat which should be of good length, but not so long that it interferes with free movement. The coat is straight, silky and should never be crimped, curled or have a woolly undercoat. The head and expression of the Maltese is important, the skull and muzzle being of equal length and with a well-defined stop. The muzzle should be broad, and never mean or pointed. The head should be nicely filled under the eyes, which should be oval, dark-brown, and never prominent. As with the Bichon, there should be black eye-rims and haloes, which are the areas of darkly pigmented skin around the eyes.

The Maltese should have fairly long ears, which hang close to the head, and they are profusely feathered – the hair of the ears blending with the hair on the neck and shoulders. The neck is moderately long, the forelegs short and straight, and the feet round with black pads, which judges should always confirm. The Maltese body has good spring of rib and a level back, the well-feathered tail being carried well over in an arch. The breed should move freely, holding a level topline, with a gait that almost suggests it is actually gliding – rather like an ice-skater. Slight lemon markings are allowed in the coat.

THE MINIATURE PINSCHER

A breed with a decidedly hackney gait, which should exude confidence and spirit. It is a very compact dog, short-coupled and very elegant. Its head should be quite long, and the cheeks should be clean. The skull appears flat and the muzzle is proportionately rather strong. The dark eyes should be not too full and rounded, but neither should they be small and slanting. The ears are set high, small, and can be either erect or dropped. Some judges forget the provision for drop-ears.

The neck is strong, yet gracefully arched, and free of dewlap. There should be good development of forechest, the forehand being quite broad, with straight and parallel forelegs of moderate bone, and neat cat-feet with dark nails. The elbows should be close to the chest. The Min Pin is square, with a straight topline, which has a distinct gradual slope to the rear. The ribs are well sprung and deep, and there is reasonable tuck-up. The tail is carried high, and the hindquarters should be well muscled with good turn of stifle. The coat of the Min Pin is smooth, hard and short, close-fitting, and free from ridges of hair or cow-licks.

The breed's characteristic movement is free, totally co-ordinated and with a definite hackney action. In colour, Min Pins can be solid red of various shades, or black, blue or chocolate with distinct tan markings on the cheeks, lips, underjaw, throat, spots over the eyes and on the chest, lower half of the forelegs, inside the hindlegs and under the tail, on the lower part of the hocks and feet. These colours will have black pencilling on the toes, but no thumb-marks like the ETT. A white chest spot may be tolerated. The nose should always be black, except for chocolates and blues in which it can be self-coloured.

THE PAPILLON

The breed's name means "butterfly", and essentially it should always be a dainty dog, free of lumber and coarseness. The breed takes its name from the shape and position of the ears, and when they are erect and fully fringed, they are held obliquely like spread butterfly wings. In view of the fact that this breed characteristic gave the breed its name, it should be considered very important. The breed may also have completely dropped ears, in which case the breed is known as the Phalene (moth). In Britain, the two are shown as one breed, whereas in Europe the Phalene is given its own classes.

When I was judging at Monmouth County Kennel Club in the USA I awarded Best of Winners in Papillons to Roseann Fucillo's owner-handled Cilloette Grand Marnier. This dog puppy was sired by the English export, Ch. & Can. Ch. Caswell Copernicus, while his dam was a daughter of another English export, Ch. & Am. Ch. Melchester Bowman of Lordsrake.

John Ashbey.

The Papillon should be lively and alert, its movement being light, free and positive without any restriction. It should move true up and down, and in profile display ground-covering qualities without any hackneying. The head should be gently rounded between the ears, and the muzzle should be contrastingly finely pointed, and about one-third of the length of the head. Some Papillons tend to be rather thick and blocky in muzzle, which gives a very untypical head. The stop is well defined and the nose should be black. The eyes are rounded but not too full, medium size, and they are rather low in the skull. The eye rims should be black. The ears are large, mobile and with rounded tips, very well fringed and set towards the back of the skull wide enough apart to show the gently rounded top-skull. The markings of the head should be symmetrical, and a clear white blaze is desirable if not essential. The neck is moderately long, the forelegs straight and parallel, slender and fine in bone, with fine hare-feet well tufted with hair. The elbows should be close to the chest, which is rather deep. The body is fairly long (a lot of judges expect Papillons to be square and short-backed, which they are not) with a level topline and good rib spring. The loins should be strong and the tail high-set, long and very well fringed. It should fall over the back in a graceful arch, with the fringes falling to the side in a plume. A tight tail, flat on the back, will destroy an otherwise typical outline.The hindquarters show good turn of stifle and are well developed. The coat has no undercoat but should be plentiful, flowing, long, fine and silky, falling quite flat on the back and sides. There is a profuse frill on the chest, and the forelegs, tail and thighs should be well feathered as, of course, should be the ears fringed. Some Papillons have rather thick stand-off coats, which is not at all typical. The breed should be white with patches in any colour other than liver. Tricolours should have tan in spots over the eyes, inside the ears, on the cheeks and under the tail.

THE PEKINGESE

Of all breeds, with perhaps the exception of the Bulldog, judges seem to have most difficulty with Pekingese, maybe because they are so far removed from the "average" kind of construction. The fact that they are invariably heavily-coated, and consequently judges have to use their hands and brains as well as their eyes, does not make it any easier. Imagine the Pekingese as a concrete pear and you are halfway to understanding its body shape. The Pekingese should look small but be amazingly heavy when picked up. Judges must remember that heavy bone and a well-built, sturdy body are essential, and they might find it surprising that the Pekingese Standard contains the phrase "soundness essential" more times than any other.

The Pekingese is a dignified breed, and its head and expression should convey that fact. The head should be massive and envelope-shaped, in that it is wide and shallow. The skull is flat between the ears and wide between the eyes, with the large open-nostrilled nose well up between them. The muzzle should be wide, well-wrinkled (this wrinkle being at the side of the muzzle, and not to be confused with the over-nose wrinkle, which should never be too heavy or prominent), and nicely cushioned, with plenty of strength of underjaw and level lips. The eyes are large, round, dark and full of character, yet tranquil, and the head profile of the Pekingese should be quite flat.

When I judged my first Best in Show All Breeds at Championship level, at the South Wales Kennel Association show of 1988, I gave a first Toy Group and later Best in Show to the Thomas family's Pekingese, Ch. Jonsville Daytime Lover, who went on to take two more such awards that year and ended up as Top Toy. Subsequently, the dog was sold to Germany where he continued his campaign throughout Europe. *Thomas Fall.*

The nose, lips and eye rims should always be dark-pigmented. Ears are heart-shaped, set level with the skull (never low and "houndy", but never too high and flying) and the profuse feathering should merely emphasise the width of skull, being groomed out level with the top-skull.

The neck is very short and thick, the forelegs being short, thick and heavily-boned with a slight bow, yet always firm at the shoulder. The forefeet are large and flat, not round and neat, and turn out slightly. The chest is low-slung with great breadth and good spring of ribs, and it is vital that the forehand should be sound, and not slack with loose elbows. The body has a distinct waist and a level back – roach backs are a major fault which appear frequently.

The hindquarters are much lighter than the fore, have slight angulation, but they should always be firm and sound. When the Pekingese moves it should display a neat "scissor" action behind, being rather close, while its body shape and bowed forehand result in a rolling gait in front. This roll should not be confused with loose elbows and general unsoundness. The Pekingese judge should be sure to pick up the dogs when he judges and check weight-for-size, also ascertaining that the dog's centre of gravity is nearer the front than the rear.

The Pekingese coat should act merely as the icing on the cake and not be of paramount importance. It should enhance the body shape and not mask it, and this leonine shape is emphasised by the profuse mane which extends beyond the shoulders. The top coat is rather coarse and there should be a thick undercoat. There is lavish feathering on the ears, backs of legs, tail and toes. Ideally, Pekingese should not weigh more than 12lbs, and any colour other than albino and liver is acceptable, particolours being evenly broken

THE POMERANIAN

This a small Spitz breed with an intelligent and foxy head and expression, very little neck, a short body, and a rather stand-off coat which all help to create the typical "puff ball" outline. The skull is slightly flat, much larger than the muzzle, which is finely finished and tight-lipped. The eyes should be medium in size, rather oval, bright and dark, and full of intelligence. The ears are small,

When I awarded Ann Winter's Ch. Ringlands Gaiety Girl at Rosskear one of her twenty-one CCs she was nearing veteran age. In this photogpraph she illustates so beautifully correct Pomeranian type, and the typical outline for the breed. Essential to correct balance in this breed is the rather short neck and backward head carriage.
Diane Pearce.

carried perfectly erect and have moderate distance between them. The neck is short and the resulting head carriage is such that the head is rather thrown-back.

The forelegs are finely boned, straight and parallel, of medium length and with small, compact cat-feet. The back is short and the body compact, well ribbed up, and the chest quite deep without being too wide. The hindquarters are moderately angulated and again fine-boned. The tail is a characteristic of the breed, being high-set and carried flat over the back, so profusely covered with long, harsh and spreading hair that it appears to cover the back and reach virtually to the back of the head.

The Pom's action is buoyant, free and brisk. There is a soft, fluffy undercoat and a harsh, straight top coat which covers the body, and is particularly plentiful around the neck, shoulders and chest. The Pomeranian Standard says that all colours are permissible, but it goes on to point out that whites should be free of lemon or any other colour, and that white or tan markings are highly undesirable (there is currently a move afoot to get black-and-tans accepted in Britain). While particolours are allowed, preference should be given to whole-coloured specimens where dogs are otherwise equal. White, orange, shaded sable and cream dogs should have black eye-rims and noses. In other colours the nose can be self-coloured, but never particolour or flesh-coloured. The maximum ideal weight for dogs is 4.5lbs and bitches 5.5lbs.

THE PUG

The Pug's catch-phrase is "multum in parvo" (much in little), and the breed should exude substance from a small frame. It should be hard muscled, compact and well boned, with a characteristic twist – the high-set, tightly-curled tail. The Pug has a large head, which is essentially round but not domed. The muzzle is short, blunt and square, but not up-faced like the Bulldog. The wrinkles on the forehead should be clearly defined. The eyes are dark, rather large and globular, lustrous and full of fire. Even so, the eyes must not be wild and showing the white. The ears are thin and velvety, either rose or button. The rose ear is folded back like the Bulldog; the button folds neatly forward with the tip lying close to the skull, and this is the preferred ear carriage.

The mouth is slightly undershot with a wide underjaw and lower incisors in as straight a line as possible. The neck is crested, thick, but has enough length to elevate the head proudly. The body is short-backed, cobby, wide-chested and well-ribbed. The topline is level and the hindquarters quite well angulated. The feet have well split-up toes with black nails. The twist is curled as tightly as possible over the hip with a double curl being highly prized. In movement, the Pug should be true up and down, with plenty of reach in front and good rear drive. The hindquarters should have a slightly rolling gait. The coat is fine and smooth, short and glossy, and Pugs can be black, silver, apricot or fawn. Ideally, there is a black line from occiput to tail in the non-blacks (referred to as the "trace") as well as black on the muzzle and mask, ears, cheek-moles, and the diamond of the forehead.

THE YORKSHIRE TERRIER

The Yorkie's crowning glory is its wondrous long, silky coat, with its distinctive steel-blue and three shades of tan. The importance attached to the coat has frequently been the cause of debate among judges, some feeling that coat and colour should be paramount, even at the expense of conformation. Most judges now seem to accept that, while the coat is a major characteristic, a Yorkie should have other basic attributes as well. The breed should be alert and spirited and essentially a toy terrier. Its head is rather small and flat, never too round in skull or too long in muzzle. The nose is black. The eyes are dark, medium size and sparkling, forward-looking and

Few breeds of dog require more intense pre-show preparation than the Yorkshire Terrier. Osman Sameja's Ozmilion kennel has established a phenomenal record in recent years, with many generations of home-bred Champions. Pictured is the well-named Ch. Ozmilion Dedication, who is the top-winning Yorkie of all time with fifty-two CCs to his credit – I awarded him two of these. Dedication was also the top-winning dog of all breeds in 1987.

Thomas Fall.

with black rims, always full of expression. The ears are small, neat and V-shaped, carried erect and not far apart. They should be a deep, rich tan. The neck has good reach and the forelegs are straight, parallel, with round feet and black nails. The forelegs should be well covered with long hair of a rich tan, lighter at the ends than the roots. The tan should not extend higher than the elbows. The body is compact with moderate spring of rib, a strong loin and level topline. The tail is high-set and carried high, and the hindquarters are moderately angulated, and covered with long hair of rich tan coming no higher than the stifles.

The distinctive coat should be parted from the nose to the tail, long, straight, glossy and fine. The ample fall on the head should be rich golden tan, deeper in colour at the sides of the head, at the base of the ears and on the muzzle, where it must be long. The tan on the head should not extend to the neck, and the tan must be clear without sooty or dark hairs. The body coat of dark steel-blue should run from the occiput to the tail, the tail being an even darker shade of blue, and should not have bronze, fawn or dark hairs. The chest is rich tan, and all tan hair should be darker at the roots than in the middle, and it becomes even lighter towards the tips.

Judges traditionally separate the coat to check the shades of tan by using the brush, which will be offered automatically by any experienced Yorkie exhibitor. The coat colour takes time to come through and clear, and younger dogs will often appear quite dark, so allowance should be made in the younger classes for less-than-perfect colours.

SUMMARY
As I have said before, the Toy breeds were primarily developed to serve as good-looking companions, so aesthetic qualities are important, but they must still be sound in mind and body if they are to be able to fulfil their original function satisfactorily.

Chapter Sixteen

FOREIGN BREEDS AND FOREIGN APPOINTMENTS

In the UK at the beginning of 1993, the Kennel Club recognised 137 breeds with Challenge Certificate status. There are more, of course, whose registrations and entries do not yet warrant such elevation, and yet further breeds who are still on the Kennel Club's import register and so are not as yet allowed breed classes of their own. In recent years the number of breeds in Britain has, of course, grown quite rapidly as more and more imported "new" breeds have found favour with the British fancier. In the majority of breeds, it would be fair to say that the numbers and depth of quality to be found in a typical entry at a British Championship show would be as high as found anywhere in the world. British enthusiasts are lucky to have access to large numbers of dogs in most breeds, and this exposure gives them the opportunity to develop their "eye" much more easily than in countries which may not have such depth. Consequently, it is comparatively easy to learn about most of the breeds with access to so many specimens of varying quality.

INTRODUCING NEW BREEDS

However, there will always be pioneering fanciers who wish to introduce further breeds, hitherto unknown in this country, and each year we see some new and often quite exotic breeds arriving. It is a fact that, often, the very people who seek to introduce "new" breeds to this country have failed to make any great impact in their previously chosen breeds, where competition is considerably stronger. It is not always the case, but often. The Kennel Club has, in my opinion very wisely, introduced their Import Register and this acts as a safeguard against breeds mushrooming in popularity before they have established an acceptable genetic base. It is also a welcome deterrent to those commercially minded "breeders" who see a new breed as an opportunity to make large sums of money. Only the really dedicated will spend years showing in the Import Register classes, knowing that full recognition may be many years ahead

"New" breeds will originally be imported in small quantities from other countries, not necessarily the country of the breed's origin. They are often brought in by just one or two pioneer breeders, who are naturally keen to establish their new-found breed. The process of formulating a British Breed Standard is a long and complex one, involving much correspondence with the governing body in the breed's homeland, translations, consultation with breeders, and so on. In the early stages of a Standard's development, it is vital that the British proposal is as close to the original as possible. In the past it has been suggested that, on occasions, certain clauses may have been changed to some degree in translation, and others may have been changed for convenience, if the original imports are rather lacking in some particular aspect.

Once these "new" breeds gain a foothold in Britain, they are something of a novelty and some judges seem to view their appearance as a chance to get in "on the ground floor" of judging another breed. There is nothing wrong with enthusiasm for newly introduced breeds, but I find it surprising how many multi-breed judges suddenly become instant experts on breeds whose homeland they have never even visited, much less ever having judged top-class specimens. The danger here is that the original imports in a "new" breed may not be as wholly typical as is desired, but they will be used as the blueprint for the breed in this country. It is very important that judges who presume to judge these foreign breeds should obtain as much information as possible from the country of origin, and learn as much about correct type as possible – this is not necessarily the same thing as taking everything the original importers say as gospel.

Fortunately we have in this country several top-class all-rounders of international standing, who frequently judge overseas and who will have seen many first-rate specimens of breeds which are "new" to us. Their experience and knowledge should be taken advantage of. In a breed's formative years, when it does eventually get classified as a breed, it will be judged almost exclusively by all-rounder judges. Their responsibility is great, as their early decisions as to correct type will set the pattern for the breed's future. Therefore, it is essential that these judges are familiar with the best specimens in the breed's country of origin (or country of development, as some breeds are considered to have been "adopted" and advanced by countries other than those where they originated).

INTERNATIONAL STANDING

In years gone by, British all-rounder judges led the world. Their opinions were sought in every country where dog showing was developing, and their role was almost that of disciples. Today, other countries have advanced dramatically in their dog showing activities. The United States, Canada, Australia and Japan are huge countries where the dog sport is extremely popular and sophisticated, and they have produced many well-established judges of their own who now travel the world, having acheived 'All Breeds' approval much more quickly than their British counterparts. Closer to home, dog showing is a popular activity all over Europe, and the Scandinavian nations, in particular, have proved to be extremely conscientious in their breeding of excellent dogs in many breeds. They too have produced their own judges, and a relatively tiny country like Finland can now take pride in the fact that it has produced some of the best international all rounders of our generation. While the international standing of the British all rounder may not be as omnipotent as in past times, happily this country still has many judges who are capable of judging many breeds to a very high standard, and our top judges are regularly invited to officiate in foreign lands.

OVERSEAS APPOINTMENTS

Overseas appointments will come eventually to the best judges. Throughout the year we see many foreign visitors at our shows. Often such visitors are officials of show-running clubs overseas, and they are always keen to discover new talent which they can employ in their own country. Once a judge has established a reputation for judging knowledgeably and fairly, he will soon be recognised by other countries. Judging overseas can be a great pleasure. Some countries are less advanced than others in their dog showing, and the systems will vary, but the same fundamentals apply in that the judge is required to find and reward the best dogs in his entry.

QUALITY GRADING

Most of the countries who come under the umbrella of the Federation Internationale Cynologique

Cropped ears can dramatically change the head, expression and outline of breeds which are shown with natural ears in the U.K., the Boxer being a typical example, and consequently judges have to adjust their eye somewhat. I awarded Best of Breed to Dr and Mrs. William Truesdale's Ch. Hi-Tech's Arbitrage. Arbitrage was the Number One Boxer in the U.S.A. in 1993 with many All Breeds Bests in Show and Groups to his credit.

John Ashbey.

John Hambleton of the famous Marbleton Boxers judged this Boxer, Impressiveness Naughty But Nice, on a trip to Sweden. This is a soundly constructed dog – but the tail has a significant effect on the outline.

(FCI) employ systems which demand that a written critique be given by the judge on every dog, and also a quality grading. This type of competition involves judging on two different levels. Firstly, each dog is judged against its own Breed Standard, and graded accordingly. Secondly, those who have achieved maximum grading ("First" or "Excellent", depending on where you happen to be) will reappear to compete in the relative competition class.

Such judging requires a lot of thought and knowledge on the judge's part. The exhibitors in these countries are used to receiving written critiques every weekend, and they are much more accustomed to forthright assessments. They are also well aware of their own dogs' faults, and find it rather strange when a judge refrains from mentioning obvious shortcomings. They expect a critique to contain their dogs' greatest merits, and major faults. Many British judges, because of our own attitude towards critiques, tend to be rather cautious when dictating their thoughts overseas. They sometimes, very much mistakenly, believe that if they are unduly flattering in their critiques, they will be popular and get invited back. This is not the case at all. Many overseas exhibitors are much more responsive to constructive criticism than their British counterparts and are much more realistic about their own dogs' failings.

Judging under this type of system for the first time can be a little daunting, as it can be very difficult to gauge the level of overall quality in a breed. I recall one of my first overseas appointments when I had been quite hard on many of the dogs in the earlier classes, grading lots of them Second for quality. Later in the day when the Champions class came in, I realised that some of those Second dogs were a lot better than the Champions! In some countries they schedule the Champions class first, so that judges can get an idea of the overall quality. Other countries have now abandoned the Champions class altogether as they found many judges were tending to "play safe" and automatically select their Best of Breed from that class!

The grouping and classification at dog shows will vary to an extent from country to country, but regardless of the system, there is nothing terribly difficult about placing the dogs which present themselves in the ring in your desired order of merit. British judges sometimes have problems in European countries where all dogs graded "of Certificate Quality" reappear in the Best of Breed class, regardless of whether or not they have been beaten in their earlier class. That strikes us as being rather illogical. The Certificate Quality grading indicates that the judge feels the dog would be worthy of the title of Champion, and there are no restrictions as to how many such gradings can be given.

NEW HORIZONS

Personally, I am a great admirer of the Scandinavian dog scene, and I find judging with the critique and grading system very rewarding. Other countries are not that keen to have critiques at all. At general Championship shows in Australia and the United States, for example, a judge is only required to place dogs and make awards. They have no facility for written critiques, not even for the canine press, though some breed club events do ask judges to write on their winners for a club newsletter or magazine.

In the USA, timing is critical because of the strict schedule of any show. With so many professional handlers involved, they need to know precisely which dog is required where and when, and so before the show each exhibitor receives an accurately timed schedule. Consequently, slow judges can really be a problem, and the AKC requires all judges to mark on their judge's book at what time they start, and finish, each class. Procedure is considered very important in America, and Field Representatives from the Kennel Club are required to report on visiting judges, as well as their own. The style of judging in the United States tends to be rather more regimented than in Britain, and most judges adopt very similar patterns. It is customary to place a line-up, and then ask the winners to circuit the ring, motioning them to the place boards as they complete the send-round.

Judging overseas is a great learning experience for the serious dog judge. It will broaden his outlook as to his own breed, and also others which he may not customarily see in any great numbers at home. Sometimes the overall quality of a breed will give a judge a real jolt and make him realise that the breed is not what it could be at home. I remember finding the most marvellous

Min Pins in Thailand, and superb Papillons in Australia, which had exactly that effect on me.

While your initial overseas invitation will have resulted from your being a specialist judge of your breed in your own country, and the host club would expect you to judge in accordance with your background, it should at the same time be remembered that the Breed Standard in the country where you are to judge may differ slightly from that in Britain. It is vital that you obtain a copy and study it before you judge. The chances are that differences may be relatively minor and refer to size, colour or markings, rather than anything too dramatic. Yet only a fool would undertake a foreign assignment without first having checked the local Breed Standard. When in Rome!

CROPPING AND DOCKING

Apart from subtle differences in the Breed Standards, there can be an extra worry for the British judge when overseas which concerns breeds which have been traditionally either cropped or docked. The cropping of ears has been illegal in the UK for many years, but up until now we have been allowed to continue with tail docking (the arguments about which could in themselves fill a book, so I shall refrain from commenting here). In some countries, ear cropping is still permitted, whereas in others both ear cropping and tail docking have been outlawed.

It might sound quite easy to judge cropped dogs when you are only used to seeing natural, dropped ears, but the effect which cropping can have on the head and expression and the overall "sharpness" of a dog's outline can be quite startling. The head, when cropped, immediately takes on a much cleaner appearance and the expression is logically more alert. Cropped ears can also create an optical illusion in making a head appear longer than it would seem with natural ears. Judging cropped dogs requires the judge to completely re-adjust his eye, and it can take some time. It is a fact that the most ordinary dog can appear "smart" when cropped, so the judge has to work extra hard to assess that dog objectively.

There is perhaps an even greater adjustment of the eye required for judging traditionally docked breeds with tails, and this is something we may well have to get accustomed to in the UK before too long. The entire balance of a docked breed changes when its tail is left at full length. Breeds such as Boxers, Dobermanns and Rottweilers owe much of their appeal and overall balance to their short tails, and with full tails of varying length, thickness and carriage, such breeds present a previously unencountered difficulty for the judge.

Old English Sheepdogs with tails suddenly take on a more Bearded Collie-like appearance. Cockers and American Cockers tend to be reminiscent of Setters rather than Spaniels. Some of the Terrier breeds become quite alien with curling tails, whilst some breeds (Schipperkes I find the most obvious example) which revert to a Spitz-type tail carriage, do not seem to lose too much of their outline with a tail. British judges have no difficulty in sorting out the Cardigan from the Pembroke Corgi, but when the Pembroke has a tail, would they then find it quite so easy? So, should you find yourself judging overseas breeds which may be cropped or presented with tails, a good deal of preparation is necessary as you could be in for a shock!

SUMMARY

It is important that judges who officiate overseas remember that they are representing their country, and that their behaviour and performance reflects on the system which allowed them to progress thus far. It only takes a few rotten apples to give an entire country a bad name. Many people will be invited to a foreign country at some stage. The proof of the pudding is whether or not they are invited back!

IN CONCLUSION

Dogs are amazing animals who give so much and ask so little. They are extremely tolerant of our human shortcomings, understand our moods and humours, and never criticise. We should always remember this when we judge, and try to do our very best by them. The hobby, or lifestyle, of showing and breeding dogs can be a totally satisfying one, provided the individual is prepared to adopt a balanced attitude towards it. Dog shows are to be taken seriously, but they are not life or death. There is always another show, always another judge with another opinion, and it is wise that the exhibitor should remember that the dog he takes home from the show is exactly the same dog he brought that morning.

Judging dogs is one aspect of the sport which can be equally rewarding but, again, maintaining the right perspective is vitally important. Anyone who wishes to judge dogs should take the job seriously and resolve to do his best by the dogs, rather than their owners. He should also be genuine in his desire to do the best possible job, and he should guard his independence fiercely. A judge who is not independent, or who is keener to cultivate any individual or organisation than judge dogs as dispassionately as he is able, will never reach his full potential as he will be spending too much time worrying about irrelevancies. Total independence is not as commonplace as it could be, with far too many people in the dog sport concluding that the politics of the scene are perhaps more important than the dogs themselves. Judges who are seen to be unbiased and knowledgeable will maintain respect and rise to the top; of that you can be sure. The crux of the matter when judging is that all dogs should be judged in isolation – regardless of ownership, pedigree, nationality, sponsorship or political acceptability. Great judges assess dogs "cold" and are able to dismiss any factors other than the dog's physical merits completely from their mind

There have been many suggestions as to why people want to exhibit dogs in the first place, and the psychological implications of such reasons are quite fascinating. It is very true that many find in the dog world an opportunity to become "a big fish in a little pond", and they lose sight of the fact that, in the great scheme of things, the dog world is really just a very small microcosm. It remains, however, for many of us, a way of life which is very dear to us. Once the spirit of the dog world enters the soul of a true fancier, it will never disappear. It gets under your skin and you can never be completely rid of it.

Consequently, it is the wish of the dedicated enthusiast to see the highest standard of dogs, of shows, and of judging, and we can all do our bit to contribute to that end. Reading this book will not turn you into a talented dog judge overnight, but I hope that it will make you think seriously about aspects of the role which you may not before have considered too deeply. If that is the case, then my efforts have been worthwhile.